CH

# A Tale

Since its publication in 1859, *A Tale of Two Cities* has remained the best-known fictional recreation of the French Revolution and one of Charles Dickens's most exciting novels. *A Tale of Two Cities* blends a moving love story with the familiar figures of the Revolution: Bastille prisoners, a starving Parisian mob and an indolent aristocracy.

Taking the form of a sourcebook, this guide to Dickens's dramatic novel offers:

- extensive introductory comment on the contexts and many interpretations of the text, from publication to the present
- annotated extracts from key contextual documents, reviews, critical works and the text itself
- cross-references between documents and sections of the guide, in order to suggest links between texts, contexts and criticism
- suggestions for further reading.

Part of the *Routledge Guides to Literature* series, this volume is essential reading for all those beginning detailed study of *A Tale of Two Cities* and seeking not only a guide to the novel, but a way through the wealth of contextual and critical material that surrounds Dickens's text.

**Ruth Glancy** is Associate Professor of English at Concordia University College of Alberta, Canada, and has published widely on Dickens.

# Routledge Guides to Literature*

**Editorial Advisory Board:** Richard Bradford (University of Ulster at Coleraine), Jan Jedrzejewski (University of Ulster at Coleraine), Duncan Wu (St. Catherine's College, University of Oxford)

**Routledge Guides to Literature** offer clear introductions to the most widely studied authors and literary texts.

Each book engages with texts, contexts and criticism, highlighting the range of critical views and contextual factors that need to be taken into consideration in advanced studies of literary works. The series encourages informed but independent readings of texts by ranging as widely as possible across the contextual and critical issues relevant to the works examined and highlighting areas of debate as well as those of critical consensus. Alongside general guides to texts and authors, the series includes 'sourcebooks', which allow access to reprinted contextual and critical materials as well as annotated extracts of primary text.

### Available in this series:

*Geoffrey Chaucer* by Gillian Rudd
*Ben Jonson* by James Loxley
*William Shakespeare's The Merchant of Venice: A Sourcebook* edited by S. P. Cerasano
*William Shakespeare's King Lear: A Sourcebook* edited by Grace Ioppolo
*William Shakespeare's Othello: A Sourcebook* edited by Andrew Hadfield
*John Milton* by Richard Bradford
*John Milton's Paradise Lost: A Sourcebook* edited by Margaret Kean
*Alexander Pope* by Paul Baines
*Mary Wollstonecraft's A Vindication of the Rights of Woman: A Sourcebook* edited by Adriana Craciun
*Jane Austen* by Robert P. Irvine
*Jane Austen's Emma: A Sourcebook* edited by Paula Byrne
*Jane Austen's Pride and Prejudice: A Sourcebook* edited by Robert Morrison
*Mary Shelley's Frankenstein: A Sourcebook* edited by Timothy Morton
*The Poems of John Keats: A Sourcebook* edited by John Strachan
*Charles Dickens's David Copperfield: A Sourcebook* edited by Richard J. Dunn
*Charles Dickens's Bleak House: A Sourcebook* edited by Janice M. Allan
*Herman Melville's Moby-Dick: A Sourcebook* edited by Michael J. Davey
*Harriet Beecher Stowe's Uncle Tom's Cabin: A Sourcebook* edited by Debra J. Rosenthal
*Walt Whitman's Song of Myself: A Sourcebook and Critical Edition* edited by Ezra Greenspan
*Robert Browning* by Stefan Hawlin

---

* Some books in this series were originally published in the Routledge Literary Sourcebooks series, edited by Duncan Wu, or the Complete Critical Guide to English Literature series, edited by Richard Bradford and Jan Jedrzejewski.

Charles Dickens's
# *A Tale of Two Cities*
## A Sourcebook

*Edited by Ruth Glancy*

Routledge
Taylor & Francis Group

LONDON AND NEW YORK

First published 2006
by Routledge
2 Park Square, Milton Park, Abingdon, Oxon OX14 4RN

Simultaneously published in the USA and Canada
by Routledge
270 Madison Avenue, New York, NY 10016

*Routledge is an imprint of the Taylor & Francis Group*

© 2006 Edited by Ruth Glancy

Typeset in Sabon and Gill Sans by RefineCatch Limited, Bungay, Suffolk
Printed and bound in Great Britain by
TJ International Ltd, Padstow

*British Library Cataloguing in Publication Data*
A catalogue record for this book is available from the British Library.

*Library of Congress Cataloging in Publication Data*
Charles Dickens's A tale of two cities : a sourcebook /
edited by Ruth Glancy.
      p.  cm. – (Routledge guides to literature)
Includes bibliographical references.
    1. Dickens, Charles, 1812–1870. Tale of two cities.    2. France – History –
Revolution, 1789–1799 – Literature and the revolution.    I. Glancy, Ruth F.,
1948–   II. Series.
    PR4571.C484 2006
    823'.8 – dc22                                                        2005022657

ISBN 10: 0–415–28759–6    ISBN 13: 9–78–0–415–28759–3    (hbk)
ISBN 10: 0–415–28760–X    ISBN 13: 9–78–0–415–28759–3    (pbk)

# Contents

# 2: Interpretations

# 3: Key Passages

## Key Passages                                                        115

## 4: Further Reading

# Illustrations

# Annotation and Footnotes

Annotation is a key feature of this series. Both the original notes from reprinted texts and new annotations by the editor appear at the bottom of the relevant page. The reprinted notes are prefaced by the author's name in square brackets, e.g. [Robinson's note].

# Acknowledgements

Extract from *Confessions* by Jean-Jacques Rousseau, translated by Angela Scholar, and edited by Patrick Coleman (2000), pp. 159–60. By permission of Oxford University Press.

"Judicial Special Pleading" (1848) from Charles Dickens, *The Amusement of People and Other Papers*, edited by Michael Slater. Reproduced by kind permission of Michael Slater.

"To Sir Edward Bulwer Lytton, 5 June 1860" from Charles Dickens, *Pilgrim Edition of the Letters of Charles Dickens*, edited by H. House, G. Storey and K. Tillotson (1997), pp. 258–60. By permission of Oxford University Press.

"Charles Dickens" from *Decline of the English Murder* by George Orwell, copyright © George Orwell. By permission of Bill Hamilton as the Literary Executor of the Estate of the Late Sonia Brownwell Orwell and Secker & Warburg Ltd.

Excerpt from "Charles Dickens" in *Dickens, Dali and Others: Studies in Popular Culture*, copyright © 1946 by George Orwell and renewed 1974 by Sonia Orwell, reprinted by permission of Harcourt, Inc.

Excerpts from Taylor Stoehr, *Dickens: The Dreamer's Stance*, Ithaca, NY: Cornell University Press (1965), pp. 3–33. Reproduced by kind permission of the author.

Excerpts from Ana Laura Zambrano, "Charles Dickens and Sergei Eisenstein: The Emergence of Cinema," *Style Journal* 9 (1975). Reproduced by kind permission of *Style Journal*.

Excerpts from John P. McWilliams, Jr., "Progress without Politics: *A Tale of Two Cities*," *Clio* 7: 1 (1977). Reproduced by kind permission of the author.

Excerpts from Albert Hutter, "Nation and Generation in *A Tale of Two Cities*," *PMLA* (1978) pp. 448–62. Reprinted by permission of the Modern Language Association.

Extract from Garrett Stewart, *Death Sentences: Styles of Dying in British Fiction*, Cambridge, Mass.: Harvard University Press, pp. 83–4, 86–8, 91–2, 93, copyright © 1984 by the President and Fellows of Harvard College. Reprinted by permission of the publisher.

Extract from Chris Brooks, "Recalled to Life," *Signs for the Times*, London and New York: Routledge (1984), pp. 85–95. Reproduced by permission of the publisher.

Extract from Cates Baldridge, "Alternatives to Bourgeois Individualism in *A Tale of Two Cities*," *SEL Studies in English Literature 1500–1900*, 30, 4 (autumn 1990). Reprinted with permission.

Extract from Lisa Robson, "The 'Angels' in Dickens's House: Representation of Women in *A Tale of Two Cities*," *The Dalhousie Review* 72(3), 1992. Reprinted, with permission.

Extract from Arthur Hopcraft, "The Spirit of Revolution," *The Listener*, May 18, 1989. Reproduced by permission of The Rod Hall Agency Limited.

Illustrations courtesy of the Dickens House Museum.

# Introduction

"It was the best of times, it was the worst of times." With these famous words, Charles Dickens struck what he liked to call the "keynote" of his 1859 novel, *A Tale of Two Cities*. The "times" that were both the best and the worst were the years leading up to the French Revolution of 1789–93, a cataclysmic event that saw the overthrow of feudal privilege and whose repercussions were still being felt throughout Europe seventy years later. In two cities – London and Paris – and through two heroes, doubles, who love the same woman, Dickens set a private story of self-sacrificing love against the lurid public events of a violent revolution that took the world largely by surprise. These two threads of action, the private and the public, are woven throughout the novel until they mesh in the equally famous conclusion, when Sydney Carton does a "far, far better thing" than he has ever done by going to the guillotine in the place of his rival, Charles Darnay. Just as Dickens's 1843 novella *A Christmas Carol* has become an essential part of the English-speaking world's celebration of Christmas, many people's conception of the French Revolution is coloured by Dickens's dramatic retelling of its main events in *A Tale of Two Cities*.

In calling the novel a "tale," Dickens was deliberately concentrating on plot rather than on his more characteristic strengths – character and dialogue – to carry his theme that oppression brutalizes humanity and can lead only to greater brutality. Although his friend and biographer, John Forster, was later to write that this new emphasis on plot could "hardly be called an entirely successful experiment" (see Early Critical Reception, **p. 66**), Dickens himself considered *A Tale of Two Cities* the "best story" that he had written (it was his twelfth novel).[1] He recognized that he was striking out in a new direction when he wrote to Forster,

I set myself the little task of making a *picturesque*[2] story, rising in every chapter with characters true to nature, but whom the story itself should

---

1   Letter to François Régnier, in G. Storey (ed.) *The Letters of Charles Dickens*, vol. IX, Oxford: Clarendon Press, 1997, p. 132.
2   The "picturesque" was a movement in art and literature during the late eighteenth century that recognized the value of scenery, especially the quaintness and neatness of rural England rather than the "sublime" rugged landscapes of continental Europe. Dickens is thinking here of his reliance on settings: a quiet house in Soho, London, the turbulent streets of Paris, a musty old English bank, a Parisian wine-shop.

express, more than they should express themselves, by dialogue. [. . .] If you could have read the story all at once, I hope you wouldn't have stopped halfway.[3]

John Forster was unable to read the story "all at once" because *A Tale of Two Cities* was written and published in instalments. While most of Dickens's novels appeared in monthly parts that contained a sizable chunk of the story, several of them, including *A Tale of Two Cities*, appeared in weekly journals and thus in much smaller portions. In 1850 Dickens had established his own magazine, *Household Words*, in which he published *Hard Times* in 1854. On April 30 1859 he launched a new journal, *All the Year Round*, with *A Tale of Two Cities* as the front-page serial. It ran there in weekly instalments until November 26 and ensured the success of the new venture; a steady 100,000 copies sold each week. Recognizing that some people did not like reading in "teaspoons,"[4] Dickens decided to publish the story in simultaneous monthly numbers as well, each number containing two illustrations by Dickens's regular illustrator, Hablot Knight Browne. When the weekly and monthly instalments concluded in November 1859, the novel was published in one volume with a preface (see Key Passages, **p. 115**) and a dedication to a close friend, Lord John Russell (1792–1878), liberal parliamentary reformer and twice prime minister.

As an historical novel, *A Tale of Two Cities* has not always been well received by literary critics, who debate Dickens's success in having characters carry the weight of enacting a personal love story while taking on political significance as actors in the events of the French Revolution. But in many ways the novel deserves its reputation as consistently one of Dickens's most popular works. *A Tale of Two Cities* exemplifies his lifelong sympathy with the victims of tyranny (and his recognition that victims can readily turn into tyrants themselves). It was always Dickens's method to remind readers that behind political processes are the individuals involved in them. If Madame Defarge acts from a personal need for revenge, so did the real-life Revolutionaries storm the Bastille out of intensely personal suffering.

The characters in *A Tale of Two Cities* exemplify Dickens's acute understanding of human nature and the workings of the mind under stress. Central to the story, for example, is his harrowing portrayal of the detrimental effects of long-term imprisonment. The novel opens with an English banker, Mr. Lorry, and Lucie Manette, a young Frenchwoman now living in England, on their way to Paris to find Lucie's father, who has just been released from the Bastille prison after being held in solitary confinement for eighteen years. Doctor Manette's connection to Charles Darnay, Lucie's future husband, and to Madame Defarge, wife of Manette's old servant with whom he is now staying, is the secret that haunts Doctor Manette's disturbed brain and casts a dark shadow over the novel until its final and tragic revelation. Equally vivid is the characterization of that implacable revolutionary, Thérèse Defarge. Prowling the streets of Paris like a tiger hunting down her prey or silently knitting her enemies' names into a register

---

3   Letter to John Forster, in Storey, *Letters*, pp. 112–13.
4   Thomas Carlyle made this complaint. See Dickens's letter to Mrs. William Howitt, in Storey, *Letters*, p. 113.

of condemned men, she has become as synonymous with the English-speaking world's French Revolution as Scrooge has with Christmas. While lacking the genial humor of Dickens's earlier works – the highly comic characters such as Mr. Pickwick and Mr. Micawber – *A Tale of Two Cities* exemplifies Dickens's characteristic comic vision, borne out of his essential vitality and optimism, and out of his eye for the incongruous and contradictory in human affairs. G.K. Chesterton shared in this vision when he famously remarked that Sydney Carton "is never so happy as when his head is being cut off."[5]

*A Tale of Two Cities* was written at a particularly difficult time in Dickens's life. In 1857 he acted in his friend Wilkie Collins's play *The Frozen Deep* and fell in love with one of the young professional actresses who performed with them. Unhappily married for some time, Dickens left his wife in 1858, shortly before beginning *A Tale of Two Cities*. The novel's love triangle of Sydney Carton, Charles Darnay, and Lucie Manette derived from the plot of the play in which Dickens acted the part of an unlikable hero who sacrifices his own life to save that of his rival. Dickens wrote in his preface to *A Tale of Two Cities* that the idea that became Sydney Carton possessed him completely and that in his own life he had "done and suffered" his hero's troubled story. The "Contexts" section of this sourcebook places the novel in these turbulent years.

As an historical novel set in Revolutionary France, *A Tale of Two Cities* requires an understanding of the factual background that informed Dickens's plot and themes. In the "Contexts" section the reader will find a short history of the French Revolution as well as extracts from Dickens's sources and an overview explaining how the novel grew out of his admiration for Thomas Carlyle's epic history, *The French Revolution*, his reading of contemporary eyewitness accounts of the Revolution, and his fascination with prisons. The reader will also find a detailed chronology of Dickens's life and times (1812–70), extracts from his letters, and other materials that help to explain Dickens's intentions and methods.

The "Interpretations" section of the sourcebook begins with an overview of the responses to the novel from the first periodical reviews in 1859 (some written before the novel was finished) to the often contradictory interpretations of the late twentieth century. Extracts from some early reviews are followed by a selection of twentieth-century views, which shed new light on this very familiar story and offer a variety of approaches – feminist, psychoanalytic, historical – as well as close readings of some of the important passages. "The Novel in Performance" introduces the reader to the major stage and screen versions of *A Tale of Two Cities* and includes comments on the most acclaimed film versions by directors, actors, and critics.

The third section of the sourcebook, "Key Passages," begins with a plot summary and chronology of the novel and the French Revolution. The most important passages from the novel are excerpted here, with commentary and explanatory notes. The passages are cross-referenced to the contextual and source materials as well as to the critical excerpts so that readers can easily find relevant comment on important historical or thematic details. The sourcebook concludes with a short guide to the best editions of *A Tale of Two Cities*, as well as to other books and articles helpful to the study of Dickens's revolutionary novel.

# 1
# Contexts

# Contextual Overview

Before reading this section, which provides an overview of the composition of *A Tale of Two Cities* and the historical and biographical events that influenced it, readers unfamiliar with the novel might wish to read the plot summary provided at the beginning of the Key Passages, **p. 114**.

In the Preface to the first edition of *A Tale of Two Cities* (see Key Passages, **p. 115**), Dickens cites two main sources for the novel: Thomas Carlyle's dramatic history, *The French Revolution*, published in 1837 (see Contemporary Documents, **pp. 31–7**) and Wilkie Collins's play *The Frozen Deep* (see Contemporary Documents, **pp. 44–5**), in which Dickens had acted a leading role in 1857. These two very different works by Dickens's friends recognize the public and private influences on a novel that is built around the relationship between these two spheres of human life. Dickens went to Carlyle for the events of the Revolution and the rhetoric in which to recount them, but in Collins's play (and his own life) he found the inspiration for the story of two heroes, Charles Darnay and Sydney Carton, and Lucie Manette, the woman they both love, that was to play out against the backdrop of historic events. Central also to *A Tale of Two Cities* was Dickens's lifelong interest in prisons and the disastrous effects of long incarceration, especially solitary confinement, on the human mind. Eighteen years of imprisonment endured by Lucie's father, Doctor Manette, have just ended when the novel opens (see Key Passages, **pp. 122–4**), but those years inexorably haunt the story and bring about its tragic conclusion.

## Overview of the French Revolution, 1789–93 [1]

*A Tale of Two Cities* is an "historical novel." While most novels are set in a recognizable place and time and sometimes refer to real people and events, in an historical novel, people from real life are represented as taking part in the narrative, often speaking with the fictional characters and engaging in the action. The author of an historical novel wishes to dramatize a particular time in history

---

1   For a chronology of the French Revolution and the events in *A Tale of Two Cities*, see Key Passages, p. 114.

for the reader – to bring historical moments and people to life by blending an imaginative reconstruction of events with facts known from contemporary accounts and other historical sources. The historical novelist usually has a point to make about the historical processes that brought about the events, or about the psychological complexities of the people involved. When Dickens chose the French Revolution of 1789–93 as the background for the action in *A Tale of Two Cities*, it had already been the subject of many plays and novels, partly because it was an historic event of world-changing proportions that involved not just armies and governments but also ordinary citizens with whom the reader could identify – farmers, merchants, shopkeepers, businessmen, professionals – people very like Dickens's 1859 audience.[2] The events of the French Revolution – uplifting and exciting but at the same time horrifyingly violent and out of control – lent themselves to romantic stories of heroic action, self-sacrifice, and suffering. Some knowledge of those events is helpful to a full understanding of *A Tale of Two Cities* and Dickens's imaginative dramatization of this turbulent time.

The Revolutionary period, its causes and effects, extended for many years, but the main events of the French Revolution occurred between 1789, the storming of the Bastille prison in Paris (see Key Passages, **pp. 139–43**) and 1793, the execution of King Louis XVI. Most of the events of *A Tale of Two Cities* take place during these years. But as Dickens's opening chapter makes clear, the roots of the French Revolution lay deep in the soil of feudal France. While the eighteenth century was "the best of times" (see Key Passages, **p. 117**) for many in France, as a result of its enviable position as a leading world power at the beginning of the Industrial Revolution, for many others it was "the worst of times" as a result of a long-standing feudal system of government. All political power lay in the hands of the King and those who held about two-thirds of the land – the clergy (or "First Estate") and the aristocracy (the "Second Estate"). The vast majority of the citizens made up the "Third Estate," which included not just peasants but the entire middle class of businessmen and professionals – the "bourgeoisie" (including Dickens's Doctor Manette) – and the many city workers, such as the novel's wineshop owner, Ernest Defarge. The clergy and aristocracy benefited from many rights and privileges, including exemption from most of the taxes levied on the members of the Third Estate, who had virtually no political power. These crippling taxes enforced by the State and the Church included the salt tax, or *gabelle*, a requirement that everyone over the age of seven had to buy a certain amount of salt per year at a fixed price. Dickens named Charles Darnay's faithful servant after this tax (see Key Passages, **p. 136**). Failure to pay taxes and other very minor infringements resulted in harsh punishments, and many innocent people found themselves abandoned in dismal cells through the infamous *lettres de cachet* (sealed letters), which allowed the nobility to request the King to imprison anyone without trial and even without cause. Even troublesome children could find themselves committed to jail by their parents (and one of the seven prisoners released in the storming of the Bastille was such a son). A *lettre de cachet* condemns Doctor Manette to the Bastille for eighteen years in *A Tale of*

---

2   Other novels about the French Revolution include Edward Bulwer Lytton's *Zanoni* (1842), Alexandre Dumas's *Le Chevalier de Maison Rouge* (1845–6), and Anthony Trollope's *La Vendée* (1850); See below, **p. 17–18**.

*Two Cities.* While the vast majority of the French population suffered under these unjust taxes and practices, many members of the aristocracy lived idle and luxurious lives, enjoying enormous wealth and privilege and supported by King Louis XVI and his wife Marie Antoinette from their grand palace of Versailles near Paris. After the Revolution, this state of affairs became known as the *ancien régime* (old regime, or system), the corrupt feudal ways that the Revolution abolished.

The injustices of the *ancien régime* were deeply resented by the educated middle classes (professional people such as doctors and lawyers), who were much better off than the peasants but who were denied any political power. Several of the greatest philosophers (known as *philosophes*) of the eighteenth century were Frenchmen who railed against the feudal system and argued for basic human rights (the right to liberty, equality, and fraternity that became one of the battle cries of the Revolution). While some of these writers, such as Voltaire (1694–1778), were harshly critical of the Church and the aristocracy without advocating democracy, others, and Jean-Jacques Rousseau (1712–78) in particular, encouraged the movement toward democracy through their writings (see Rousseau, Contemporary Documents, **pp. 30–1**). These writers were also influenced by the example of the American Revolution of 1776, and France aided the American colonies in their successful revolution against British rule. Although the most vivid impressions of the French Revolution are of the peasantry rising up in hunger-driven mania (an impression that is strong in *A Tale of Two Cities*), their revolt would not have happened without the growing shift in attitudes encouraged by the middle-class writers and intellectuals. Their sympathy with the plight of the lower classes is evident in many of the cartoons of the time which show well-fed clergymen and nobility cheerfully riding on the backs of worn-down peasants.

The immediate causes of the Revolution were many and were chiefly economic. A series of wars had led to a huge national debt that had increased with France's support of the American colonies in the American Revolution. The extravagance of the royal court, combined with the exemption of so many wealthy landowners (and the Church) from paying taxes had brought France to bankruptcy. King Louis XVI's financial advisers (and especially the popular Controller-General of Finance, Jacques Necker) recommended tax reform, but the King and his nobles were resistant to change. Adding to the misery of the common people were rising prices and serious bread shortages due to a disastrous harvest in 1788, followed by a severely cold winter. In May of 1789, King Louis XVI recalled the old Estates-General, an assembly of deputies elected by each of the three estates which had not met since 1614. He asked for lists of grievances (*cahiers*) from the people and received over 60,000 demands for the abolition of the feudal system and the *lettres de cachet*, for tax reform, and for a constitution. When the Third Estate asked that the three estates meet together and each deputy have a vote (under the old system the estates had met separately and voted as a group, so the Third Estate was always outvoted by the other two), the King refused their request. The deputies for the Third Estate under Count Mirabeau (a rebellious nobleman) then declared themselves the National Assembly of France with the intention of writing a constitution (following the example of the new United States of America). When the King banished them from Versailles, the deputies (joined by the deputies in favour of reform from the First and Second Estates, which now included most of the clergy) met on a tennis court and swore what became known as the Tennis Court Oath: a promise to remain united until a constitution was written.

Although the movement toward reform had thus begun at the state level, for the people in the streets progress was much too slow. Fearing that the mustering of troops around Paris meant that the King was going to close down the National Assembly, the people of Paris took matters into their own hands on July 14, 1789, by storming not only the Bastille prison, long a symbol of the *ancien régime* but also the munitions store.[3] The Prison Governor Bernard-René de Launay fired on the crowd but soon surrendered, allowing the crowd to pour in and release the prisoners – who turned out to number just seven. For graphic descriptions of the storming of the Bastille and the subsequent murder of de Launay, see Thomas Carlyle's *The French Revolution*, Contemporary Documents, **pp. 33–7**, and Dickens's *A Tale of Two Cities*, Key Passages, **pp. 139–43**.

Following the storming of the Bastille, the peasants in rural France set about their own revolution in a frenzied response that became known as the Great Fear. A general climate of suspicion, fostered by wandering vagrants, led to the burning and looting of châteaux in an attempt to overthrow the feudal aristocrats (see Key Passages, **pp. 146–8**). The National Assembly, in an impromptu all-night session on August 4–5, voted to abolish most of the feudal rights of the nobility; many of the members were noblemen themselves.[4] By the end of August they had adopted the Declaration of the Rights of Man, asserting the human rights of liberty, property, security, and resistance to oppression.[5] The Parisian crowd continued to take matters into their own hands, however, because they saw no improvement in their living conditions. Food prices were still very high and the hunger so vividly described in *A Tale of Two Cities* (see Key Passages, **p. 126**) was still the lot of the common people. When the King seemed reluctant to approve the National Assembly's decisions, a deputation of several thousand women marched to Versailles to confront him (see Fitzgerald, Contemporary Documents, **p. 46**). He and his family were brought back to Paris where they remained until their executions in 1793. The power of the crowd was once again demonstrated and would continue to influence the course of the Revolution.

By 1791, the National Assembly had removed most of the privileges of the Catholic Church and had adopted a constitution that created a parliamentary government with King Louis XVI as head of a hereditary monarchy. Under the constitution, all citizens were guaranteed equal rights. This constitutional monarchy did not suit the extremists on either side, however; many noblemen (*émigrés*) fled France (in *A Tale of Two Cities* they congregate at Tellson's Bank in London; see Book II, Chapter 24), and the more radical of the Revolutionaries (known as Jacobins) demanded further reforms. In 1792, France went to war

---

3   The lower-class Parisian Revolutionaries were known as *sans-culottes* (without breeches) because they wore trousers rather than aristocratic knee-breeches and hose. They included laborers, storekeepers, and artisans such as joiners and locksmiths.

4   See Dickens's letter to Edward Bulwer Lytton, Contemporary Documents, p. 48, for Dickens's comment on this session.

5   A leading member of the National Assembly was the Marquis de Lafayette, who had been a hero of the American Revolution and had brought many of the ideals of that democratic movement to France.

with Austria, who wished to restore the power of King Louis XVI. Again, the people of France rallied in defense of the gains they had made, and a patriotic movement swept the country, instituting the national anthem, the "Marseillaise," and the revolutionary slogan, "Liberty, Equality, and Fraternity." On August 10, the people overthrew King Louis XVI, who was forced to seek refuge in a prison. Under the leadership of Maximilien Robespierre, a lawyer and founder of the Jacobins, the Legislative Assembly (which had replaced the National Assembly) was replaced by an elected National Convention.

The militant side of the Revolutionaries continued to take the law into their own hands. On September 2, 1792, Jean-Paul Marat (1743–93) and others organized the brutal slaying of the inhabitants of the prisons of Paris – nobility, clergy, and criminals – fearing that they were involved in a counter-revolution, aided by France's enemies, the Prussians and Austrians, with whom they were at war. Over the three days of the "September Massacres," over 1,400 people were taken out of the prisons and murdered in the streets, a terrifying slaughter that Dickens graphically describes in the novel (see Key Passages, **pp. 148–9**).[6] Soon after, on September 21, 1792, King Louis XVI was officially deposed and the first French Republic declared. Tried and found guilty of treason for conspiring with émigrés to overturn the revolution, the King was executed on January 21, 1793 by a new (and supposedly more humane) method of punishing capital crimes: the guillotine.[7]

After the regicide, the French Revolution moved into its most infamous stage, the Reign of Terror. Government was now essentially in the hands of a new Committee of Public Safety controlled by Robespierre and other extremists, who searched out any supposed enemies of the Republic and sent them to the guillotine, from Queen Marie-Antoinette to innocent commoners such as Dickens's seamstress, who goes to the guillotine with Sydney Carton at the end of *A Tale of Two Cities* (see Key Passages, **pp. 161–2**). The "Law of Suspects," passed by the Convention in September 1793, gave a sweepingly broad definition of "enemy" and created a climate of fear and suspicion (Charles Darnay is arrested by this law in Book III, Chapter 7). Spies were everywhere, and no one could be trusted, an aspect of the Revolution that is central to Dickens's portrayal of events. The Reign of Terror swept through France, taking many thousands of lives, between September 1793 and July 1794, when Robespierre and his associates were guillotined in their turn. *A Tale of Two Cities* concludes during this violent time, the bloody conclusion to the first stage of the French Revolution.

6   The causes of the September Massacres are complex and have been the subject of much debate. See, for example, Simon Schama, *Citizens: A Chronicle of the French Revolution*, New York: Alfred A. Knopf, 1989, pp. 627–37. Schama concludes that the event of the September Massacres "more than almost any other exposed a central truth of the French Revolution: its dependence on organized killing to accomplish political ends" (p. 637).
7   Dr. Joseph-Ignace Guillotin (1738–1814), a member of the National Assembly, had recommended the institution of an Italian device that beheaded the condemned person quickly. Hanging was much more traumatic, for both spectator and victim alike. France had used the guillotine for several public executions that year, but it became identified with the "Terror" of 1793–4 in Paris.

# Dickens's Sources for his Portrayal of the French Revolution

In *A Tale of Two Cities*, Dickens's main purpose is to argue that injustice and deprivation irreparably damage the sufferers, transforming them into tyrants in their turn. In the last chapter he reminds us that the horrors we are now seeing being perpetrated by the Revolutionaries in the infamous Reign of Terror are the result of this long history of cruelty and neglect: "Crush humanity out of shape once more, under similar hammers, and it will twist itself into the same tortured forms. Sow the same seed of rapacious licence and oppression over again, and it will surely yield the same fruit according to its kind" (Key Passages, **p. 160**). In preparing to write his novel, Dickens went to historical sources that would inform him about the conditions under which the French working classes lived in the years preceding the Revolution and also the attitudes of the ruling classes at that time.

Contemporary reviewers such as Sir James Fitzjames Stephen were quick to find the novel's criticism of the aristocracy grossly overstated (see Early Critical Reception, **p. 64**), but Dickens claimed several contemporary sources as his authority for his condemnation. In 1848 he had defended the English working man's reform movement, known as Chartism,[8] by quoting the French historian Adolphe Thiers (1797–1877) on the subject of the widespread oppression of the French people (see Contemporary Documents, **pp. 40–1**). Other evidence was provided to him by Thomas Carlyle, whose history had depended upon literally hundreds of eye-witness accounts of France before and during the Revolution (see Contemporary Documents, **pp. 31–2**). Dickens joked about receiving "two cartloads"[9] of Carlyle's suggested books from the London Library, and later he told his friend John Forster that while he was writing the novel he "read no books but such as had the air of the time in them."[10] In his letter to Edward Bulwer Lytton (see Contemporary Documents, **pp. 48–9**), Dickens cites as his authorities the famous French philosopher Jean-Jacques Rousseau (1712–78; see Contemporary Documents, **pp. 30–1**) and a Parisian writer, Louis-Sébastien Mercier (1740–1814), both well-known commentators on pre-Revolutionary France. Dickens also read another of Carlyle's sources, *Travels in France during the Years 1787, 1788, and 1789*), a popular book by Arthur Young (1741–1820), an English agricultural theorist and clergyman. When it came to writing the historical scenes in the novel, however, Dickens turned to Carlyle's rendering of eye-witness accounts in *The French Revolution* rather than to the original sources for his inspiration (see Contemporary Documents, **pp. 31–7** and Key Passages, **pp. 139–43**).

8  The Chartist movement began in the late 1830s with the aim of peacefully bringing about more political reform than was accomplished by the First Reform Act of 1832. Its six-point charter demanding electoral reforms and signed by several million people was rejected by the House of Commons in 1839, 1842 and 1848, after which the movement died out. Five of their six demands were eventually realized by 1928. Dickens sympathized with the Chartists when their methods were peaceful, but he never approved of violent protest.
9  Charles Dickens the Younger, "Introduction," *A Tale of Two Cities*, London and New York: Macmillan, 1893, p. xx.
10 Letter to John Forster, in Storey, *Letters*, p. 245.

# The French Revolution and England

In writing about Revolutionary France, Carlyle and Dickens were struck by the similarities in attitude between the members of the *ancien régime* in France and the ruling classes of nineteenth-century England (see also Key Passages, **p. 116**). Rather than concentrating on specific examples of French feudal privilege, both writers were concerned to reveal the lofty arrogance and hypocritical insensitivity to the sufferings of the lower classes that marked the aristocracy of France in 1780 and England in 1850. While the Industrial Revolution was gradually improving the lives of the British people, and while political reform was even more gradually giving every person a voice, the living conditions of the urban poor were as appalling as those suffered by the peasantry and urban workers of pre-Revolutionary France. Overcrowding, disease, hunger, and long hours of work were the lot of most people, and the ruling classes appeared to be making little effort to address their problems. When the "People's Charter" (see above, n. 8) was presented to Parliament in 1838, 1842, and 1848, it was unceremoniously thrown out and their demands were met with condescension by many, much to Dickens's annoyance (see "Judicial Special Pleading," Contemporary Documents, **pp. 39–41**). Writing in 1855, Dickens suggested that the apparent lack of protest among the working classes following the collapse of the Chartist movement in 1848 was actually an "awful symptom of the advanced state of their disease." He went on:

> I believe the discontent to be so much the worse for smouldering instead of blazing openly, that it is extremely like the general mind of France before the breaking out of the first Revolution, and is in danger of being turned by any one of a thousand accidents – a bad harvest – the last straw too much of aristocratic insolence or incapacity – a defeat abroad – a mere chance at home – into such a Devil of a conflagration as has never been beheld since.

Like the aristocrats in Monseigneur's salon in Book II, Chapter 7 of *A Tale of Two Cities*, the English ruling classes were willfully oblivious of the plight of the poor:

> So, every day the disgusted millions with this unnatural gloom and calm upon them, are confirmed and hardened in the very worst of moods. Finally, round all this is an atmosphere of poverty, hunger, and ignorant desperation, of the mere existence of which, perhaps not one man in a thousand . . . has the least idea.[11]

The arrogant (and dangerous) blindness of the upper classes was also the subject of an essay on pre-Revolutionary Paris by Percy Fitzgerald, a young colleague of Dickens and contributor to his journal *Household Words* (see Contemporary Documents, **pp. 45–8**). If Dickens oversimplified the causes of the Revolution

11 Letter to A.H. Layard, in G. Storey, K. Tillotson and N. Burgis (eds) *The Letters of Charles Dickens*, vol. VII, Oxford: Clarendon Press, 1993, p. 587.

in the novel, it was partly because government inaction in the face of bread shortages, disease, and inadequate housing was a reality that he saw around him every day, and like many of his fellow Victorians, he both admired the French peasantry for demanding relief from their suffering and feared that their English counterparts might descend to the violence he depicted so vividly in *A Tale of Two Cities*.

## The Frozen Deep and Other Biographical Influences

The hero of *A Tale of Two Cities* is Sydney Carton, an English lawyer whose wasted life is redeemed when he gives it up to save the husband of the woman he loves. Carton was the embodiment of Dickens's personal identification with heroic action and self-sacrifice that developed at this time, partly in response to his growing dissatisfaction with his marriage (he had married Catherine Hogarth in 1836) and his deep restlessness and sense of emotional loss. This new concern with heroism was encouraged by his friendship with Wilkie Collins, a younger but rising fellow novelist who had joined the staff of Dickens's journals *Household Words* and *All the Year Round* and who had become a close collaborator with him. Dickens and Collins had written several short pieces for *Household Words* on the topic of heroism and male friendship, partly in response to the publicity surrounding the expedition of Sir John Franklin and his crew to find the North-west Passage across northern Canada, linking the Atlantic with the Orient. Franklin and the Scottish naturalist Sir John Richardson had twice explored the Arctic, and when Franklin's 1845 expedition did not return, Sir John Richardson commanded an unsuccessful search party in 1848–9. A later expedition brought back reports from natives that Franklin's crew had resorted to cannibalism before their deaths. Dickens and others were outraged that noble Englishmen could be accused of such a crime, and he defended them vehemently in *Household Words*.[12]

Central to Dickens's collaborations with Wilkie Collins and the plot of *A Tale of Two Cities* were accounts of the friendship between Sir John Franklin and Sir John Richardson. Dickens wrote of this friendship to John Forster in 1856: "Lady Franklin sent me the whole of that Richardson memoir; and I think Richardson's manly friendship, and love of Franklin, one of the noblest things I ever knew in my life. It makes one's heart beat high, with a sort of sacred joy."[13] Dickens and Collins turned this "manly friendship" into the 1856 Christmas number for *Household Words*, *The Wreck of the Golden Mary*, in which a captain and his mate take turns narrating the story of their heroic rescue from a shipwreck. The survival of the whole party depends upon the bravery of the captain (whose narrative was written by Dickens) and his loyal mate (written by Collins), who takes over command when the captain collapses. The story looked ahead to *A Tale of Two Cities* in the "manly friendship" of the heroic captain and mate, and a golden-haired heroine called Lucy, who acts as the spiritual guide.

12  "The Lost Arctic Voyagers" appeared in *Household Words* on December 2 and 9, 1854.
13  Letter to John Forster, in G. Storey and K. Tillotson (eds) *The Letters of Charles Dickens*, vol. VIII, Oxford: Clarendon Press, 1995, p. 66.

The following year, Dickens and Collins collaborated on the production of *The Frozen Deep*, a story of a lost Arctic expedition in which the Franklin–Richardson friendship was transformed into a rivalry over the love of one woman (see Contemporary Documents, **pp. 44–5**). Franklin's name was used for the open-hearted, noble Frank Aldersley, played by Wilkie Collins; Richardson became Richard Wardour, the unlikable, brooding, and passionately jealous suitor whose beloved Clara Burnham has turned her attention to the deserving Frank. Unknown to each other, the two men are on an Arctic expedition and are eventually stranded together, allowing Wardour to discover that his companion is the hated rival on whom he has long ago sworn to take revenge. He could easily leave Frank to die, fulfilling the dream that he has brooded over for months. But when the time comes, his innate heroism rises to the fore and he carries the dying Aldersley to safety at the expense of his own life. Dickens wrote to his friend Mary Boyle that he "terrified Aldersley to that degree by lungeing at him to carry him into the Cave, and the said Aldersley always shook like a mould of jelly, and muttered 'By G—this is an awful thing!' "[14] It was this experience, Dickens tells us in the Preface to *A Tale of Two Cities* (see Key Passages, **p. 115**), repeated night after night for a rapturous audience, that suggested Sydney Carton's sacrifice for his rival Charles Darnay in order to win the eternal gratitude of the woman they both love.

The Frozen Deep was performed by Dickens's family and friends at Tavistock House, his home in London, in January 1857, to a select audience that included the Dean of St. Paul's Cathedral and some esteemed members of parliament and the judiciary. It was so successful that the cast performed it privately for Queen Victoria in July and then staged several public performances with professional actresses taking the places of the amateur women (who had included Dickens's daughters). One of these professionals was Ellen Ternan, an eighteen-year-old actress with whom Dickens fell in love during the performances of the play. She played Lucy Crayford while her sister Maria took the lead role of Clara Burnham, the woman loved by two rivals who would become Lucie Manette in *A Tale of Two Cities*. As Maria Ternan's genuine tears streamed down on the dying Wardour, "new ideas for a story" came into Dickens's mind "with surprising force and brilliancy."[15] When the performances were over, he sank into "grim despair and restlessness,"[16] and by the following March (1858) he wrote to Wilkie Collins, "I can't write, and (waking) can't rest, one minute. I have never known a moment's peace or content, since the last night of the Frozen Deep."[17] Within a year he had left his wife and begun a clandestine affair with Ellen Ternan that was often pursued in France. Biographical critics speculate that in recreating the love triangle of *The Frozen Deep*, Dickens "split" his personality into the faultless Charles Darnay (who shares Dickens's first name and initials) and the scapegoat (but more interesting) Sydney Carton, whose sacrifice allows CD to win Lucy/Lucie.[18]

---

14 Letter to Mary Boyle, in Storey and Tillotson, *Letters*, p. 277.
15 Letter to Angela Burdett Coutts, in Storey and Tillotson, *Letters*, p. 432.
16 Letter to Wilkie Collins, in Storey and Tillotson, *Letters*, p. 423.
17 Letter to Wilkie Collins, in Storey and Tillotson, *Letters*, p. 536.
18 Lucie Manette's physical characteristics were based on Ellen. The most complete account of Dickens's relationship with Ellen Ternan is Claire Tomalin's *The Invisible Woman*, London: Viking, 1990. For a biographical reading of the novel see Leonard Manheim, "A Tale of Two

Richard Wardour, Dickens's role in *The Frozen Deep*, was a kind of Byronic hero, moody, strong in his passions, but revengeful, even murderous in his thoughts. Dickens complained to his friend John Forster in August 1856 that he was tired of making his heroes conform to Victorian standards of respectability, standards he felt were hypocritical, unrealistic, and limiting to art:

> I have always a fine feeling of the honest state into which we have got, when some smooth gentleman says to me or to some one else when I am by, how odd it is that the hero of an English book is always uninteresting—too good—not natural, &c. I am continually hearing this of Scott from English people here, who pass their lives with Balzac and Sand.[19] But O my smooth friend, what a shining impostor you must think yourself and what an ass you must think me, when you suppose that by putting a brazen face upon it you can blot out of my knowledge the fact that this same unnatural young gentleman (if to be decent is to be necessarily unnatural), whom you meet in those other books and in mine, *must* be presented to you in that unnatural aspect by reason of your morality, and is not to have, I will not say any of the indecencies you like, but not even any of the experiences, trials, perplexities, and confusions inseparable from the making or unmaking of all men![20]

While editing Collins's script, Dickens tempered Collins's portrayal of Richard Wardour to make him complex rather than coarse, capable of fine instincts that have been overwhelmed by disappointment and regret. Lillian Nayder notes that Dickens changed Collins's adjectives "surly" and "mad" to the more interesting "moody," and "rough" to "abrupt." He also removed references to Wardour's violent behaviour.[21] As in his portrayal of Sydney Carton, Dickens wished to emphasize the potential for noble action that had been wasted (the "frozen deep" referred to Wardour's buried better instincts as well as to the landscape). On the page, Richard Wardour does not rise above the melodrama in which he appears; only Dickens's acting could give him any sort of stature. But in Sydney Carton, Dickens expanded upon the possibilities of Richard Wardour to create a character who has since become the central interest of the novel for later film audiences and many readers (see The Novel in Performance, **pp. 102–3**). Dickens admitted to a friend that if he had been able to act the part of Carton he "could have done something with his life and death."[22]

Characters: A Study in Multiple Projection," *Dickens Studies Annual*, I (1970), pp. 225–37; reprinted in *Critical Essays on Charles Dickens's A Tale of Two Cities*, ed. Michael A. Cotsell, New York: G.K. Hall, 1998, pp. 61–73.

19  Sir Walter Scott (1771–1832) was a Scottish novelist and the most popular writer in England at the beginning of the nineteenth century. His novels were historical romances, very different from the more realistic studies of human nature in the novels of the French writers Honoré de Balzac (1799–1850) and George Sand (1804–76, pseudonym of Amandine-Aurore Lucille Dupin).

20  Forster, *The Life of Charles Dickens*, revised by A. J. Hoppé, London: J. M. Dent, 1966, II, 267.

21  *Unequal Partners: Charles Dickens, Wilkie Collins, and Victorian Authorship*, Ithaca, N.Y. and London: Cornell University Press, 2002, p. 94.

22  Letter to Mary Boyle, in G. Storey (ed.) *The Letters of Charles Dickens*, vol. IX, Oxford: Clarendon Press, 1997, p. 177.

# The French Revolution in Literature

In the seventy years that separated the fall of the Bastille (see Contextual Overview, **p. 10**) from *A Tale of Two Cities*, the French Revolution had become a rich source of material for plays and novels. In his 1847 visit to Paris, Dickens had been very moved by a production of a melodrama entitled *The French Revolution*, and he was particularly impressed by the "power and massiveness in the Mob, which is positively awful."[23] The destructive mindlessness of mob behaviour is central to *A Tale of Two Cities* also, not just in the storming of the Bastille and the events of the Reign of Terror, but also in the bloodthirsty attitudes of the English observers at Charles Darnay's trial for treason in London (Book II, Chapter 3) and at the mock funeral of Roger Cly, who testifies against Darnay and then fakes his own death to cover his activities as a spy. In accounts of the Revolution, the depiction of the Revolutionaries varied according to the point of view of the writer, but even those sympathetic to their cause usually found their violent methods inexcusable. After the overthrow of the Bastille, optimism that democracy was going to triumph gave way to fear and revulsion with the Reign of Terror and September Massacres. This shift in sympathy is evident in Dickens's account also (see Key Passages, **pp. 148–9**).

   *A Tale of Two Cities* has remained the best known and most universally popular literary work of the many plays and novels that retold the legends of the French Revolution. Stories of last-minute substitutions at the guillotine, of buried letters, and of prisoners growing old and grey within the walls of the Bastille were hugely popular in the years following 1789 and became common property. In November 1859, three weeks before *A Tale of Two Cities* concluded its run in *All the Year Round*, a strikingly similar play appeared on the London stage. *The Dead Heart*, by an Irish playwright, Watts Phillips, told the story of Robert Landry, imprisoned in the Bastille by a cruel aristocrat who has also abducted his fiancée. Like Dickens's Doctor Manette, who is similarly imprisoned by an aristocrat, Landry is released after eighteen years and goes on to orchestrate the death of his fiancée's son because of her apparent betrayal. When at the last minute he learns of his mistake, he has no option but to die in the boy's place, just as Sydney Carton substitutes himself for Charles Darnay at the guillotine. The similarities between the two works were recognized at once (Phillips even used Dickens's phrases "buried alive" and "recalled to life") but it was impossible to say who had plagiarized from whom, if indeed either writer had been influenced by the other. At the time, the newspapers accused Phillips of the theft, but later commentators have argued that Dickens may have heard the play read as early as March 1857.[24]

   The most likely explanation is that both writers drew upon the wealth of literary works in English and French about the French Revolution. An English novel, *Zanoni* (1842), by Dickens's friend Edward Bulwer Lytton (see Contemporary Documents, **p. 48**), concluded with a substitution at the guillotine, as did a play,

---

23  Letter to the Revd Edward Tagart, in G. Storey and K. Fielding (eds) *The Letters of Charles Dickens*, vol. V, Oxford: Clarendon Press, 1980, p. 20.
24  The most complete account of this issue is found in Carl R. Dolmetsch, "Dickens and *The Dead Heart*," *Dickensian*, 55 (1959), pp. 179–87.

*Le Chevalier de Maison Rouge*, by the famous French writer Alexandre Dumas (1802–70), which was produced in London in 1853. In the 1850s and 1860s the London stage was awash with self-sacrificing Revolutionary heroes. *A Tale of Two Cities* alone appeared on the boards in three different versions (see "The Novel in Performance" p. 103). All of these fictional sacrifices could have been based on the factual case reported by Carlyle in *The French Revolution* of Lieutenant-General Loiserolles's answering the death-list in place of his son, who was asleep.[25] This anecdote is the most likely source of Dickens's transference of Richard Wardour's sacrifice for Frank Aldersley from the frozen Arctic to the streets of Paris.

## Prisons and Prisoners

When Dickens suggested "Buried Alive" as a possible title for his new novel, he asked his friend John Forster if it seemed "too grim?"[26] As early as July 1846 he had considered writing a story based on a man's long imprisonment. He wrote to Forster that "good Christmas characters might be grown out of the idea of a man imprisoned for ten or fifteen years: his imprisonment being the gap between the people and circumstances of the first part and the altered people and circumstances of the second, and his own changed mind."[27] By "Christmas characters" Dickens meant people like Scrooge in *A Christmas Carol* who undergo a change of heart from cynical or doubting isolation to renewed faith in the value of human experience and striving. Sydney Carton is such a character, but so too is Doctor Manette, "buried alive" for eighteen years in the Bastille but "recalled to life" by his daughter Lucie's love.

Dickens's understanding of the effects of long imprisonment was partly the result of his lifelong interest in prisons, inspired by his early experience of his father's incarceration in the Marshalsea Prison for debt (a common occurrence in the nineteenth century) and his own "imprisonment" in Warren's Blacking Factory at that time. A sensitive child of twelve, he was suddenly deprived of his regular activities and schooling and made to work long days pasting labels onto bottles of shoe blacking (and observed by curious passersby in the street, just as Ernest Defarge charges the Revolutionaries to watch Doctor Manette at work above the wine-shop in Book I, Chapter 5). Doctor Manette's later, painful mental lapses back to his Bastille days were something Dickens too understood. Much as he tried to blot out the memory of the blacking-factory days, they would suddenly reappear, especially in times of stress. He told John Forster that in 1857 (the year he acted in *The Frozen Deep*, met Ellen Ternan, and thought of *A Tale of Two Cities*), he found himself dwelling upon that time. Forster recalls that in June 1862, Dickens wrote to him:

25 *The French Revolution*, Vol. II, p. 412; The Penguin edition of *A Tale of Two Cities* (2000) has an excellent appendix with extracts from some of these literary substitutions.
26 Storey and Tillotson, *Letters*, vol. VIII, p. 531.
27 Letter to John Forster in K. Tillotson (ed.) *The Letters of Charles Dickens*, Vol. IV, Oxford: Clarendon Press, 1977, p. 590.

I must entreat you, to pause for an instant, and go back to what you know of my childish days, and to ask yourself whether it is natural that something of the character formed in me then, and lost under happier circumstances, should have reappeared in the last five years. The never-to-be-forgotten misery of that old time bred a certain shrinking sensitiveness in a certain ill-clad, ill-fed child, that I have found come back in the never-to-be-forgotten misery of this later time.[28]

As a child, Dickens would also have been familiar with the gory "Chamber of Horrors" at Madame Tussaud's waxwork museum in London. On display there, among the terrifying images of the French Revolution, he would have seen a grey-bearded Bastille prisoner, surrounded by rats (see Contemporary Documents, **p. 41**). He had more recent evidence of the destructive effects of incarceration as a result of his visit to the Eastern Penitentiary in Philadelphia during his 1842 tour of America (see Contemporary Documents, **pp. 37–9**). What was particularly disturbing about this prison was its solitary system, a punishment intended to reform by isolating each prisoner entirely for the duration of his or her sentence. Left alone with only their conscience, prisoners could not be influenced by the bad example of their fellow inmates. Dickens recognized that this system inflicted such deep psychic wounds that the prisoners could never be reintegrated into the community. Like Doctor Manette, these solitary prisoners held on to what shreds of sanity they had by working at handwork such as shoemaking and weaving.

For the portrayal of Doctor Manette, Dickens was also able to draw on popular accounts of long-term incarceration during the French Revolution, stories he had known since childhood (see Contemporary Documents, **p. 41**). As well as the anecdote of the Bastille prisoner Quéret Démery that appears in *The French Revolution* (see Contemporary Documents, **p. 37**), Carlyle also referred Dickens to Honoré de Riouffe's *Mémoires sur les Prisons* (1823), which gave him many of the details he needed to describe La Force and the Conciergerie, the Parisian prisons in which Charles Darnay is held. Richard Maxwell's edition of *A Tale of Two Cities* provides extracts from two other Bastille memoirs with which Dickens would have been familiar: Simon-Nicolas-Henri Linguet's *Mémoires sur la Bastille, et la détention de l'auteur dans ce château royal, depuis le 27 septembre 1780 jusq'au 19 mai 1782* (1783; reprinted 1875) and Henri Masers de Latude, *Le Despotisme dévoilé, ou mémoires de Henri Masers de Latude, détenu pendant trente-cinq ans dans diverses prisons d'état* (1790). Latude describes making ink with his blood, as Doctor Manette does, but Maxwell suggests that much of Latude's memoir is romantic fiction, "half Don Quixote, half Robinson Crusoe."[29] Dickens would also have read Alexandre Dumas's *The Count of Monte Cristo* (1844–5), in which a prisoner describes writing a memoir in blood.

The trauma of imprisonment is a favourite motif in Western literature because incarceration was, for centuries, the usual punishment for being on the wrong side of those in power. In these accounts, the released prisoners usually do not

28  Letter to John Forster, in G. Storey (ed.) *The Letters of Charles Dickens*, Vol. X, Oxford: Clarendon Press, 1998, pp. 97–8.
29  *A Tale of Two Cities*, ed. Richard Maxwell, London: Penguin, 2000, pp. 417–23.

welcome their freedom at all; in fact they are reluctant to leave the cell that has separated them from friends and family for so long. In Lord Byron's poem "Prisoner of Chillon" (1816), for example, the hero is so inured to his cell that he cannot bear to be torn from his "hermitage" and his spider friends. The Bastille prisoner that haunted Dickens's childhood (see Contemporary Documents, p. 41) is such a figure, and in his 1841 historical novel, *Barnaby Rudge*, he writes that many of the prisoners released from Newgate Prison in London are "drawn back to their old place of captivity by some indescribable attraction" (Book II, Chapter 9). The Philadelphia prisoners are similarly fearsome, and Dickens closes his essay with the startling story of a voluntary inmate (wishing to cure himself of alcoholism) who, when suddenly faced with an open gate and freedom, "with the involuntary instinct of a prisoner" turns his back on the sunlit fields (see Contemporary Documents, pp. 37–9).

One of the most moving accounts of a released Bastille prisoner is found in Louis-Sébastien Mercier's *Tableau de Paris* (1781–8). Finding his family and friends all dead long since, or moved away, this prisoner of forty-seven years enters a world much more lonely than his isolated cell and begs to be returned to his cell in the Bastille.[30] Doctor Manette, too, is unsure if he wants to be "recalled to life." Only his daughter and her resemblance to his dead wife can lure him out of his living tomb, and his mental lapses, when he thinks himself back in the Bastille, reveal the captive's mind that lies just beneath the surface of his fragile sanity. Like the Philadelphia prisoner who begs, "give me some work to do, or I shall go raving mad!",[31] Doctor Manette continues to seek the reassurance of his shoemaker's bench.

Following the Chronology of Dickens's life and times, readers will find extracts from some of the contemporary documents discussed above that are important to an understanding of Dickens's composition of *A Tale of Two Cities*. Readers wishing to know more about the French Revolution will find a listing of recommended books in the Further Reading section of this sourcebook (pp. 167–70).

---

30   Richard Maxwell extracts this passage in the Penguin edition (2000), pp. 415–17.
31   Dickens, "Philadelphia, and its Solitary Prison," *American Notes for General Circulation* (London: Chapman & Hall, 1842).

# Chronology

Bullet points indicate events in Dickens's life; asterisks refer to selected historical and literary events.

**1810**
- CD's sister Frances (Fanny) born

**1812**
- CD born February 7 in Portsmouth, second child of John and Elizabeth Dickens; of six following brothers and sisters, four survive
- Napoleon invades Russia; England and America at war

**1813**
- Family moves to Southsea
- Jane Austen, *Pride and Prejudice*

**1815**
- Family moves to London
- Napoleon defeated at the Battle of Waterloo; restoration of the Bourbon monarchy in France; Corn Laws passed (restricting the import of grain to Britain)

**1816**
- CD's sister Letitia born (died 1893)
- Jane Austen, *Emma*

**1817**
- Family moves to Chatham, Kent
- Jane Austen dies

**1819**
- Peterloo Massacre (violent break-up of a large meeting of working-class reformers in St. Peter's Fields, Manchester led to the passing of the repressive Six Acts to curtail radical movements); George Eliot (Mary Ann Evans) born; Walter Scott, *Ivanhoe*

**1820**

• CD's brother Frederick born
* Death of King George III; accession of George IV

**1821**

• CD begins school with William Giles, favourite school teacher; neighbour is Lucy Stroughill, a possible influence on Lucie Manette in *A Tale of Two Cities*
* Keats dies; Greek War of Independence

**1822**

• CD's brother Alfred born; family moves to London in financial difficulties; CD's education interrupted
* Percy Bysshe Shelley drowns in Italy

**1823**

• CD's sister Fanny enrolls at Royal Academy of Music
* Death penalty abolished for many crimes in Britain

**1824**

• CD's father imprisoned three months in the Marshalsea Prison for debt; CD employed in Warren's Blacking Factory; lodges away from family; father released May 28
* Lord Byron dies

**1825**

• CD leaves Warren's and enrolls at Wellington House Academy
* Opening of first passenger railway in UK (Stephenson's "Rocket")

**1826**

• CD's father works as parliamentary correspondent for *The British Press*

**1827**

• Family evicted for non-payment of rates; CD leaves school and starts work as a solicitor's clerk; brother Augustus born
* Battle of Navarino; British, French, and Russian fleets destroy Turkish fleet; Ludwig van Beethoven and William Blake die

**1828**

• CD's father works as reporter for *The Morning Herald*
* Greek independence declared

**1829**

• CD learns shorthand and works as freelance reporter at Doctors' Commons
* Robert Peel establishes Metropolitan Police in London; Catholic Emancipation Act (allowed Catholics to hold public office)

**1830**
- CD studies independently at the British Museum library; falls in love with Maria Beadnell
* George IV dies; accession of William IV; "July Revolution" in France and accession of Louis-Philippe

**1831**
- CD begins work as a reporter for *The Mirror of Parliament*
* Victor Hugo, *Notre Dame de Paris*

**1832**
- CD considers an acting career but misses the audition due to a bad cold; moves to *The Sun* as a parliamentary reporter
* First Reform Bill passed, extending vote to owners or renters of property worth £10 per year

**1833**
- CD's first story, "A Dinner at Poplar Walk" (later renamed "Mr Minns and His Cousin"), published in *The Monthly Magazine*; ends relationship with Maria Beadnell
* First steamship crossing of the Atlantic; slavery abolished in the British Empire; Thomas Carlyle, *Sartor Resartus*

**1834**
- CD moves to *The Morning Chronicle* as a reporter; publishes twelve sketches and stories; meets Catherine Hogarth, daughter of George Hogarth, editor of the *Evening Chronicle*
* Poor Law Amendment Act (establishes workhouses); Samuel Taylor Coleridge dies

**1835**
- CD becomes engaged to Catherine Hogarth; publishes thirty-two stories and sketches

**1836**
- CD marries Catherine Hogarth, April 2; leaves staff of *Morning Chronicle*; publishes several more stories and sketches; first collection of previously published stories and sketches appears as *Sketches by Boz* in February; *Pickwick Papers* begins publishing in monthly numbers (March 31); *Sketches by Boz, Second Series* appears December 17; two plays, *The Strange Gentleman* and *Village Coquettes*, produced in London
* Chartist Movement begins (see Contextual Overview, **p. 12**)

**1837**
- Charles Jr. (Charley), born, first of ten children; *Pickwick Papers* concludes; sister-in-law Mary Hogarth dies unexpectedly in Dickens's house (48 Doughty Street, London; now the Dickens House Museum); CD becomes editor of *Bentley's Miscellany* and begins *Oliver Twist* for monthly publication in the journal

\*    King William IV dies; accession of Queen Victoria; Thomas Carlyle, *The French Revolution*

**1838**

• CD begins *Nicholas Nickleby* in monthly parts for Chapman & Hall; *Oliver Twist* concludes; daughter Mary ("Mamie") born in March

\*    Anti-Corn Law League founded (to protest duties on imported foodstuffs); the Working Men's Association publishes the People's Charter demanding six electoral reforms

**1839**

• CD resigns from *Bentley's Miscellany*; *Nicholas Nickleby* concludes in October; second daughter, Kate, born in October; family moves to 1 Devonshire Place

\*    First Opium War between Britain and China leads to Britain acquiring Hong Kong

**1840**

• CD begins a weekly journal, *Master Humphrey's Clock*, for Chapman & Hall; *The Old Curiosity Shop* serialized in it over forty weeks

\*    Queen Victoria marries Albert; introduction of the penny post

**1841**

• *Barnaby Rudge* runs in *Master Humphrey's Clock*; fourth child, Walter, born

\*    Robert Peel succeeds Melbourne as prime minister; Thomas Carlyle, *On Heroes and Hero Worship*

**1842**

• CD tours North America with Catherine, January to June; visits the Eastern Penitentiary in Philadelphia; *American Notes* published in October; *Martin Chuzzlewit* begins in monthly parts

\*    Second Chartist petition rejected

**1843**

• *A Christmas Carol* published in December

\*    Thomas Carlyle, *Past and Present*

**1844**

• CD quarrels with Chapman & Hall and moves to publishers Bradbury & Evans; *Martin Chuzzlewit* concludes; family moves to Italy; *The Chimes* (Christmas book) published in December; Dickens returns to London briefly to read it to friends, including Thomas Carlyle; fifth child, Francis, born

**1845**

• CD and family return to England in July; sixth child, Alfred, born; Christmas book *The Cricket on the Hearth* published in December; CD involved in amateur theatricals

1846
- CD briefly editor of *The Daily News;* lives in Switzerland for five months, and then in Paris; *Pictures from Italy* published in May; begins *Dombey and Son* in monthly parts; writes an account of Christ's life for his children (first published in 1934 as *The Life of our Lord*); Christmas book *The Battle of Life* published in December
* Repeal of the Corn Laws

1847
- While in Paris, CD visits the sites of the French Revolution; returns to England in February; seventh child, Sydney, born; helps Angela Burdett Coutts, a wealthy philanthropist, establish Urania Cottage, a home for fallen women; works closely with the home for the next ten years
* First Californian gold rush; Factory Act improves working conditions for women and children; Charlotte Brontë, *Jane Eyre*; Emily Brontë, *Wuthering Heights*; William Makepeace Thackeray's *Vanity Fair* begins publishing in monthly parts

1848
- *Dombey and Son* concludes in April; Christmas book *The Haunted Man* published in December; sister Fanny dies
* Outbreak of revolutions in Europe; Louis-Philippe abdicates; Second French Republic proclaimed; cholera epidemic in London; end of the Chartist movement; Elizabeth Gaskell, *Mary Barton*; William Makepeace Thackeray's *Pendennis* begins publishing in monthly parts

1849
- *David Copperfield* begins in monthly parts; eighth child, Henry, born;
* Charlotte Brontë, *Shirley*

1850
- CD establishes a new journal, *Household Words; David Copperfield* concludes; third daughter, Dora, born; with Edward Bulwer Lytton, CD establishes the Guild of Literature and Art to benefit struggling writers and artists
* Wordsworth dies and Alfred Tennyson succeeds him as poet laureate; Tennyson's "In Memoriam" and Wordsworth's "The Prelude" published

1851
- Visits Paris; *A Child's History of England* begins in *Household Words*; Dora and John Dickens (CD's father) die; family moves to Tavistock House; amateur theatricals
* The Great Exhibition in London

1852
- *Bleak House* begins in monthly parts; tenth child, Edward ("Plorn"), born; first family holiday in Boulogne
* Duke of Wellington dies; William Makepeace Thackeray, *Henry Esmond*

**1853**

- CD tours Italy and Switzerland with Wilkie Collins and Augustus Egg; *Bleak House* and *A Child's History of England* conclude; first charity reading of *A Christmas Carol*; summer holiday in Boulogne
* Outbreak of cholera; Charlotte Brontë, *Villette*; William Makepeace Thackeray, *The Newcomes*

**1854**

- *Hard Times* serialized weekly in *Household Words*; summer holiday in Boulogne
* Outbreak of Crimean war; Elizabeth Gaskell, *North and South*, serialized in *Household Words*

**1855**

- *Little Dorrit* begins in monthly parts; CD directs and acts in Wilkie Collins's play *The Lighthouse*; Dickens family lives in Paris from October
* Palmerston succeeds Aberdeen as prime minister; Anthony Trollope, *The Warden*

**1856**

- CD buys Gad's Hill Place, Kent; returns from France; collaborates on *The Wreck of the Golden Mary* for the *Household Words* Christmas number
* Crimean War ends

**1857**

- CD collaborates with Wilkie Collins on *The Frozen Deep* and plays the lead role; Meets Ellen Ternan; *Little Dorrit* concludes; walking tour of the Lake District with Wilkie Collins results in *The Lazy Tour of Two Idle Apprentices* for *Household Words*; collaborates with Wilkie Collins on *The Perils of Certain English Prisoners* for the *Household Words* Christmas number
* Indian Mutiny; Thomas Hughes, *Tom Brown's Schooldays*; Anthony Trollope, *Barchester Towers*; Elizabeth Barrett Browning, *Aurora Leigh*; Charlotte Brontë, *The Professor*

**1858**

- CD gives first series of for-profit public readings in London, other English cities, Ireland, and Scotland; separates from Catherine; brother Augustus dies
* Abolition of the East India Company and end of the Indian Mutiny; Thomas Carlyle, *Frederick the Great*

**1859**

- CD quarrels with Bradbury & Evans and returns to Chapman & Hall; establishes new weekly journal *All the Year Round*; *A Tale of Two Cities* serialized in it (April 30 to November 26); second provincial reading tour
* Darwin, *On the Origin of Species*; Karl Marx, *Critique of Political Economy*; George Eliot, *Adam Bede*; Samuel Smiles, *Self-Help*; Alfred Tennyson, *Idylls of the King*

1860
- *The Uncommercial Traveller* serialized in *All the Year Round* followed by *Great Expectations*; brother Alfred dies
- * Wilkie Collins, *The Woman in White* (in *All the Year Round*); George Eliot, *The Mill on the Floss*

1861
- *Great Expectations* concludes in August; public readings in London and the provinces
- * Prince Albert dies; American Civil War; George Eliot, *Silas Marner*

1862
- CD gives public readings in London
- * Victor Hugo, *Les Misérables*; John Ruskin, *Unto this Last*

1863
- Elizabeth Dickens (CD's mother) dies; Walter, CD's fourth child, dies in India; CD gives charity readings in Paris
- * William Makepeace Thackeray dies

1864
- *Our Mutual Friend* begins in monthly parts
- * John Henry Newman, *Apologia pro vita sua*; Leo Tolstoy's *War and Peace*

1865
- *Our Mutual Friend* concludes; CD and Ellen Ternan are involved in a train derailment at Staplehurst, Kent, returning from Paris, June 9; *The Uncommercial Traveller* (second series)
- * President Lincoln assassinated; Elizabeth Gaskell dies; Lewis Carroll, *Alice in Wonderland*

1866
- CD gives public readings in London and the provinces
- * Fyodor Dostoevsky, *Crime and Punishment*; George Eliot, *Felix Holt*

1867
- CD gives reading tour of England, Ireland, and America; collaborates with Wilkie Collins on *No Thoroughfare* for *All the Year Round* Christmas number
- * Henrik Ibsen, *Peer Gynt*; Karl Marx, *Das Kapital*, Vol. I

1868
- CD begins farewell reading tour in England; "George Silverman's Explanation" and "Holiday Romance" (short stories) published in America; CD's brother Frederick dies.
- * Wilkie Collins, *The Moonstone*; Fyodor Dostoevsky, *The Idiot*; Louisa May Alcott, *Little Women*

1869
- CD's reading tour curtailed due to failing health
* Suez Canal opened; Matthew Arnold, *Culture and Anarchy*; John Stuart Mill, *On the Subjection of Women*

1870
- CD begins *The Mystery of Edwin Drood* in April; twelve public readings in London; CD dies at Gad's Hill on June 9; Buried in Westminster Abbey, June 14
* Franco-Prussian War; end of the Second French Empire; establishment of Third Republic

# A TALE

## OF

# TWO CITIES,

### BY

## CHARLES DICKENS.

*Figure 1*  **Vignette from the original title page, by Hablot Knight Browne; Doctor Manette in his Bastille Cell.**

# Contemporary Documents

From **Jean-Jacques Rousseau, *Confessions*** (1781–8), ed. Patrick Coleman, trans. Angela Scholar (Oxford: Oxford University Press, 2000), pp. 159–60

The radical ideas of the French philosopher Jean-Jacques Rousseau (1712–78) were enormously influential in nineteenth-century Europe. Rousseau argued that civilization corrupted the naturally good man, and that children were best educated in natural surroundings. (For Rousseau's views of women see Robson, Modern Criticism, **p. 100**.) His support of equality and universal justice made him popular with the proponents of the French Revolution, and Dickens found in the following passage from Rousseau's autobiography (published post-humously) an example of the economic oppression of the poor by the ruling classes in pre-Revolutionary France. Dickens slightly alters Rousseau's account when he incorporates it into the document Doctor Manette writes while imprisoned in the Bastille (*A Tale of Two Cities*, Book III, Chapter 10). Recalling the events he witnessed at the Evrémonde château, Doctor Manette writes that the peasant boy (Madame Defarge's brother) told him how his family had to barricade their house so that the Evrémonde "people" would not take away their "bit of meat." But Rousseau's lifelong sympathy with the generous peasant described in this passage, forced like thousands of others to live in fear and deprivation because of unjust taxes (see Contextual Overview, **p. 8**), was shared by Dickens in his portrayal of the Revolution as the inevitable overthrow of corruption and privilege by a hardworking and miserable peasantry. Dickens acknowledged his debt to Rousseau in his letter to Edward Bulwer Lytton (see Contemporary Documents, **pp. 48–9**). Rousseau's encounter with the peasant occurred in 1731, as he returned on foot to Lyons from Paris. He wrote of it with the same sense of resentment and pity forty years later.

One day, having left the path on purpose to explore a place that had seemed delightful from afar, I liked it so well and roamed about for so long that at length I became completely lost. After several hours of fruitless wandering, weary and dying of hunger and thirst, I stopped at a cottage belonging to a peasant, which did not look very inviting but which was the only one I could see round about. I thought it would be as in Geneva and Switzerland, where all the inhabitants who are comfortably off are in a position to offer hospitality. I asked him if I could pay for some dinner. He offered me skimmed milk and coarse barley-bread, saying that it was all he had. I drank the milk with enjoyment and I ate the bread, husks and all; but it was not enough to restore a man worn out with fatigue. The peasant, who was watching me closely, no doubt judged the truth of my story from the size of my appetite; for, saying that he could see[1] very well that I was a kind and good young man, who would not give him away, he opened a little trapdoor just outside his kitchen, disappeared, and returned a minute later with some good brown bread made from pure wheat, a piece of ham which, although already broached, looked appetizing, and a bottle of wine, the sight of which rejoiced my heart more than all the rest. To this he added a thick omelette, and I enjoyed a dinner such as only a walker can ever have known. When it was time to pay, he was again seized with worry and anxiety; he would have nothing to do with my money; he refused it with a display of extraordinary distress; the entertaining part about it was that I could not begin to imagine what there was to be afraid of. At length, trembling, he uttered the terrible words "excisemen" and "cellar-rats".[2] He gave me to understand that he was hiding his wine because of the excise duty, and that he was hiding his bread because of the tax, and that he was a lost man if anyone should suspect that he was not dying of hunger. Everything he said on this subject, of which I had previously not had the least idea, made an impression on me so profound as never to be erased. Here was the germ of that inextinguishable hatred which has since grown up in my heart against the vexations endured by the wretched populace and against their oppressors. This man, although comfortably off, dared not eat the bread he had won with the sweat of his brow, and could only avoid ruin by displaying the same misery as prevailed all around him. I left his house full of compassion and indignation, and deploring the fate of those delightful regions upon whom nature has lavished gifts only in order that they may become a prey to barbarous publicans.[3]

From **Thomas Carlyle, The French Revolution** (1837), ed. K. J. Fielding and David Sorensen (Oxford: Oxford University Press, 1989), Vol. I, Book 5, pp. 198–208

The Scottish writer Thomas Carlyle (1795–1881) was one of the most powerful critics of the leading political ideas of his day. From his home in Chelsea, London, he earned the title of "The Sage of Chelsea" for his prophetic and

1  [Rousseau's note.] Apparently I had not yet acquired the physiognomy they have since given me in my portraits.
2  No one was more hated than the army of tax collectors hired by the crown and the landowners to collect the assorted taxes levied on grain, wine, salt, and other essentials. They were "cellar-rats" presumably because they would search the peasants' cellars for hidden goods. The *fermiers-généraux*, or farmers-general, was a group of speculators who bought the right to collect taxes for a fixed sum. See *A Tale of Two Cities*, Book II, Chapter 7, for Dickens's attack on the wealth and corruption of the farmers-general.
3  Tax collector.

searching analyses of industrialism and its disastrous effects on the working poor of nineteenth-century England. Dickens shared Carlyle's belief that laissez-faire economics and statistical, utilitarian attitudes to human affairs[1] denied the spiritual and emotional core of human nature; mutual trust and obligation between classes was being replaced by the "cash-nexus," a purely monetary exchange that isolated workers and bosses alike in a mechanical system of profit and a factory dominated by machines. In his most polemical works – *A Christmas Carol* (1843), *The Chimes* (1844), *Hard Times* (1854), and *A Tale of Two Cities* – Dickens sought the approval of the older writer, and generally received it. He dedicated *Hard Times* to Carlyle. In the preface to *A Tale of Two Cities* Dickens acknowledges his debt to Carlyle's *The French Revolution* (see Key Passages **p. 115**), a book which he carried about with him for years and knew almost by heart. Carlyle wrote in an idiosyncratic, rhetorical style that is often called "Carlylese." His intention was to wake up his complacent (and often hypocritical) fellow Britons to an awareness of the conditions under which the working poor lived and died. In Dickens's novels, Carlyle's authoritative voice can often be heard condemning the indifferent ruling classes for allowing such misery to happen in a so-called Christian land. Carlyle's language is often biblical (he was raised in a Calvinistic rural family), but it also reflects his knowledge of classical and modern languages, especially German, because he was strongly influenced by the German Romantic writers of the time. (See Fitzgerald, Contemporary Documents, **pp. 45–8**, for a contemporary response to Carlyle's book.) In the following passages from Volume I, Book 5 of *The French Revolution* we can see that Dickens had Carlyle's text at his elbow (or perhaps ringing in his mind) as he wrote about the fall of the Bastille and the killing of De Launay (see Key Passages, **pp. 139–43**). In Carlyle's account we find the same rhetorical style – choppy, abrupt, breathless sentences, intended to convey the urgency and drama of the scene – and many details of the event. Claude Cholat the wine merchant becomes, in *A Tale of Two Cities*, Ernest Defarge, at the centre of a personified Saint-Antoine, a poor and densely populated district surrounding the Bastille. The dominant metaphor is of a surging sea of people caught up in a whirlpool. And in Carlyle's miserable Bastille prisoner, Quéret-Démery, we can see the germ of Dickens's Alexandre Manette. For more information on Dickens's debt to Carlyle see the Contextual Overview (**p. 12**). See also the Contextual Overview, **pp. 7–11**, for an historical summary of the French Revolution. For commentary on Dickens's debt to Carlyle see McWilliams, Jr. Modern Criticism, **pp. 79–82**. In the following extracts, Carlyle's footnotes identifying his sources are not included.

---

1   Laissez-faire, a French term meaning "let do," means lack of government regulation. In the early days of industrialism it meant that the markets determined wages and prices, often to the detriment of the working class. Jeremy Bentham (1748–1832), the leading proponent of utilitarianism, argued that all human relations could be given a quantifiable value, and that the greatest happiness of the greatest number was the measure of right and wrong.

## From Chapter 6 "Storm and Victory"

All morning, since nine, there has been a cry everywhere: To the Bastille! Repeated "deputations of citizens"[2] have been here, passionate for arms; whom De Launay[3] has got dismissed by soft speeches through port-holes. Towards noon, Elector Thuriot de la Rosière[4] gains admittance; finds De Launay indisposed for surrender; nay disposed for blowing up the place rather. Thuriot mounts with him to the battlements: heaps of paving-stones, old iron and missiles lie piled; cannon all duly levelled; in every embrasure a cannon,—only drawn back a little! But outwards, behold, O Thuriot, how the multitude flows on, welling through every street: tocsin[5] furiously pealing, all drums beating the *générale*:[6] the Suburb Saint-Antoine rolling hitherward wholly, as one man! Such vision (spectral yet real) thou, O Thuriot, as from thy Mount of Vision,[7] beholdest in this moment: prophetic of what other Phantasmagories, and loud-gibbering Spectral Realities, which thou yet beholdest not, but shalt! "*Que voulez-vous?*"[8] said De Launay, turning pale at the sight, with an air of reproach, almost of menace. "Monsieur," said Thuriot, rising into the moral-sublime,[9] "what mean *you*? Consider if I could not precipitate *both* of us from this height",—say only a hundred feet, exclusive of the walled ditch! Whereupon De Launay fell silent. Thuriot shows himself from some pinnacle, to comfort the multitude becoming suspicious, fremescent:[10] then descends; departs with protest; with warning addressed also to the Invalides,[11]—on whom, however, it produces but a mixed indistinct impression. The old heads are none of the clearest; besides, it is said, De Launay has been profuse of beverages (*prodigua des buissons*). They think, they will not fire,—if not fired on, if they can help it; but must, on the whole, be ruled considerably by circumstances.

Woe to thee, De Launay, in such an hour, if thou canst not, taking some one firm decision, *rule* circumstances! Soft speeches will not serve; hard grape shot is questionable; but hovering between the two is *un*questionable. Ever wilder swells the tide of men; their infinite hum waxing ever louder, into imprecations, perhaps into

---

2  Most of the crowd that stormed the Bastille were artisans living in the Saint Antoine district of Paris. Fearing that the King had sent troops to quell them and that the guns on the top of the Bastille were trained on them, they went to the prison, hoping to take over the gunpowder that had been moved there.

3  Bernard-René Jordan de Launay (1740–89), Governor of the Bastille Prison. When faced with the angry mob he hoped to turn them back by threatening to blow up the prison (and its surroundings).

4  Jacques Alexis Thuriot de la Rosière (1753–1829), one of the elected deputies in the new National Assembly, was called in to demand of de Launay that the guns and powder be handed over to the Paris militia, but de Launay felt he could do nothing without the permission of the King.

5  Alarm bell.

6  A call to arms sounded on drums and trumpets.

7  Thuriot went up on the battlements with de Launay to see that the guns were withdrawn, but de Launay maintained that the guns were not trained on the mob. Carlyle is referring to Thuriot's vision of the coming Revolution, and possibly to "La Montagne" (The Mountain), the term given to the Revolutionaries in the National Assembly, so called because they occupied the highest benches on the left.

8  What do you want?

9  Continuing the mountain metaphor, Carlyle refers to Thuriot's moral high ground as "sublime," a word used at the time to denote uplifting mountain scenery.

10  Muttering or growling with impatience; a word more commonly used in French.

11  Retired soldiers or veterans. According to Simon Schama, de Launay had eighty-two *invalides* in the Bastille to help defend the gunpowder. See *Citizens: A Chronicle of the French Revolution*, New York: Alfred A. Knopf, 1989, pp. 399–400.

crackle of stray musketry,—which latter, on walls nine feet thick, cannot do exe-cution. The Outer Drawbridge[12] has been lowered for Thuriot; new *deputation of citizens* (it is the third, and noisiest of all) penetrates that way into the Outer Court: soft speeches producing no clearance of these, De Launay gives fire; pulls up his Drawbridge. A slight sputter;—which has *kindled* the too combustible chaos; made it a roaring fire-chaos! Bursts forth Insurrection, at sight of its own blood (for there were deaths by that sputter of fire), into endless rolling explosion of musketry, distraction, execration;—and overhead, from the Fortress, let one great gun, with its grape shot, go booming, to show what we *could* do. The Bastille is besieged!

On, then, all Frenchmen, that have hearts in your bodies! Roar with all your throats, of cartilage and metal, ye Sons of Liberty; stir spasmodically whatsoever of utmost faculty is in you, soul, body, or spirit; for it is the hour! [. . .]

To describe this Siege of the Bastille (thought to be one of the most important in History) perhaps transcends the talent of mortals. [. . .] Flesselles[13] is "pale to the very lips", for the roar of the multitude grows deep. Paris wholly has got to the acme of its frenzy; whirled, all ways, by panic madness. At every street-barricade, there whirls simmering a minor whirlpool,—strengthening the barricade, since God knows what is coming; and all minor whirlpools play distractedly into that grand Fire-Mahlstrom[14] which is lashing round the Bastille.

And so it lashes and it roars. Cholat the wine-merchant has become an impromptu cannoneer. [. . .]

Blood flows; the aliment of new madness. The wounded are carried into houses of the Rue Cerisaie; the dying leave their last mandate not to yield till the accursed Stronghold fall. And yet, alas, how fall? The walls are so thick! Deputations, three in number, arrive from the Hôtel-de-Ville; Abbé Fauchet[15] (who was of one) can say, with what almost superhuman courage of benevolence. These wave their Town-flag in the arched Gateway; and stand, rolling their drum; but to no pur-pose. In such Crack of Doom, De Launay cannot hear them, dare not believe them: they return, with justified rage, the whew of lead still singing in their ears. What to do? The Firemen are here, squirting with their fire-pumps on the Invalides' cannon, to wet the touchholes; they unfortunately cannot squirt so high; but produce only clouds of spray. Individuals of classical knowledge propose *catapults*. Santerre, the sonorous Brewer of the Suburb Saint-Antoine, advises rather that the place be fired, by a "mixture of phosphorous and oil-of-turpentine spouted up through forcing pumps": O Spinola-Santerre,[16] hast thou the mixture *ready?* Every man his own engineer! And still the fire-deluge abates not: even

---

12  There were two drawbridges, one over the moat and one over the ditch.
13  Jacques de Flesselles (1721–89), a Parisian magistrate murdered outside the Hôtel de Ville (town hall).
14  More commonly spelt maelstrom, a whirlpool.
15  Claude Fauchet (1774–93), Bishop of Caen and a radical clergyman on the side of the Revolution.
16  Compares the brewer Santerre to Ambrogio Spinola (1569–1630), Spanish general who fought in Holland and survived long sieges.

women are firing, and Turks; at least one woman[17] (with her sweetheart), and one Turk. Gardes Françaises have come: real cannon, real cannoneers. Usher Maillard[18] is busy; half-pay Elie, half-pay Hulin[19] rage in the midst of thousands.

How the great Bastille Clock ticks (inaudible) in its Inner Court there, at its ease, hour after hour; as if nothing special, for it or the world, were passing! It tolled One when the firing began; and is now pointing towards Five, and still the firing slakes not.[20]—Far down, in their vaults, the seven Prisoners hear muffled din as of earthquakes; their Turnkeys[21] answer vaguely.

[. . .]

For four hours now has the World-Bedlam roared: call it the World-Chimæra,[22] blowing fire! The poor Invalides have sunk under their battlements, or rise only with reversed muskets: they have made a white flag of napkins; go beating the *chamade*,[23] or seeming to beat, for one can hear nothing. The very Swiss at the Portcullis[24] look weary of firing; disheartened in the fire-deluge: a porthole at the drawbridge is opened, as by one that would speak. See Huissier Maillard, the shifty man! On his plank, swinging over the abyss of that stone Ditch; plank resting on parapet, balanced by weight of Patriots,—he hovers perilous: such a Dove towards such an Ark![25] Deftly, thou shifty Usher: one man already fell; and lies smashed, far down there, against the masonry! Usher Maillard falls not: deftly, unerring he walks, with outspread palm. The Swiss holds a paper through his porthole; the shifty Usher snatches it, and returns. Terms of surrender: Pardon, immunity to all! Are they accepted?—"*Foi d'officier*, On the word of an officer", answers half-pay Hulin,—or half-pay Elie, for men do not agree on it, "they are!" Sinks the drawbridge,—Usher Maillard bolting it when down; rushes-in the living deluge: the Bastille is fallen! *Victoire! La Bastille est prise!*

---

17  In *A Tale of Two Cities*, Dickens places Madame Defarge at the head of a group of armed women. Carlyle is probably more accurate in depicting their role as limited at this time; they became involved in later negotiations, and they helped in earlier protests again high grain prices. Dickens rightly stresses the women's motivation as their children's hunger (see Key Passages **p. 126**). For Carlyle's view of the Revolutionary women see Robson, Modern Criticism **p. 98**.

18  Stanislas Maillard (1763–94) became famous for claiming that it was he who crawled across the plank to retrieve de Launay's note asking the Revolutionaries to capitulate, as Carlyle describes later in this account. Carlyle refers to him as an usher or *huissier* (the French word for usher), someone who guards a door. Simon Schama thinks it is more likely that Hulin crossed the plank. See *Citizens* (see note 11), p. 461.

19  Jacob Elie (1746–1825) and Pierre-Augustin Hulin were French soldiers who had fought on the American side in the American War of Independence. According to Simon Schama, they brought organization and arms to the assault on the Bastille. See *Citizens* (see note 11), pp. 402–3.

20  The Bastille was protected by two drawbridges. After Thuriot's visit, two members of the crowd severed the chains of the outer drawbridge, allowing the crowd to pour into the inner courtyard. For four hours shooting took place on both sides until de Launay waved a white handkerchief and posted a message on the wall, which was retrieved by Maillard or someone else. De Launay's troops had stopped firing so the mob charged the inner drawbridge and gained entry.

21  Minor prison guards. The seven prisoners included four forgers, two lunatics, and a young aristocrat imprisoned by his family (see Contextual Overview, **p. 10**).

22  Bedlam was a lunatic asylum in London (originally Bethlehem Royal Hospital); the Chimæra was a mythical fire-breathing monster with a lion's head, serpent's tail, and goat's body.

23  A drum or trumpet call for surrender.

24  Swiss guards manned the portcullis or grating that was let down to close the drawbridge over the moat (the Bastille was originally a fortress). According to Simon Schama, thirty-two Swiss guards were called in to help de Launay on July 7. See *Citizens* (note 11), pp. 399–400.

25  To mark the conclusion of his deluge metaphor, Carlyle ironically refers to the dove that appears to Noah, signaling the end of the flood in Genesis 8. Maillard the dove is not bringing peace, however.

## From Chapter 7 "Not a Revolt"

[. . .] As we said, it was a living deluge, plunging headlong: had not the Gardes Françaises,[26] in their cool military way, "wheeled round with arms level-led", it would have plunged suicidally, by the hundred or the thousand, into the Bastille-ditch.

And so it goes plunging through court and corridor; billowing uncontrollable, firing from windows—on itself; in hot frenzy of triumph, of grief and vengeance for its slain. The poor Invalides will fare ill; one Swiss, running off in his white smock, is driven back, with a death-thrust. Let all Prisoners be marched to the Townhall, to be judged!—Alas, already one poor Invalide has his right hand slashed off him; his maimed body dragged to the Place de Grève, and hanged there. This same right hand, it is said, turned back De Launay from the Powder-Magazine, and saved Paris.[27]

De Launay, "discovered in grey frock with poppy-coloured riband", is for killing himself with the sword of his cane. He shall to the Hôtel-de-Ville; Hulin Maillard and others escorting him; Elie marching foremost "with the capitulation-paper on his sword's point". Through roarings and cursings; through hustlings, clutchings, and at last through strokes! Your escort is hustled aside, felled down; Hulin sinks exhausted on a heap of stones. Miserable de Launay! He shall never enter the Hôtel-de-Ville: only his "bloody hair-queue, held up in a bloody hand"; that shall enter, for a sign. The bleeding trunk lies on the steps there; the head is off through the streets; ghastly, aloft on a pike.

Rigorous De Launay has died; crying out, "O friends, kill me fast!" Merciful De Losme must die; though Gratitude embraces him, in this fearful hour, and will die for him; it avails not. Brothers, your wrath is cruel! Your Place de Grève[28] is become a Throat of the Tiger; full of mere fierce bellowings, and thirst of blood. One other officer is massacred; one other Invalide is hanged on the Lamp-iron; with difficulty, with generous perseverance, the Gardes Françaises will save the rest. Provost Flesselles, stricken long since with the paleness of death, must descend from his seat, "to be judged at the Palais Royal":[29]—alas, to be shot dead, by an unknown hand, at the turning of the first street!—

O evening sun of July, how, at this hour, thy beams fall slant on reapers amid peaceful woody fields; on old women spinning in cottages; on ships far out in the silent main; on Balls at the Orangerie of Versailles, where high-rouged Dames of the Palace are even now dancing with double-jacketted Hussar-Officers;[30]—and

---

26  The local militia was trying to keep order outside the Bastille, although some were on the side of the rioters.
27  Simon Schama identifies this *invalide* as Béquard, who had argued against blowing up the prison but who was mistaken for a prison warder and then for one of the cannoneers. See *Citizens* (note 11), pp. 403–4.
28  Site of the Hôtel de Ville, the town hall.
29  Formerly the gardens of Cardinal Richelieu, the Palais-Royal had been turned by the Duke of Orléans and of Chartres into a pleasure grounds for the people of Paris. See also note 2, p. 40.
30  Versailles was the lavish palace of the French monarchy. Carlyle's references to orange trees and hussars (troops from other European countries, such as Queen Marie-Antoinette's Austria) draw attention to the monarchy's non-French sympathies. In *A Tale of Two Cities*, Dickens emphasizes the obliviousness of the ruling classes to the mood of the French people. See also Percy Fitzgerald, Contemporary Documents, **pp. 46–8.**

also on this roaring Hell-porch of a Hôtel-de-Ville! [. . .] Denunciation, vengeance; blaze of triumph on a dark ground of terror: all outward, all inward things fallen into one general wreck of madness!

[. . .]

Along the streets of Paris circulate Seven Bastille Prisoners, borne shoulder-high; seven Heads on pikes; the Keys of the Bastille; and much else. See also the Gardes Françaises, in their steadfast military way, marching home to their barracks, with the Invalides and Swiss kindly enclosed in hollow square. [. . .]

Likewise ashlar stones of the Bastille continue thundering through the dusk; its paper archives shall fly white. Old secrets come to view; and long-buried Despair finds voice. Read this portion of an old Letter:[31] "If for my consolation Monseigneur would grant me, for the sake of God and the Most Blessed Trinity, that I could have news of my dear wife; were it only her name on a card, to show that she is alive! It were the greatest consolation I could receive; and I should for ever bless the greatness of Monseigneur". Poor Prisoner, who namest thyself *Quéret Démery*, and hast no other history,—she is *dead*, that dear wife of thine. and thou art dead! 'Tis fifty years since thy breaking heart put this question; to be heard now first, and long heard, in the hearts of men.

## From **Charles Dickens, "Philadelphia, and its Solitary Prison"**
(1842) in *American Notes for General Circulation*. (London: Chapman & Hall, 1842), pp. 116–18

Dickens's knowledge of prison life began with his father's incarceration in London's Marshalsea Prison when Dickens was twelve (see Contextual Overview, **p. 18**). Like many Victorians, John Dickens was imprisoned for the crime of being in debt, and in his novel *Little Dorrit* (1855–7), Dickens explored both the experience of living for years in the Marshalsea (although Mr. Dickens was there for only a few months) and also the impossibility of freeing oneself from that mental imprisonment even after physical release. Prisons and criminals feature prominently in Dickens's work, but the psychology of the prisoner finds its fullest expression in William Dorrit and Doctor Manette, neither of them criminals, but both imprisoned for many years. Mr. Dorrit enjoys considerable status in his prison – he is the Father of the Marshalsea – but Doctor Manette derives from the pitiable prisoners that Dickens encountered at the Eastern Penitentiary in Philadelphia while touring America and Canada in 1842. As an ardent social reformer, Dickens was vitally interested in the penal system, one of the hot topics of the day. While seeing the need for incarceration as a method of reforming criminals and keeping them off the street (he had no time for systems that pampered them), he was also concerned that they be reintegrated into society and not inhumanely treated. His interest in the Philadelphia prison was to see the effects of the "solitary system," an

---

31 [Carlyle's note.] *Dated*, à la Bastille, 7 Octobre 1752; *signed* Quéret-Démery. *Bastille Dévoilée*; in Linguet, *Mémoires sur la Bastille* (Paris, 1821), p. 199.

experiment that isolated each prisoner entirely from human contact, often for years. In this essay Dickens argues that while this system is well intentioned, its proponents have no idea of the mental suffering they are inflicting on the inmates: "I hold this slow and daily tampering with the mysteries of the brain, to be immeasurably worse than any torture of the body." In the following extract in which Dickens describes meeting one of the inmates we see the origins of Doctor Manette, another man "buried alive," his old life forgotten, his menial task his only hold on reality.

Standing at the central point, and looking down these dreary passages, the dull repose and quiet that prevails is awful. Occasionally there is a drowsy sound from some lone weaver's shuttle, or shoemaker's last, but it is stifled by the thick walls and heavy dungeon door, and only serves to make the general stillness more profound. Over the head and face of every prisoner who comes into this melancholy house a black hood is drawn; and in this dark shroud, an emblem of the curtain dropped between him and the living world, he is led to the cell from which he never again comes forth until his whole term of imprisonment has expired. He never hears of wife or children; home or friends; the life or death of any single creature. He sees the prison officers, but, with that exception, he never looks upon a human countenance, or hears a human voice. He is a man buried alive; to be dug out in the slow round of years; and in the meantime dead to everything but torturing anxieties and horrible despair.

His name, and crime, and term of suffering are unknown, even to the officer who delivers him his daily food. There is a number over his cell door, and in a book of which the governor of the prison has one copy, and the moral instructor another: this is the index to his history. Beyond these pages the prison has no record of his existence: and though he live to be in the same cell ten weary years, he has no means of knowing, down to the very last hour, in what part of the building it is situated; what kind of men there are about him; whether in the long winter nights there are living people near, or he is in some lonely corner of the great gaol, with walls, and passages, and iron doors between him and the nearest sharer in its solitary horrors.

Every cell has double doors: the outer one of sturdy oak, the other of grated iron, wherein there is a trap through which his food is handed. He has a Bible, and a slate and pencil, and, under certain restrictions, has sometimes other books, provided for the purpose, and pen and ink and paper. His razor, plate, and can, and basin hang upon the wall, or shine upon the little shelf. Fresh water is laid on in every cell, and he can draw it at his pleasure. During the day, his bedstead turns up against the wall, and leaves more space for him to work in. His loom, or bench, or wheel is there; and there he labours, sleeps and wakes, and counts the seasons as they change, and grows old.

The first man I saw was seated at his loom, at work. He had been there six years, and was to remain, I think, three more. He had been convicted as a receiver of stolen goods, but even after this long imprisonment denied his guilt, and said he had been hardly dealt by. It was his second offence.

He stopped his work when we went in, took off his spectacles, and answered freely to everything that was said to him, but always with a strange kind of pause first, and in a low, thoughtful voice. He wore a paper hat of his own making, and was pleased to have it noticed and commended. He had very ingeniously manufactured a sort of Dutch clock[1] from some disregarded odds and ends; and his vinegar bottle served for the pendulum. Seeing me interested in this contrivance, he looked up at it with a great deal of pride, and said that he had been thinking of improving it, and that he hoped the hammer and a little piece of broken glass beside it "would play music before long." He had extracted some colours from the yarn with which he worked, and painted a few poor figures on the wall. One, of a female, over the door, he called "The Lady of the Lake."

He smiled as I looked at these contrivances to while away the time; but, when I looked from them to him, I saw that his lip trembled, and could have counted the beating of his heart. I forget how it came about, but some allusion was made to his having a wife. He shook his head at the word, turned aside, and covered his face with his hands.

"But you are resigned now?" said one of the gentlemen after a short pause, during which he had resumed his former manner. He answered with a sigh that seemed quite reckless in its hopelessness, "Oh yes, oh yes! I am resigned to it." "And are a better man, you think?" "Well, I hope so: I'm sure I hope I may be." "And time goes pretty quickly?" "Time is very long, gentlemen, within these four walls!"

He gazed about him—Heaven only knows how wearily!—as he said these words; and, in the act of doing so, fell into a strange stare as if he had forgotten something. A moment afterwards he sighed heavily, put on his spectacles, and went about his work again.

From **[Charles Dickens], "Judicial Special Pleading"** (1848) *The Examiner*, December 23. Reprinted in *The Amusements of the People and Other Papers: Reports, Essays and Reviews 1834–51*, ed. Michael Slater. *The Dent Uniform Edition of Dickens' Journalism*, Vol. II (London: J. M. Dent; Columbus: Ohio State University Press, 1996), pp. 137–42

In 1848, the "year of revolutions," the democratic movement flared up across Europe, leading to revolts in every country except Great Britain and Russia. In France, the monarchy that had been reestablished in 1814 was overthrown for the last time with the abdication of King Louis-Philippe. In England, members of the Chartist movement (see Contextual Overview, **p. 13**), having failed in 1839 and 1842, once again attempted to bring about democratic reforms in England by presenting a People's Charter, signed by over a million people, to Parliament. Generally peaceful reformers, the Chartists alarmed the nation when they gathered en masse for the presentation of the Charter. In April 1848, the more vocal representatives of the movement were arrested and tried by a judiciary that overreacted, fearful that a violent revolution might occur. In the following extracts, Dickens is responding to Sir Edward Alderson's charge to

---

1 Small wall clock, among the first clocks to employ a pendulum.

the jury hearing the case in Chester, one of the many trials that were held. Alderson, a staunch Conservative, had told the jury that the revolutionaries in France had no justification for their actions and that poor people were created that way so that the better off could exercise Christian charity. Alderson's comments typified the upper-class attitudes most deplored by Dickens (see Contextual Overview, **pp. 13–14**).

Mr Baron Alderson informed the grand jury, for their edification, that "previous to the Revolution in France, of 1790, the physical comforts possessed by the poor greatly exceeded those possessed by them subsequent to that event." Before we pass to Mr Baron Alderson's proof in support of this allegation,[1] we would inquire whether, at this time of day, any rational man supposes that the first Revolution in France was an event that could have been avoided, or that is difficult to be accounted for, on looking back? Whether it was not the horrible catastrophe of a drama, which had already passed through every scene and shade of progress, inevitably leading on to that fearful conclusion? Whether there is any record, in the world's history, of a people among whom the arts and sciences, and the refinements of civilised life existed, so oppressed, degraded, and utterly miserable, as the mass of the French population were before that Revolution? Physical comforts! No such thing was known among the French people – among *the people* – for years before the Revolution. They had died of sheer want and famine, in numbers. The hunting-trains of their kings had ridden over their bodies in the Royal Forests. Multitudes had gone about, crying and howling for bread, in the streets of Paris. The line of road from Versailles to the capital had been blocked up by starvation and nakedness pouring in from the departments. The tables spread by Égalité Orléans[2] in the public streets had been besieged by the foremost stragglers of a whole nation of paupers, on the face of every one of whom the shadow of the coming guillotine was black. An infamous feudality and a corrupt government had plundered and ground them down, year after year, until they were reduced to a condition of distress which has no parallel. As their wretchedness deepened, the wantonness and luxury of their oppressors heightened, until the very fashions and customs of the upper classes ran mad from being unrestrained, and became monstrous.

'All,' says Thiers,[3] 'was monopolised by a few hands, and the burdens bore upon a single class. The nobility and the clergy possessed nearly two-thirds of the landed property. The other third, belonging to the people, paid taxes to the king, a multitude of feudal dues to the nobility, the tithe to the clergy, and was,

1   Alderson's "proof" consisted of figures showing that the average quantity of meat consumed by men in Paris was higher in 1789 than at any later date. Dickens pointed out that in 1789, the population of Paris was largely members of the court and the aristocracy, and that several upper-class events were held in Paris that year: "in short, the meat-eating classes were all in Paris, and all at high-feasting in the whirl and fury of such a time!" (p. 141)
2   Louis-Philippe-Joseph, Duke of Orléans and of Chartres (1747–93) was known as Philippe-Egalité. He established the Palais-Royal gardens as pleasure grounds for the people of Paris in 1785, but the area quickly became overrun with petty criminals. (See note 29, p. 36.)
3   Louis-Adolphe Thiers, *History of the French Revolution*, trans. F. Shoberl (5 vols, 1838). This book was included in an inventory of Dickens's library in 1844.

moreover, liable to the devastations of noble sportsmen and their game. The taxes on consumption weighed heavily on the great mass, and consequently on the people. The mode in which they were levied was vexatious. The gentry might be in arrear with impunity; the people, on the other hand, ill-treated and imprisoned, were doomed to suffer in body, in default of goods. They defended with their blood the upper classes of society, without being able to subsist themselves.'

Bad as the state of things was which succeeded to the Revolution, and must always follow any such dire convulsion, if there be anything in history that is certain, it is certain that the French people had NO physical comforts when the Revolution occurred. And when Mr Baron Alderson talks to the grand jury of that Revolution being a mere struggle for "political rights," he talks (with due submission to him) nonsense, and loses an opportunity of pointing his discourse to the instruction of the chartists. It was a struggle on the part of the people for social recognition and existence. It was a struggle for vengeance against intolerable oppressors. It was a struggle for the overthrow of a system of oppression, which in its contempt of all humanity, decency, and natural rights, and in its systematic degradation of the people, had trained them to be the demons that they showed themselves, when they rose up and cast it down for ever.

## From [Charles Dickens], "Where We Stopped Growing" (1853)
*Household Words*, 6 (January 1), p. 363

In this delightful and very Dickensian New Year's Day essay, Dickens reiterates his firmly held belief in the importance of keeping alive the child's imaginative view of the world. Among his catalogue of books, events, and stories that captured his imagination as a child and still haunt him (the places where he stopped growing), he includes the following description of a Bastille prisoner, one of several sources for Doctor Manette in the novel. The passage suggests the strong hold that imprisonment had on Dickens's imagination long before he wrote *A Tale of Two Cities* or read a similar story in Mercier's *Tableau de Paris* (See Contextual Overview, **p. 20** and Contemporary Documents, **p. 49**). It is likely that this "old man of the affecting anecdote" was the fictional Comte de Lorges, invented by a journalist as an eighth released prisoner from the Bastille and exhibited in wax form at Madame Tussaud's famous waxwork museum in London with other horrors of the French Revolution. Dickens would probably have seen the exhibit as a small boy, and he wrote about it in grimly comic detail in *All the Year Round* (on January 7, 1860, shortly after completing the novel). Dickens would also have known Laurence Sterne's account of an (imaginary) Bastille prisoner in his *A Sentimental Journey* (1768), one of the books Dickens loved as a child. For other Bastille prisoners, see Contextual Overview, **p. 19**.

[. . .] We have never outgrown the wicked old Bastille. Here, in our mind at this present childish moment, is a distinct groundplan (wholly imaginative and resting on no sort of authority), of a maze of low vaulted passages with small black doors; and here, inside of this remote door on the left, where the black cobwebs hang like a veil from the arch, and the jailer's lamp will scarcely burn, was shut up, in black silence through so many years, that old man of the affecting anecdote, who was at last set free. But, who brought his white face, and his white hair, and his phantom figure, back again, to tell them what they had made him—how he had no wife, no child, no friend, no recognition of the light and air—and prayed to be shut up in his old dungeon till he died.

## From *Charles Dickens' Book of Memoranda: A Photographic and Typographic Facsimile of the Notebook Begun in January 1855*, ed. Fred Kaplan. (New York: The New York Public Library, 1981.)

Starting in January 1855, Dickens jotted down ideas, characters' names, and possible book titles for his novels and stories in a small notebook. The entries are undated, but Fred Kaplan has used a variety of sources to establish a time-line. The second of the "memoranda," as Dickens called his entries, was the idea of the lawyer Mr. Stryver and his junior, Sydney Carton, as the lion and the jackal. It was commonly believed that the jackal hunted down prey for the lion and thus came to mean the person who did the dirty work for his superior. After he wrote *A Tale of Two Cities*, Dickens noted "(*Done in Carton*)" after the entry.
  Kaplan added explanatory symbols to the entries as follows:

< >letters or words deleted by Dickens, or titles canceled
^ ^ insertions or revisions by Dickens
[ ]editorial insertions
x illegible letter
xx illegible word

  The drunken?—dissipated?—what?
  —LION—and his JACKALL and Primer—stealing down to him at unwonted hours. (*Done in Carton*)

Another early entry suggests Sydney Carton's redemption through resurrec-tion. Carton's wasted life gains purpose only when he dies on the guillotine in place of Charles Darnay. The novel abounds in examples of resurrection, some serious, some macabre, as in Jerry Cruncher's nighttime pursuit of grave-robbing. The biblical metaphor of sowing and harvesting is central to *A Tale of Two Cities*, as it was to Dickens's 1854 novel *Hard Times*. See, for example, the closing chapter of *A Tale of Two Cities* (Key Passages **p. 160**).

  "There is some virtue in him too."
  "Virtue! Yes. So there is in any grain of seed in a seedsman's shop—but you must put it in the ground, before you can get any good out of it."
  "Do you mean that *he* must be put in the ground before any good comes of *him*?"

"Indeed I do. You may call it burying him, or you may call it sowing him, <but> ^ as you like.^ <y> YOu must set him in the earth, before you get any good of him."

---

Dickens took the naming of characters and novels very seriously, and he usually mulled over a long list of possible titles before hitting on the right one. This early list for a novel in two time periods was compiled in 1855, before he was thinking specifically of the story that would become *A Tale of Two Cities*, but he returned to Memory Carton for Stryver's nickname for Sydney Carton. "Two Generations" suggests that Dickens also had in mind the importance of father–son relationships. See Hutter, Modern Criticism **pp. 83–7**.

---

How as to a story in two periods—with a lapse of time between, like a French Drama?

_____

Titles for such a notion—TIME!

| | |
|---|---|
| THE LEAVES OF THE FOREST | FIVE AND TWENTY YEARS |
| SCATTERED LEAVES | YEARS AND YEARS. |
| THE GREAT WHEEL | ROLLING YEARS. |
| ROUND AND ROUND. | DAY AFTER DAY. |
| ✓OLD LEAVES. | <MEMORY CARTON.> |
| <OLD AND NEW LEAVES.> | ROLLING STONES. |
| <LEAVES OF YEARS> | <DRIED LEAVES.> |
| <LEAVES> | FALLEN LEAVES. |
| LONG AGO | TWO GENERATIONS. |
| FAR APART | <MANY YEARS' LEAVES.> |
| <THE LUMBER ROOM> | |

_____

[right]
FELLED TREES.

---

On September 5, 1857, Dickens wrote to his friend Angela Burdett Coutts that the previous night he had recorded in his memoranda book some of the thoughts that had come to him while lying on the stage at the end of his performance of Richard Wardour in *The Frozen Deep* (see Contemporary Overview, **pp. 14–16** and Contemporary Documents, **pp. 44–5**). The entries for this time do not directly relate to *A Tale of Two Cities* as it came to be written eighteen months later, with the exception of the following idea, which became Jerry Cruncher, messenger for Tellson's Bank, and his long-suffering wife. In Book II, Chapter 14 of *A Tale of Two Cities*, Jerry beats his wife for praying, accusing her of undermining his attempts to earn an honest living. (He is actually robbing recent graves and selling the bodies for medical research: a "resurrection man.")

A man, and his wife—or daughter—or Niece. The man, a reprobate and ruffian; the woman (or girl), with good in her, and with compunctions. He <be> believes nothing, and defies everything; yet has suspicions always, that she is "praying against" his evil schemes, and making them go wrong. He is very much opposed to this, and is always angrily harping on it. "<If wh> If she *must* pray, why can't she pray in their favor, instead of going against 'em? She's always ruining me—she always is—and calls that, Duty! There's a religious person! Calls it Duty to fly in my face! Calls it Duty to go sneaking against me!"

From **Wilkie Collins, *The Frozen Deep*** (1857), in *Under the Management of Mr. Charles Dickens: His Production of "The Frozen Deep"*, ed. Robert Louis Brannan (Ithaca, NY: Cornell University Press, 1966), pp. 158–60

The following passage concludes the play to which Dickens refers in his Preface to *A Tale of Two Cities* (see Key Passages, **p. 115**). For a discussion of the importance of the play to Dickens's conception of Sydney Carton see the Contextual Overview, **pp. 14–16**. Dickens played the part of Richard Wardour, and his friend Wilkie Collins was Frank Aldersley. Clara Burnham, the girl beloved by both men, was played originally by Dickens's daughter Mary. When the play was performed for paying audiences, professional actresses took the women's parts. Clara was played by Maria Ternan. Her sister, Ellen, with whom Dickens was soon to form a relationship, played Lucy Crayford. In this closing scene, the audience learn that their fears that Wardour has carried out his plan to murder his rival or leave him to die are groundless. Instead, he has brought him safely back at the cost of his own life. Dickens described Maria Ternan's acting in a letter to a friend:

> But when she had to kneel over Wardour dying, and be taken leave of, the tears streamed out of her eyes into his mouth, down his beard, all over his rags—down his arms as he held her by the hair. At the same time she sobbed as if she were breaking her heart, and was quite convulsed with grief. It was of no use for the compassionate Wardour to whisper "My dear child, it will be over in two minutes—there is nothing the matter—don't be so distressed!" She could only sob out, "O! It's so sad, O it's so sad!" [. . .][1]

(For Sydney Carton's death see Key Passages, **pp. 162–3**.)

WARDOUR: I took him away alone—away with me over the waste of snow—he on one side, and the tempter on the other, and I between them, marching, marching, till the night fell and the camp-fire was all aflame. If you can't kill him, leave him when he sleeps—the tempter whispered me—leave him when he sleeps! I set him his place to sleep in apart; but he crept between the Devil and me, and nestled

---

1 Letter to Angela Burdett Coutts, in G. Storey and K. Tillotson (eds), *The Letters of Charles Dickens*, Vol. VIII, Oxford: Clarendon Press, 1997, pp. 432–3.

his head on *my* breast, and slept *here*. Leave him! Leave him!—the voice whispered—Lay him down in the snow and leave him! Love him—the lad's voice answered, moaning and murmuring *here*, in his sleep—Love him, Clara, for helping me! love him for my sake!—I heard the night-wind come up in the silence from the great Deep. It bore past me the groaning of the ice-bergs at sea, floating, floating past!—and the wicked voice floated away with it—away, away, away for ever! Love him, love him, Clara, for helping *me!* No wind could float that away! Love him, Clara,—(*His voice dies away and his head sinks.*)

ALDERSLEY: Help me up! I *must* go to him! Clara, come with me. (*Advances between Clara and Steventon.*) Wardour! Oh help Wardour! Clara, speak to him!

CLARA: Richard! (*No answer.*)

ALDERSLEY: Richard!

WARDOUR: Ah, poor Frank! I didn't forget you, Frank, when I came here to beg. I remembered you, lying down outside in the shadow of the rocks. I saved you your share of food and drink. Too weak to get at it now! A little rest, Frank! I shall soon be strong enough to carry you down to the ship!

ALDERSLEY: Get something to strengthen him, for God's sake! Oh, men! men! I should never have been here but for him! He has given all his strength to my weakness; and now, see how strong *I* am, and how weak *he* is! Clara! I held by his arm all over the ice and snow. *His* hand dragged me from the drowning men when we were wrecked. He kept watch when I was senseless in the open boat. Speak to him, Clara,—speak to him again!

CLARA: Richard, dear Richard, look at your old playmate! Have you forgotten me?

(*Music "River, River," merging at "kiss me before I die!" into "Those Evening Bells" which lasts until the Curtain has fallen.*)

WARDOUR: Forgotten you? (*Lays his hand on Frank's head.*)—Should I have been strong enough to save him, if I could have forgotten you? Stay! Some one was here and spoke to me just now. Ah! Crayford! I recollect now. (*Embracing him*) Dear Crayford! Come nearer! My mind clears, but my eyes grow dim. You will remember me kindly for Frank's sake? Poor Frank! Why does he hide his face? Is he crying? Nearer, Clara—I want to look my last at *you*. My sister, Clara!—Kiss me, sister, kiss me before I die!

## From **[Percy Fitzgerald], "The Eve of a Revolution"** (1858)
*Household Words*, 17 (5 June), pp. 589–95

Percy Fitzgerald (1834–1925) was a regular contributor to Dickens's two journals, *Household Words* and *All the Year Round*. As the "conductor" of the journals, Dickens took a personal interest in every item that appeared in them, and he spent hours correcting and altering them to assure liveliness of style and an adherence to his opinions on the matters of the day. This essay shows signs of

Dickens's editorial hand and foreshadows *A Tale of Two Cities* in many details, such as the acknowledgement of Carlyle's history *The French Revolution* (see Contextual Overview, **p. 12** and Contemporary Documents, **pp. 31–7**) and the comparison between the Revolution and Belshazzar's feast (see Key Passages, **pp. 124–6**). It also reveals that in *A Tale of Two Cities* Dickens drew upon materials that were commonly available to English readers. Fitzgerald gives as his sources Dr. John Moore, a Scottish doctor, and Arthur Young, an English writer on agricultural subjects, both of whom visited France around the time of the Revolution and recorded their observations. Fitzgerald also mentions the many pamphlets and memoirs – the "trustworthy witnesses" to whom Dickens refers in his Preface (see Key Passages, **p. 115**) – that helped to form the dominant impressions of the Revolution seventy years on. Although he does not mention Louis-Sebastien Mercier, Fitzgerald, like Dickens, relies on him for many of his scenes. His description of the dangerous driving of the aristocrats' coaches is taken directly from the *Tableau de Paris* (see Key Passages, **pp. 132–3**).[1] Fitzgerald's dominant metaphor of the aristocrats arrogantly and blindly dancing on a volcano is central also to Dickens's portrayal of the Revolution as building silently but relentlessly to its sudden and irreversible explosion. For the history of the French Revolution see Contextual Overview, **pp. 7–11**.

For a period so near to us as that of the great French Revolution of seventeen hundred and eighty-nine—upon which a few octogenarians can even now, as it were, lay their hand—it is surprising what a dim veil of mystery, horror, and romance seems to overhang the most awful convulsion of modern times. While barely passing away, it had of a sudden risen to those awful and majestic dimensions which it takes less imposing events centuries to acquire, and towered over those within its shadow as an awful pyramid of fire, blinding those who look. It requires no lying by, or waiting on, posterity for its proper comprehension. It may be read by its own light, and by those who run; and is about as intelligible at this hour as it is ever likely to be. It is felt instinctively: and those whose sense is slow, may have it quickened by Mr. Carlyle's flaming torch—flaring terribly through the night. He might have been looking on in the crowd during that wild night march to Versailles,[2] or standing at the inn door in the little French posting town, as the sun went down, waiting wearily for the heavy berline to come up. Marvellous lurid torch that of his. Pen dipped in red and fire, glowing like phosphoric writing. His history of the French Revolution, the most extraordinary book, to our thinking, in its wonderful force, picturesqueness, and condensation, ever written by mere man. There is other subsidiary light, too, for such as look back—light from tens of thousands of pamphlets, broadsides, handbills[3]—all honest, racy of the time, writ

---

1    Mercier's version (translated into English) can be found in R. Maxwell (ed.), *A Tale of Two Cities*, London: Penguin, 2000, pp. 410–12.
2    The women's march to Versailles on October 5, 1789. See Contextual Overview, **p. 10**. A berline is a four-wheeled covered carriage with a seat behind, possibly the royal coach that took King Louis XVI and his family back to Paris with the deputation of women.
3    Cheap, popular, and often ribald political publications that flooded Paris after the Fall of the Bastille and helped to fuel the Revolution.

by furious hearts, by hands trembling with frensy and excitement—hands streaked with blood and dust of the guillotine: read by mad wolfish eyes at street corners on the step of the scaffold by lamplight. Hawked about, too, by hoarse-mouthed men and women, to such horrible tune as Le Père Duchesne est terriblement enragé aujourd'hui.[4] An awful, repulsive cloud, darkening the air for such as look back at it. Vast shower of ribaldry, insane songs, diatribe, declamation—all shot up from that glowing crater. An inexhaustible study!

[. . .]

To take up, then, that mysterious subject of Paris sleeping unconsciously on the eve of eruption—dim, strange vision, that makes one hold the breath, and brings up thoughts of that ten minutes' suspense before the criminal comes out upon the drop—and turning to the fiddlings and disporting that went forward while that smithy light was seen through the chinks. It is surprising in the midst of what gay, sprightly rioting and bacchanalian[5] festivity that day of wrath surprised them. It was Belshazzar's feast over again, and the handwriting on the wall. The king was on his throne, and Paris population feasting merrily, and sight-seeing—such, at least, as were coming fast to their last sous.[6] To have taken a walk then through the city, with eyes and ears open, would have been only helping one to the conclusion, that this was a well-kept, thriving, light-hearted, innocent people—if ever there was innocent people on the earth. [. . .]

[. . .] There are terrible dangers in these same streets of Paris. For it is customary to drive at full speed, and his ears will be deafened with an eternal Gare! Gare! look out! M. le Prince comes thundering along with six horses. He used to have two couriers running on in front, whose white silk stockings some way never showed a speck; but now the mode is to have dogs, monster dogs, bounding in front, howling, barking, and certain to overthrow every unguarded passenger. Poor Jean Jacques[7] was once knocked down by a huge Danish dog on the Menil road, and was left there while the owner of the carriage passed on. [. . .] Should Provincial be run down, his chance of redress will altogether depend on the wheel that has done the mischief—say, broken Provincial's leg. The coachman has only to look to his fore wheel. The larger one he is not accountable for: so he may with comfort bid an unholy person take that hindermost. [. . .]

This laquais[8] fever was then raging too, and every person of quality kept up a cloud of retainers for no profit or use in the world beyond standing in rich liveries in their masters' halls for pure ostentation's sake. Unpaid, most likely, according to the golden rule then flourishing; never likely to be paid. Our farmers-general[9]— the only folk at that time with full money-bags—kept four-and-twenty footmen, not counting coachmen, cooks and their aides-de-camp, to say nothing either of

4  "Father Duchesne is terribly angry today." Le Père Duchesne was the newspaper of the extreme Revolutionaries, edited by Jacques René Hébert.
5  Drunken, after the Roman god of wine, Bacchus.
6  French five-centime piece (100 centimes in a franc).
7  Rousseau. For Rousseau see Contemporary Documents, pp. 30–1.
8  Footman or valet to a wealthy person.
9  See p. 31, note 2. Dickens describes the wealthy farmers-general in Book II, chapter 7 of A Tale of Two Cities.

Madame's six ladies-maids. These gentlemen wore jewellery like their masters. [...]

At about nine o'clock the day may be said practically to begin, and whoever may be walking abroad at that hour is pretty sure of being jostled by myriads of hair-dressers, all tripping along with wig in one hand and curling-irons in the other—they hurrying to be in time for Monsieur and Madame's toilet, who are just done sipping their chocolate. [...]

## From **letter from Charles Dickens to Edward Bulwer Lytton**, 5 June 1860, in **The Letters of Charles Dickens**, ed. Graham Storey (Oxford: Clarendon Press, 1997), Vol. IX, pp. 258–60

Dickens was always anxious that his novels be as accurate as possible when referring to actual places or events. He often addressed criticism of his facts in later prefaces, famously defending, for example, the spontaneous combustion of a character in *Bleak House* in the 1853 Preface to the novel. In the following letter to his friend and fellow novelist Sir Edward Bulwer Lytton, he answered his friend's criticism of his portrayal of the French aristocracy. Louis-Sebastien Mercier's twelve-volume *Tableau de Paris* was a well-known series of essays on Parisian life before the Revolution. For Jean-Jacques Rousseau's recollections see Contemporary Documents **pp. 30–1**. For Madame Defarge's death see Key Passages, **pp. 158–60**. For Sydney Carton's death see Key Passages, **pp. 162–3**.

My Dear Bulwer Lytton,

I am very much interested and gratified by your letter concerning "A Tale of Two Cities." I do not quite agree with you on two points, but that is no deduction from my pleasure.

In the first place, although the surrender of the feudal privileges (on a motion seconded by a nobleman of great rank) was the occasion of a sentimental scene,[1] I see no reason to doubt, but on the contrary, many reasons to believe, that some of these privileges had been used to the frightful oppression of the peasant, quite as near to the time of the Revolution as the doctor's narrative, which, you will remember, dates long before the Terror.[2] And surely when the new philosophy was the talk of the salons and the slang of the hour, it is not unreasonable or unallowable to suppose a nobleman wedded to the old cruel ideas, and representing the time going out, as his nephew represents the time coming in; as to the condition of the peasant in France generally at that day, I take it that if anything

---

1  On August 4, 1789, the Viscount de Noailles proposed various reforms to taxation and the abolition of feudal privilege. He was seconded by the Duke d'Aiguillon. In calling the scene "sentimental" Dickens is referring to the anxiety of some noblemen to be seen to be democratic. Simon Schama calls the Viscount's speech "a set piece of revolutionary oratory." See *Citizens. A Chronicle of the French Revolution*, New York: Alfred A. Knopf, 1989, pp. 437–8. See also Contextual Overview, **p. 10**.

2  Doctor Manette began writing his narrative in December 1767, twenty-five years before the Terror.

be certain on earth it is certain that it was intolerable. No *ex post facto*[3] enquiries and provings by figures will hold water, surely, against the tremendous testimony of men living at the time.

There is a curious book printed at Amsterdam, written to make out no case whatever, and tiresome enough in its literal dictionary-like minuteness, scattered up and down the pages of which is full authority for my marquis. This is "Mercier's Tableau de Paris." Rousseau is the authority for the peasant's shutting up his house when he had a bit of meat. The tax-taker was the authority for the wretched creature's impoverishment.

I am not clear, and I never have been clear, respecting that canon of fiction which forbids the interposition of accident in such a case as Madame Defarge's death. Where the accident is inseparable from the passion and emotion of the character, where it is strictly consistent with the whole design, and arises out of some culminating proceeding on the part of the character which the whole story has led up to, it seems to me to become, as it were, an act of divine justice. And when I use Miss Pross[4] (though this is quite another question) to bring about that catastrophe, I have the positive intention of making that half-comic intervention a part of the desperate woman's failure, and of opposing that mean death—instead of a desperate one in the streets, which she wouldn't have minded—to the dignity of Carton's wrong or right; this *was* the design, and seemed to be in the fitness of things.

3   Retrospective.
4   Lucie Manette's loyal old servant, who represents, with the banker Mr. Lorry, English restrained good sense and faithfulness, contrasted at the end of the novel with Madame Defarge's irrational and vindictive loyalty to her family.

# 2

# Interpretations

# Critical History[1]

Like many classic novels that remain immensely popular with readers over the years, *A Tale of Two Cities* has received very mixed reviews from professional critics. Part of the blame lies with a famous and influential early review by the well-known Victorian critic Sir James Fitzjames Stephen (Early Critical Reception [ECR] **pp. 62–4**), an attack so vehement that it was referred to frequently in other contemporary reviews and colored future assessments of the early reception of the novel. In a review of *Great Expectations* in October 1861 the *Eclectic Review* told readers that Stephen's criticism had reduced Dickens to "a state of [such] hopeless lethargy, that it needed the constant application of warm flannels and bathings of mustard and turpentine, and the united influence of at least a dozen physicians, to restore him to consciousness."[2] According to the *Eclectic*, "*A Tale of Two Cities* pleased nobody*," a judgment that has been handed down through the years by scholars assessing the novel's contemporary reception. Fortunately David G. Tucker set the record straight in 1979 when he unearthed a large number of very favorable newspaper and journal reviews to conclude that "beyond doubt, the response to *A Tale of Two Cities* was overwhelmingly favorable, enthusiastic, indeed, laudatory."[3] See, for example, the reviews in the *Sun* (ECR, **pp. 60–1**) and the *Morning Chronicle* (ECR, **pp. 65–6**).

Some of Stephen's criticisms were echoed by other reviewers of the time, such as his disagreement with the novel's suggestion that the England of 1859 was superior to the England of the 1760s, and his objection to Dickens's portrayal of the French aristocracy before the Revolution. But his general condemnation of the novel as a mechanical contrivance based on artificial pathos and grotesqueness was not shared by most contemporary reviewers. His attack on the plot as "a disjointed framework for the display of the tawdry wares which form Mr. Dickens's stock-in-trade" is particularly idiosyncratic, as most readers agree with John Forster (see Early Critical Reception, **pp. 66–7**) that the tightly

---

1 This section is an updated version of the introduction to Ruth F. Glancy, *A Tale of Two Cities: An Annotated Bibliography*. New York: Garland, 1993.
2 "Charles Dickens' 'Great Expectations.' " *Eclectic Review*, N.S. 1 (1861), 458–9.
3 "The Reception of *A Tale of Two Cities*: Part I." *Dickens Studies Newsletter*, 10 (1979), pp. 8–13 and "The Reception of *A Tale of Two Cities*: Part II." *Dickens Studies Newsletter*, 10 (1979), pp. 51–6.

constructed plot is one of the novel's strengths. Wilkie Collins, who is frequently credited with influencing Dickens's later plots, including this one, referred to the novel as Dickens's "most perfect work of constructive art."[4] Dickens was quick to reject Collins's suggestion that Doctor Manette's story should be revealed early in the novel, however (see "The Novel in Performance," **p. 103.**)

Another often-repeated criticism of *A Tale of Two Cities* is that it is un-Dickensian, most favored by readers who generally dislike Dickens, but least favored by true Dickensians who miss the humor and broad range of distinctive characters that are typical of the other novels. Writing in 1871, the year after Dickens's death, the Victorian novelist and reviewer Margaret Oliphant suggested that it "might have been written by any new author, so little of Dickens there is in it," going on to argue that half a dozen writers could have written a more authentic imitation of Dickens than was evident in *A Tale of Two Cities.*[5] J.W.T. Ley, an early Dickensian scholar, called it "an almost humorless book; by no Dickensian standard can it be judged: it stands apart." Ley was writing at a time (the 1920s) when Dickens's early novels (such as *Pickwick Papers* and *Nicholas Nickleby*) were particularly favored for their broad comedy and eccentric characters. For these readers, *A Tale of Two Cities* was a disappointment. Not until the 1980s did literary criticism properly come to grips with the many strengths of the novel – its historical method, psychological complexity, and narrative skill – all, in fact, characteristically Dickensian. Those who concentrate on *A Tale of Two Cities* as an anomaly have been answered by many who assert, like Taylor Stoehr, that the novel is not un-Dickensian but "ultra-Dickensian," at least in style (see Modern Criticism, **pp. 70–6**). Not many would agree with John Gross that the style is "grey and unadorned;"[6] the descriptions of the spilt wine cask, the storming of the Bastille, Madame Defarge's sinister knitting in the wine-shop, or the September Massacres (see Contextual Overview, **p. 11**) when the grindstone turned inexorably outside Tellson's Parisian office remain in most readers' minds long after they have closed the book. As George Orwell says, "thanks to Dickens, the very word 'tumbril' has a murderous sound"[7] (see Modern Criticism, **p. 70**). Dickens's influence on the masters of film technique in the twentieth century is largely due to the literary qualities of repetition, montage, and rhythm that are characteristic of *A Tale of Two Cities*, as Ana Laura Zambrano has argued (see Modern Criticism, **pp. 76–8**). The early film classic about the French Revolution, D.W. Griffith's *Orphans of the Storm* (1921), owed a great deal to the novel's blend of theme and symbol, as did Sergei Eisenstein's film *Ten Days that Shook the World* (1927).

Although critics have deplored the artificiality of some of the dialogue (such as Lucie's first meeting with her father), stylistic studies such as Garrett Stewart's (Modern Criticism, **pp. 87–90**) have identified the skill with which Dickens has linked the themes and events of the novel through echo and repetition, while incorporating allusive words that have the multidimensional range of

4   Preface to *The Woman in White*, 1860.
5   "Charles Dickens." *Blackwood's Magazine*, 109 (1871), p. 691.
6   "A Tale of Two Cities." In *Dickens and the Twentieth Century*, ed. John Gross and Gabriel Pearson. London: Routledge & Kegan Paul, 1962, pp. 187–97.
7   Originally just a farm cart, tumbrils were used for transporting the victims to the guillotine.

Shakespearean language. Notable also is the subtlety of the speeches – both direct and indirect – in the Old Bailey trial (see Key Passages, **pp. 126–8**). More controversial is Dickens's use of fractured English to indicate a French speaker: French idiom is translated directly into English in phrases such as "That's well," "How goes it," and "Behold the manner of it." Sir James Fitzjames Stephen (see Early Critical Reviews, **p. 63**) found this speech "intolerably tiresome and affected," a "misbegotten jargon" that showed a lack of sensibility for the importance of the events described. Later more detailed analyses of this dialogue have also been critical, blaming the artificiality of the device on what is sometimes seen as Dickens's anti-French bias. A similar problem arose in the 1989 film, in which the English voices are dubbed into French for the French version, but the French actors speak a highly accented English for the English version (see The Novel in Performance, **pp. 106–7**).

Readers vary widely in their response to the Christian doctrine of resurrection that underlies the plot and symbolism of A Tale of Two Cities (see Contemporary Documents, **p. 42**). George Bernard Shaw compares Sydney Carton to the ghost in Hamlet to argue that both Dickens and Shakespeare "exploit popular religion for professional purposes without delicacy or scruple."[8] Some later critics have agreed with Shaw that the Christian ethic in the novel is not only forced but even blasphemous. John Carey, for instance, accuses Dickens of using Carton's reiteration of Christ's words "to shove his readers onto a higher plane so that they won't mind too much the injustice of Carton's death."[9] For other critics, such as Chris Brooks (see Modern Criticism, **pp. 90–3**), however, the novel is deeply imbued with Christian symbolism and thus provides a coherent allegory in which Paris and London are fallen cities redeemed by Sydney Carton. Although film versions have increasingly omitted any reference to the novel's Christian roots or the identification between Carton and Christ (see The Novel in Performance, **p. 103**), literary scholars are still finding religious interpretations fruitful and persuasive.[10]

Much has been written about Dickens's portrayal of revolutionary France and A Tale of Two Cities as an historical novel. The contemporary reviewers were generally critical of the novel's view of the French Revolution, although several were prepared to acknowledge the events as powerfully rendered, even if the portrayal of the Revolution was inaccurate. Conservative critics decried what they saw as Dickens's one-sided support of the Revolutionaries and hostility to the aristocracy, failing to note that Dickens's sympathy is greatly tempered once the Revolution is underway. Noting Dickens's acknowledgment of Thomas Carlyle's influence (see Key Passages, **p. 115**), many at the time blamed Carlyle for the inaccuracies; the subject of influence has subsequently received much detailed study.[11] The Critic argued that the novel did not show the true forces behind the

8  Preface to Man and Superman. In The Complete Prefaces of Bernard Shaw. London: Paul Hamlyn, 1965, pp. 161–2.
9  The Violent Effigy: A Study of Dickens' Imagination. London: Faber & Faber, 1973, pp. 107–8.
10 Kenneth M. Sroka, for example, finds the novel a complement to the Gospel of John, the source of Carton's words as he goes to the guillotine ("I am the Resurrection and The Life . . .") See "A Tale of Two Gospels: Dickens and John." Dickens Studies Annual, 27 (1998), pp. 145–69.
11 See, for example, Michael Goldberg, Carlyle and Dickens, Athens, Ga.: University of Georgia Press, 1972, and William Oddie, Dickens and Carlyle: The Question of Influence, London: Centenary Press, 1972.

Revolution, a view shared by later critics of the novel who accuse Dickens of totally ignoring the middle-class society of eighteenth-century France and its role in the Revolution (see Contextual Overview, **p. 9**).

The contemporary reviewers of the novel did not consider it as a warning that revolution was possible in nineteenth-century Britain, but later critics have debated at length whether Dickens intended the novel to have implications for his own society. In the 1930s, critics such as the Marxist T.A. Jackson argued that the novel conclusively showed Dickens's belief that the Revolutionaries were justified in using violence, cruelty, and revenge to overcome their oppression.[12] Gamal Abdel Nasser, on the other hand, reportedly opposed the shedding of blood in his own revolution in Egypt in the 1950s because he had learned from *A Tale of Two Cities* that "violence breeds violence".[13] More recent critics still cannot decide whether Dickens is revolutionary or not. Some see Carton as a disappointingly middle-class hero whose personal sacrifice merely indicates that the novel avoids political solutions. But according to Cates Baldridge (see Modern Criticism, **pp. 93–7**), there is a "subversive subtext to the narrator's middle-class horror at the collectivist Revolutionary ideology," and he argues that Dickens may actually prefer the community of the Revolutionaries to the isolation of middle-class bourgeois life.

Some critics have denied that *A Tale of Two Cities* can be called an historical novel at all because of its one-sided portrayal of the French aristocracy before the Revolution and because there are so few historical characters in it. For some readers this lack of scholarliness is a virtue, but many agree with George Bernard Shaw that the novel is "pure sentimental melodrama from beginning to end, and shockingly wanting in any philosophy of history."[14] The historian Georg Lukács voices the frequently heard criticism that the novel fails to connect the personal adventures of the characters with the revolutionary background: "Dickens, by giving pre-eminence to the purely moral aspects of causes and effects, weakens the connection between the problems of the characters' lives and the events of the French Revolution."[15] In his famous biography of Dickens, Edgar Johnson finds that "instead of merging, the truth of revolution and the truth of sacrifice are made to appear in conflict."[16] How can Sydney Carton's personal sacrifice for Charles Darnay bring an end to the anarchy that was flaring in the Terror? Is Madame Defarge representative of her class or merely a monster driven by the desire for personal revenge? Those who see the novel as a warning for contemporary Britain usually find the fusion of the personal and historical both deliberate and successful, however. Andrew Sanders, who has worked on the novel more extensively than anyone else, defends it on the grounds that Dickens deliberately offers a solution based not on political means but on the value of private lives and

12  *Charles Dickens: The Progress of a Radical*, New York: International Publishers, 1938, pp. 170–88.
13  Robert Stephens, *Nasser: A Political Biography*, Harmondsworth: Penguin, 1971, p. 33.
14  Foreword to *Great Expectations*, reprinted in Dan H. Laurence and Martin Quinn (eds) *Shaw on Dickens*, New York: Frederick Ungar, 1985, p. 46.
15  *The Historical Novel* 1962; rpt Lincoln, Nebr. and London: University of Nebraska Press, 1983, p. 243.
16  *Charles Dickens: His Tragedy and Triumph*, 2 vols, Boston, Mass.: Little Brown; London: Hamish Hamilton, 1952, Vol. II, 981–2.

human love.[17] John P. McWilliams, Jr. (see Modern Criticism, **pp. 79–83**) is more critical of Dickens's avoidance of political issues in the novel, suggesting that Dickens was hoping to allay his fears of revolution in England by removing social progress and individual conduct from any connection with political action.

Most Dickens scholars date the genesis of modern approaches to Dickens – approaches that pay close attention to the darker, psychological aspects of the novels – as Edmund Wilson's 1941 study "Dickens: The Two Scrooges."[18] Wilson takes an historical rather than psychoanalytic approach in his short note about *A Tale of Two Cities*, and it was not until the dramatic increase of academic interest in Dickens after 1970 (the centenary of his death) that *A Tale of Two Cities* received serious attention. This interest coincided with the application of the theories of psychoanalysts such as Sigmund Freud, Carl Gustav Jung, and Jacques Lacan, and the French philosophers Jacques Derrida and Michel Foucault (whose interest is with power and surveillance). Some of these theories are particularly applicable to *A Tale of Two Cities* and have sparked considerable debate. Albert D. Hutter's seminal essay on *A Tale of Two Cities* (see Modern Criticism, **pp. 83–7**) in 1978 first examined the pervasiveness of Freud's notion of "splitting"[19] in the novel as well as the relationship between the private and the public in the father–son conflicts and the central question of parricide (as the regicide of Louis XVI by his "children," the French people, was considered). Freud's writings on cannibalism have been a part of a growing body of critical theory on the iconography (symbols and pictorial representations) of the French Revolution, not just in Dickens and Carlyle, but in political writing about revolution.[20] In "The Duplicity of Doubling in *A Tale of Two Cities*," the American scholar Catherine Gallagher raises the question of Dickens's violation of the private in the public execution of Sydney Carton.[21] Central to the discussion of the very public violence of the French Revolution is the work of French philosopher Michel Foucault (1926–84), whose theories about prisons, capital punishment, and the relationship between the body and the body politic are relevant to the novel and have been explored by critics such as Jeremy Tambling in his 1995 book *Dickens, Violence and the Modern State*. Feminist criticism and recent studies of the French Revolution have drawn attention to the female iconography of the Revolution (including the attribution of the guillotine as female and the mythological females such as the gorgon that became identified with the Revolution) and reexamined the importance of the women in the novel. Lisa Robson (Modern Criticism, **pp. 97–101**) and other feminist critics draw on

---

17 *The Victorian Historical Novel, 1840–1880*, London: Macmillan, 1978, pp. 68–96.
18 In *The Wound and the Bow*, Cambridge, Mass.: Houghton Mifflin, 1941.
19 In psychoanalysis, "splitting" refers to the attempt to deal with a problematical relationship by dividing oneself into two people or by dividing the person causing the trauma. See, for example, the reading of the novel that identifies Charles Darnay and Sydney Carton as Dickens's attempt to resolve his conflict over his love for Ellen Ternan (see Contextual Overview, **p. 15**). In the novel, doublings are essential to the plot and symbolism.
20 One of the first commentaries on cannibalism in the novel and in Carlyle's *The French Revolution* is Lee Sterrenburg's "Psychoanalysis and the Iconography of Revolution," *Victorian Studies* 19 (1975), pp. 241–64. Harry Stone's *The Night Side of Dickens: Cannibalism, Passion, Necessity*, Columbus: Ohio State University Press, 1994, has an extended discussion of the topic.
21 "The Duplicity of Doubling in *A Tale of Two Cities*," *Dickens Studies Annual*, 12 (1983), pp. 125–45.

late twentieth-century studies of the role of women in the French Revolution to offer a new perspective on Madame Defarge, the seamstress, and Madame Roland, whom Dickens invokes at the end of the novel and who has been the subject of much contemporary feminist analysis.

Another recent academic interest that is important for *A Tale of Two Cities* is the reassessment of melodrama as a genre worthy of serious study. These new approaches help to readdress the long-standing intellectual condemnation of the novel for its "middlebrow" popularity (a work appealing to educated but undiscriminating readers). Because melodrama as a genre originated in post-Revolutionary French theatre (with which Dickens was very familiar), its relevance to *A Tale of Two Cities* is particularly noticeable. Melodrama is coming to be seen not as an inferior type of tragedy (relying on music and emotion rather than depth of character) but as a deliberate art form that arose as a popular entertainment in response to the politics and culture of the revolution.[22]

*A Tale of Two Cities*, more than most of Dickens's novels, has suffered critically because of these roots in popular entertainment and its wide appeal as a school text, as a film, and with the general reading public. The eminent Dickensian George Ford considers it the only one of Dickens's novels that could be dismissed as formula writing that appeals to scullery maids who would rather identify with a romantic heroine than "enter into the lives of others," as readers of other novels do.[23] Angus Wilson considers it Dickens's "great middlebrow success" because it appeals to the half-educated.[24] Such views derive from the superior position of the academic and scholar, but distaste for the novel as "middlebrow" is also felt by Marxist critics who find Dickens's portrayal of the Parisian mob typical of a middle-class syndrome that is based on fear. Also, many readers refuse to be moved by Carton's death in case they reveal a Victorian sensibility to which the modern reader should be impervious. Hedging their bets, some critics damn the novel with faint praise: a famous American professor, Edward Wagenknecht, for example, finds it "a fascinating and deeply moving story which must take very high rank indeed among productions of the second rank."[25]

Melodrama or tragedy? Subversively bourgeois or subversively revolutionary? Whatever the verdict, the increase in serious critical interest in *A Tale of Two Cities* shows no sign of abating. Perhaps the tempering of John Forster's praise that this excellent novel is still not an "entirely successful experiment" (see Early Critical Reception, **p. 66**) has remained the keynote of any final appraisal of the novel for many readers. Charles Beckwith finds it "Dickens's closest approximation to the effect of tragedy;"[26] for George Gissing it is "something like a true tragedy;"[27] for K.J. Fielding it is "an attempt at romantic tragedy, wonderfully told, but failing at complete success."[28] Writing in 1916, Wilhelm Dibelius

22 Juliet John's *Dickens's Villains: Melodrama, Character, Popular Culture*, Oxford: Oxford University Press, 2001 is a recent study on this topic.
23 *Dickens and His Readers: Aspects of Novel-Criticism since 1836*, New York: Norton, 1965, p. 37.
24 *The World of Charles Dickens*. London: Martin Secker & Warburg, 1970, p. 261.
25 "Introduction," in the 1950 Random House edition of *A Tale of Two Cities*.
26 "Introduction," in *Twentieth Century Interpretations of A Tale of Two Cities*, Englewood Cliffs, NJ: Prentice-Hall, 1972, p 14.
27 *Charles Dickens: A Critical Study*, London: Blackie, 1898, p. 61.
28 *Charles Dickens: A Critical Introduction*, London: Longmans, Green, 1958, p. 167.

considered it Dickens's masterpiece in the area of the serious novel, but also only "perhaps" destined for immortality.[29] At the beginning of the twenty-first century, we can safely remove Dibelius's reservation and assign *A Tale of Two Cities* its rightful and lasting place at the heart of the Dickens canon, not as imitation Carlyle, or Dickens on an off day, but as a powerful work of historical fiction that well justifies its author's acknowledgment, "It has greatly moved and excited me in the doing, and Heaven knows I have done my best and have believed in it."[30]

29  Charles Dickens, Liepzig and Berlin: B. G. Teubner, 1916, p. 455.
30  Letter to Wilkie Collins, in G. Storey (ed.), *The Letters of Charles Dickens*, Vol. IX, Oxford: Clarendon Press, 1997, p.128.

# Early Critical Reception

From **[Anonymous], "Charles Dickens's New Work: *A Tale of Two Cities*. Nos. I., II., and III. Chapman and Hall"** (1859), *Sun,* 11 August, n.p.

Dickens's novels were frequently reviewed after only a few numbers had appeared. This anonymous review of the first three monthly installments of the novel (up to Book II, Chapter 13) finds great promise in the story so far. The reviewer's praise for the narrator's control of the readers' emotions (and admission that he was moved to tears) is typical of many Victorian critics and now seems strangely at odds with the prevalent twentieth-century dislike of pathos and melodrama.

It is hard for modern readers to appreciate the anticipation with which Dickens's contemporaries were able to read the story and speculate on its plot. Few readers today can come to *A Tale of Two Cities* without already knowing the story and even having by heart the famous closing lines. This reviewer would have to wait for another four months to discover if Carton's "reclamation" will come about, as the reviewer so earnestly hopes.

[. . .] It[1] illustrates anew, and in a remarkable manner, his[2] extraordinary command over our emotions as a pathetic narrator. It yields additional and startling evidence of his rare and comparatively speaking but recently developed genius as a master of Terror. [. . .]

[. . .] Not to loiter over the minute touches of humour which are as usual scattered abundantly about him by our novelist—bringing out localities and individualities with all the distinctness of photography when viewed through the stereoscope—let us, before we close this notice of the three first instalments of this charming *Tale of Two Cities*, enumerate briefly a few of the incidents already depicted in it, and the "pick" of some among the principal characters introduced. [. . .] "The Wine Shop," and "The Shoemaker," the two chapters in

1 *A Tale of Two Cities.*
2 Dickens's.

which the unfortunate prisoner[3] is restored to the world, and drawn, at last, to the recognition, and into the arms, of his young daughter, are among the most exquisite things Charles Dickens has ever yet written. We read words like these through our tears—we have for them no less spontaneous a tribute of appreciative admiration. Scarcely less pathetic, or less beautiful, in its way (though the pathos is here in a lesser degree) is the incident described in the third number [. . .] "The Stoppage at the Fountain."[4] Besides these Parisian incidents there are others hardly less attractive in their general interest—a trial, for example, of Monsieur, one of the young heroes, at the Old Bailey, ending in his acquittal[5] —a supercilious piece of brutality, on the part of Monseigneur, ending in his assassination[6]— and several proposals for Mademoiselle, the heroine,[7] ending, at any rate, in two casual refusals: one of the rejected suitors being "A Fellow of Delicacy," the other "A Fellow of no Delicacy." The two gentlemen last mentioned are among the most striking delineations in the numbers of the work yet published—Sydney Carton, a young barrister of brilliant parts, but no address, and of a baulked ambition, who acts as jackal to that self-asserting lion at the bar, Mr. Stryver.[8] [. . .] Our preference unquestionably treads in the direction of poor Sydney—and we long for the reclamation of that waste land of promise! Mr. Lorry,[9] by the way, has raised himself wonderfully in our estimation by his gallant contest with the Lion, when visited by the latter in his own little den at Tellson's. Yet in the end Mr. Lorry too, like Sydney Carton, seems to have given way at last to the "shouldering." Charles Darnay as yet, we confess—we don't much care for—Charles Darnay being, nevertheless, the hero of the story, and the all but accepted lover of that charming, golden–haired heroine, Lucie Manette. [. . .]

It[10] is the key note of the story. It is new evidence that the Novelist is—true Poet also in the depth of his human sympathies and in the picturesque vividness of his imagination. It renders obvious at a glance the significance of this *Tale of Two Cities*—the loves and the lives of the Manettes seen by the glare of that tremendous Revolution!

From **[Anonymous],** *A Tale of Two Cities* (1859), *Observer,* 11 December, p. 7

This anonymous reviewer concentrates on Dickens's preface (see Key Passages, **p. 115**), which had just appeared with the first edition of the novel in book form. In taking issue with Dickens's knowledge of history, the reviewer shares a commonly held view that Dickens was badly educated and ill informed.

---

3  Doctor Manette.
4  The scene in which the Marquis (Charles Darnay's uncle) callously runs over Gaspard's child (Key Passages, **p. 115**). For comment on this scene see Contemporary Documents, **p. 46.**
5  See **pp. 132–3.**
6  See pp. 135–6.
7  Lucie Manette.
8  For Dickens's thoughts on the lion and jackal see Contemporary Documents, **p. 42.**
9  The elderly employee of Tellson's Bank and loyal friend of Lucie Manette and her father.
10  "It" refers to the chapter "Hundreds of People," Book II, Chapter 6. See pp. **pp. 128–31.**

This volume contains, in a complete form, the "Tale of Two Cities" published by Mr. Dickens in weekly portions, for some time past, in his new periodical. He states that the idea of the story occurred to him while acting with his children and friends in Mr. W. Collins's drama of the "Frozen Deep," and that it took an especial hold of his imagination. That the work has been, as he avers, an object of particular care and interest to him, is no doubt true, but it is equally true that the work is, perhaps, the feeblest that he has given to the public. Mr. Dickens states that in his references to the French Revolution he has acted on the statements of the most trustworthy witnesses. Nevertheless he has gone widely astray in his appreciation of that great historical event, and has written of it as though he were imbued with all the prejudices of the days of Pitt,[1] against the actors and the drama. He thinks he may do something to add to the popular means of understanding that terrible time, but he has done nothing, because he has mainly depended for his facts upon a work which he calls wonderful, but which the world calls by a different epithet, Carlyle's *History of the French Revolution*.[2] If Mr. Dickens would only read Villaume's history in four post 8vo. volumes, he would understand that period much better, to say nothing of Louis Blanc's really wonderful history, now in progress of publication.[3]

From **[Sir James Fitzjames Stephen],** *A Tale of Two Cities* (1859), *Saturday Review of Politics*, December 17, pp. 741–3

Sir James Fitzjames Stephen (1829–94), uncle of the novelist Virginia Woolf, was a barrister and later a high-court judge. He wrote essays on a wide variety of topics for the journals of his day, but none is more famous than this savage attack on *A Tale of Two Cities*. Stephen begins by comparing Dickens to the Scottish novelist Sir Walter Scott. Whereas the faults of Scott's later novels can be excused because he was writing to get out of debt, *A Tale of Two Cities* has no such redeeming feature, complains Stephen. If Scott's novels are cold soup, raw mutton, and tough fowls, at least they are food; Dickens's novel is "puppy pie and stewed cat." After summarizing the plot, Stephen opines "it would perhaps be hard to imagine a clumsier or more disjointed framework for the display of the tawdry wares which form Mr. Dickens's stock-in-trade." Dickens's popularity rests on "his power of working upon the feelings by the coarsest stimulants, and his power of setting common occurrences in a grotesque and unexpected light." Stephen then decimates Dickens's tendency to pathos, which he finds overdone and mechanical, and his reliance on grotesque tricks of character,

---

1   William Pitt, known as Pitt the Younger (1759–1806), who served as Prime Minister from 1783 to 1801. Britain at this time was generally nervous about the Republican movement in France following the violence of the Revolution. See Contextual Overview, pp. 13–14.
2   See pp. 31–7.
3   Villaume's history included original material about Jean-Paul Marat, one of the leaders of the Revolution. The French radical politician Louis Blanc (1811–82) wrote his thirteen-volume history of the French Revolution between 1847 and 1862, while in exile in England. Neither of these histories is now as well known as Carlyle's.

such as Jerry Cruncher's spiky hair. Stephen concludes his attack by noting that Dickens based Darnay's English trial on the trial of a French aristocrat, Francis Henry de la Motte, who was found guilty of spying and executed in 1781 (see Key Passages, **pp. 126–8**). Stephen's vitriolic review was probably motivated by a personal dislike of Dickens and his politics. He may have been angered also by what he saw as an attack on his father in Tite Barnacle of *Little Dorrit*, the novel that preceded *A Tale of Two Cities* and that ridiculed, through the Barnacle family, the red tape and nepotism of public life. Unfortunately this review became widely known and helped to create the misconception that the novel was universally disliked (see Critical History, **p. 53**).

One special piece of grotesqueness introduced by Mr. Dickens into his present tale is very curious. A good deal of the story relates to France, and many of the characters are French. Mr. Dickens accordingly makes them talk a language which, for a few sentences, is amusing enough, but which becomes intolerably tiresome and affected when it is spread over scores of pages. He translates every French word by its exact English equivalent. For example, "Voilà votre passe-port" becomes "Behold your passport"—"Je viens de voir," "I come to see," &c. Apart from the bad taste of this, it shows a perfect ignorance of the nature and principles of language. The sort of person who would say in English, "Behold," is not the sort of person who would say in French "Voilà;" and to describe the most terrible events in this misbegotten jargon shows a great want of sensibility to the real requirements of art. If an acquaintance with Latin were made the excuse for a similar display, Mr. Dickens and his disciples would undoubtedly consider such conduct an inexcusable pedantry. To show off familiarity with a modern language is not very different from similar conduct with respect to an ancient one.

The moral tone of the *Tale of Two Cities* is not more wholesome than that of its predecessors, nor does it display any nearer approach to a solid knowledge of the subject-matter to which it refers. Mr. Dickens observes in his preface—"It has been one of my hopes to add something to the popular and picturesque means of understanding that terrible time, though no one can hope to add anything to the philosophy of Mr. Carlyle's wonderful book." The allusion to Mr. Carlyle confirms the presumption which the book itself raises, that Mr. Dickens happened to have read the History of the French Revolution, and, being on the look-out for a subject, determined off-hand to write a novel about it. Whether he has any other knowledge of the subject than a single reading of Mr. Carlyle's work would supply does not appear, but certainly what he has written shows no more. It is exactly the sort of story which a man would write who had taken down Mr. Carlyle's theory without any sort of inquiry or examination, but with a comfortable conviction that "nothing could be added to its philosophy." The people, says Mr. Dickens, in effect, had been degraded by long and gross mis-government, and acted like wild beasts in consequence. There is, no doubt, a great deal of truth in this view of the matter, but it is such very elementary truth that, unless a man had something new to say about it, it is hardly worth mentioning;

and Mr. Dickens supports it by specific assertions which, if not absolutely false, are at any rate so selected as to convey an entirely false impression. It is a shameful thing for a popular writer to exaggerate the faults of the French aristocracy in a book which will naturally find its way to readers who know very little of the subject except what he chooses to tell them; but it is impossible not to feel that the melodramatic story which Mr. Dickens tells about the wicked Marquis who violates one of his serfs and murders another, is a grossly unfair representation of the state of society in France in the middle of the eighteenth century. That the French *noblesse* had much to answer for in a thousand ways, is a lamentable truth; but it is by no means true that they could rob, murder, and ravish with impunity.

[. . .]

England as well as France comes in for Mr. Dickens's favours. He takes a sort of pleasure, which appears to us insolent and unbecoming in the extreme, in drawing the attention of his readers exclusively to the bad and weak points in the history and character of their immediate ancestors. The grandfathers of the present generation were, according to him, a sort of savages, or very little better. They were cruel, bigoted, unjust, ill-governed, oppressed, and neglected in every possible way. The childish delight with which Mr. Dickens acts Jack Horner, and says What a good boy am I, in comparison with my benighted ancestors, is thoroughly contemptible. England some ninety years back was not what it now is, but it was a very remarkable country. It was inhabited and passionately loved by some of the greatest men who were then living, and it possessed institutions which, with many imperfections, were by far the best which then existed in the world, and were, amongst other things, the sources from which our present liberties are derived. There certainly were a large number of abuses, but Mr. Dickens is not content with representing them fairly. He grossly exaggerates their evils.

[. . .] In the early part of his novel he introduces the trial of a man who is accused of being a French spy, and does his best to show how utterly corrupt and unfair everybody was who took part in the proceedings. The counsel for the Crown is made to praise the Government spy, who is the principal witness, as a man of exalted virtue, and is said to address himself with zeal to the task of driving the nails into the prisoner's coffin. In examining the witnesses he makes every sort of unfair suggestion which can prejudice the prisoner, and the judge shows great reluctance to allow any circumstance to come out which would be favourable to him, and does all in his power to get him hung, though the evidence against him is weak in the extreme. It so happens that in the State Trials for the very year (1780) in which the scene of Mr. Dickens's story is laid, there is a full report of the trial of a French spy—one De la Motte—for the very crime which is imputed to Mr. Dickens's hero. One of the principal witnesses in this case was an accomplice of very bad character; and in fact it is difficult to doubt that the one trial is merely a fictitious "rendering" of the other. The comparison between them is both curious and instructive. It would be perfectly impossible to imagine a fairer trial than De la Motte's, or stronger evidence than that on which he was convicted. [. . .] It is surely a very disgraceful thing to represent such a transaction as an attempt to commit a judicial murder.[. . .]

From **[Anonymous], "A Tale of Two Cities"** (1860), *Morning Chronicle*, 2 January, p. 7

This very favourable review begins by taking issue with those critics who condemn Dickens because of his popularity. Dickens is widely read, the reviewer argues, because the experience from which he writes is recognized by many readers. The reviewer goes on to defend the theatricality of the story and the shifts in time and place. He concludes with a long quotation from the first chapter of Book III, "In Secret," in which Darnay is challenged at the barrier to Paris and arrested.

[. . .] If judged by the rules which false criticism has set up, "A Tale of Two Cities" is not faultless, but it is a gross injustice to deny to it the applause to which the genius of the author entitles all his works. There are evidences of thoughtfulness and care in it which are not to be found in every one of its predecessors. As a rule, Dickens is inclined to sacrifice common sense to a taste for dramatic situations, but we doubt whether, were he to abjure this tendency, his books would be by any means so agreeable. It may be true that, in consequence of the exaggeration, a reader may be unable to lose himself in the reality which exists in some of his creations, but the pleasure derived is often so great, and the absorption for the time so complete, that no impartial reader can grudge the thanks to which the labours of the most versatile of modern writers attest a just claim. The mechanism of his present story suffers to a certain extent from want of unity in time and place, but the exigencies of its historical foundation render this almost unavoidable; and were any attempt made to combat or avoid them, the natural sequence of events would have to be sacrificed. As it happens, however, there is nothing new in sudden transitions of time and scene in the relation of stories. If anything, this course, when well supported, adds to the interest and renders the situations more striking. [. . .] But there is one merit exhibited by the book under discussion which does not seem to have been noticed by those who have subjected it to criticism. It is, that no one is prepared for the *dénouement*. Accustomed as we are to digest works of fiction—good, bad, and indifferent—we can say, in all truth and honesty, that we were not prepared for the part which Sydney Carton plays at the end of the story. It might, perhaps, have been guessed, but the uninterrupted flow of the tale seems never to suggest it; and when the reader draws near its accomplishment, he is perfectly amazed at a solution so unexpected, and withal so natural. The great attraction of the tale will, after all, be found in the isolated pictures of life which abound in its pages. In this respect we have never seen Mr. Dickens so strong or so true to himself. As he remarks in the introduction, he has thoroughly thrown himself into his work, and has, so to speak, written as if he were a living actor in, not a narrator of, the events. [. . .]

Taken as a whole, this is about the most complete story that has proceeded from Mr. Dickens's pen. It is short, concise, and displays plain purpose throughout. Not a moment seems to be lost or a page wasted in the recital. Its essential feature is, that it is a story well told; and its success serves to show that, however severely the mine afforded by the French revolutionary epoch has been worked, its treasures are not yet exhausted. There are, however, few hands able to pluck jewels from its recesses so successfully as Mr. Dickens. He is *par excellence* the professor of romance, and his last production is not a whit behind his early fame.

From **John Forster, *The Life of Charles Dickens*** (1872–4), revised by A.J. Hoppé, (London: J.M. Dent, 1966), Vol. II, 282–3

John Forster (1812–76) was Dickens's best friend and literary adviser. His biography, begun two years after Dickens's death, is a vital and unique source of information about Dickens's life and personality, but it is also unequaled in the glimpses it gives us of Dickens's literary methods. Although trained for the law, Forster spent his life in the arts as a literary and dramatic critic, editor for eight years of the influential journal the *Examiner*, historian, and biographer. He was at the centre of literary life in London, where he supported many philanthropic projects to aid struggling writers. Dickens valued Forster's advice and opinions during the writing of his novels, even allowing his friend to make changes to the manuscripts when Dickens was abroad. The following evaluation of the novel in Forster's biography is preceded by Dickens's letter to Edward Bulwer Lytton (see Contemporary Documents, **pp. 48–9**.) Later critics have been more strident than Forster in faulting Dickens's reliance upon incident rather than character and dialogue, but Forster's judicious appraisal raises many of the questions that later critics have addressed. See John P. McWilliams, Jr., for example, on the merging of the public and the private (Modern Criticism **pp. 79–83**).

These are interesting intimations of the care with which Dickens worked; and there is no instance in his novels, excepting this, of a deliberate and planned departure from the method of treatment which had been pre-eminently the source of his popularity as a novelist. To rely less upon character than upon incident, and to resolve that his actors should be expressed by the story more than they should express themselves by dialogue[1], was for him a hazardous, and can hardly be called an entirely successful, experiment. With singular dramatic vivacity, much constructive art, and with descriptive passages of a high order everywhere (the dawn of the terrible outbreak in the journey of the marquis from Paris to his country seat, and the London crowd at the funeral of the spy, may be instanced for their power), there was probably never a book by a great humorist, and an artist so prolific in the conception of character, with so little humour and so few rememberable figures. Its merits lie elsewhere. Though there are excellent traits and touches all through the revolutionary scenes, the only full-length that stands out prominently is the picture of the wasted life saved at last by heroic sacrifice. Dickens speaks of his design to make impressive the dignity of Carton's death, and in this he succeeded perhaps even beyond his expectation. [. . .] its[2] distinctive merit is less in any of its conceptions of character, even Carton's, than as a specimen of Dickens's power in imaginative story-telling. There is no piece of fiction

---

1  Forster is quoting Dickens's own description of the novel.
2  The novel's.

known to me, in which the domestic life of a few simple private people is in such a manner knitted and interwoven with the outbreak of a terrible public event, that the one seems but part of the other. When made conscious of the first sultry drops of a thunderstorm that fall upon a little group sitting in an obscure English lodging, we are witness to the actual beginning of a tempest which is preparing to sweep away everything in France. And, to the end, the book in this respect is really remarkable.

# Modern Criticism

From **George Orwell, "Charles Dickens"** (1940), in *Decline of the English Murder and Other Essays* (Harmondsworth: Penguin, 1965), pp. 89–93

In this lively long essay on Dickens, the political writer and novelist George Orwell (1903–50) argues that all art is propaganda because the writer has an argument to present. He was particularly interested in *A Tale of Two Cities* because of its examination of revolution and the gradual descent into tyranny of the Revolutionaries, a descent that was the subject of Orwell's political allegory about the Russian Revolution of 1917, *Animal Farm* (1945). In "Charles Dickens," he considers Dickens's novels as social criticism. What was Dickens's attitude to class, and was he truly a revolutionary? Orwell argues that although Dickens did not advocate the overthrow of the existing systems and had little to offer in the way of solutions to society's ills, his belief that common decency could correct most of the problems "is not such a platitude as it sounds" (p. 98). If the French aristocracy had been more like Charles Darnay the Revolution would not have been necessary. Orwell's discussion of *A Tale of Two Cities* is one of the best accounts of the overall impression that the book leaves with a reader, an impression often derived from reading the novel in school. For another reading that stresses Dickens's apolitical stance see John P. McWilliams, Jr. (Modern Criticism, **pp. 79–83**).

The one thing that everyone who has read *A Tale of Two Cities* remembers is the Reign of Terror.[1] The whole book is dominated by the guillotine – tumbrils thundering to and fro, bloody knives, heads bouncing into the basket, and sinister old women knitting as they watch. Actually these scenes only occupy a few chapters, but they are written with terrible intensity, and the rest of the book is rather slow going. But *A Tale of Two Cities* is not a companion volume to *The Scarlet Pimpernel*.[2] Dickens sees clearly enough that the French Revolution was

---

1   See Contextual Overview, **p. 11.**
2   A novel published in 1905 by Baroness Orczy (1865–1947) in which a band of Englishmen goes to the rescue of the victims of the Reign of Terror.

bound to happen and that many of the people who were executed deserved what they got. If, he says, you behave as the French aristocracy had behaved, vengeance will follow. He repeats this over and over again. We are constantly being reminded that while "my lord" is lolling in bed, with four liveried footmen serving his chocolate and the peasants starving outside, somewhere in the forest a tree is growing which will presently be sawn into planks for the platform of the guillotine, etc., etc., etc. The inevitability of the Terror, given its causes, is insisted upon in the clearest terms. [. . .]

In other words, the French aristocracy had dug their own graves. But there is no perception here of what is now called historic necessity. Dickens sees that the results are inevitable, given the causes, but he thinks that the causes might have been avoided. The Revolution is something that happens because centuries of oppression have made the French peasantry sub-human. If the wicked nobleman could somehow have turned over a new leaf, like Scrooge, there would have been no Revolution, no jacquerie,[3] no guillotine – and so much the better. This is the opposite of the "revolutionary" attitude. From the "revolutionary" point of view the class-struggle is the main source of progress,[4] and therefore the nobleman who robs the peasant and goads him to revolt is playing a necessary part, just as much as the Jacobin[5] who guillotines the nobleman. Dickens never writes anywhere a line that can be interpreted as meaning this. Revolution as he sees it is merely a monster that is begotten by tyranny and always ends by devouring its own instruments. In Sydney Carton's vision at the foot of the guillotine, he foresees Defarge and the other leading spirits of the Terror all perishing under the same knife – which, in fact, was approximately what happened.

And Dickens is very sure that revolution *is* a monster. That is why everyone remembers the revolutionary scenes in *A Tale of Two Cities*; they have the quality of nightmare, and it is Dickens's own nightmare. Again and again he insists upon the meaningless horrors of revolution – the mass-butcheries, the injustice, the ever-present terror of spies, the frightful blood-lust of the mob. The descriptions of the Paris mob – the description, for instance, of the crowd of murderers struggling round the grindstone to sharpen their weapons before butchering the prisoners in the September massacres[6] – outdo anything in *Barnaby Rudge*.[7] The revolutionaries appear to him simply as degraded savages – in fact, as lunatics. He broods over their frenzies with a curious imaginative intensity. He describes them dancing the "Carmagnole", for instance.[8] [. . .]

It[9] and others like it show how deep was Dickens's horror of revolutionary hysteria. Notice, for instance that touch, "with their heads low down and their

3 The name attached to the French peasants who took part in the French Revolution, derived from Jacques Bonhomme (Goodman Jack), a name often derisively used in France for peasants.
4 Orwell is referring here to the Marxist theory of dialectical materialism, which states that everything in the universe, including human systems, is in a constant state of change brought about through the continual conflict of opposites. Class struggle is one aspect of this dialectic and leads to progress toward communism.
5 Members of the Revolutionary party led by Danton, Marat, and Robespierre (see Contextual Overview, pp. 7–18). The name derives from their meeting place, the convent of St. Jacques in Paris.
6 See pp. 148–9.
7 See p. 20.
8 See p. 148.
9 The passage.

hands high up", etc., and the evil vision it conveys. Madame Defarge is a truly dreadful figure, certainly Dickens's most successful attempt at a *malignant* character. Defarge and others are simply "the new oppressors who have risen in the destruction of the old", the revolutionary courts are presided over by "the lowest, cruellest and worst populace", and so on and so forth. All the way through Dickens insists upon the nightmare insecurity of a revolutionary period, and in this he shows a great deal of prescience. "A law of the suspected, which struck away all security for liberty or life, and delivered over any good and innocent person to any bad and guilty one; prisons gorged with people who had committed no offence, and could obtain no hearing" – it would apply pretty accurately to several countries today.

The apologists of any revolution generally try to minimize its horrors; Dickens's impulse is to exaggerate them – and from a historical point of view he has certainly exaggerated. Even the Reign of Terror was a much smaller thing than he makes it appear. Though he quotes no figures, he gives the impression of a frenzied massacre lasting for years, whereas in reality the whole of the Terror, so far as the number of deaths goes, was a joke compared with one of Napoleon's battles. But the bloody knives and the tumbrils rolling to and fro create in his mind a special sinister vision which he has succeeded in passing on to generations of readers. Thanks to Dickens, the very word "tumbril" has a murderous sound; one forgets that a tumbril is only a sort of farm-cart. To this day, to the average Englishman, the French Revolution means no more than a pyramid of severed heads. It is a strange thing that Dickens, much more in sympathy with the ideas of the Revolution than most Englishmen of his time, should have played a part in creating this impression.

From **Taylor Stoehr, Dickens: The Dreamer's Stance** (Ithaca, NY: Cornell University Press, 1965), pp. 1–33

Taylor Stoehr's famous examination of style in A Tale of Two Cities is the most comprehensive of several essays on this subject. In his discussion of Dickens's style in general, Stoehr chooses A Tale of Two Cities for his analysis because he finds the novel "ultra-Dickensian" – highly rhetorical but in the best sense. He selects four scenes from the novel to demonstrate three characteristics of Dickens's style that he considers typical of Dickens at his most brilliant: the use of detail to paint the scene and advance the plot; the use of rhetorical devices such as anaphora (beginning successive phrases with the same words) and metonymy (naming a thing by the name of something related to it) to connect the details; and the effect of detail and repetition on characterization and plot. The scenes Stoehr examines closely are the breaking of the wine cask outside the Defarges' shop (see Key Passages, **pp. 124–6**), the murder of the Marquis (see Key Passages, **pp. 134–6**), the storm scene in Soho Square (see Key Passages, **pp. 128–31**), and the storming of the Bastille (not included here; see Zambrano, Modern Criticism, **pp. 76–8**, for a detailed discussion of this scene). Lengthy quotations from these scenes are not duplicated here. Stoehr defends Dickens from the criticism of heavy-handedness by arguing that behind the realistic detail of Dickens's scenes lies a dreamlike intensity whose effect on the reader is almost subliminal. He also answers the frequently heard criticism that the plot relies too heavily on coincidence by arguing that Dickens implies a cosmic rationale (the role of Providence in human events).

## [The Wine-Cask Scene]

The beginning of interest lies in the concrete object, the thing; Dickens sets the scene, almost cinematically, by focusing on such particulars. Here the effect is that of a high-angle view, centered on the splintered cask, slowly moving down on the square. As we are brought closer, description slides into narration, still determined by the objects in the setting. [. . .]

Everything "run[s] to the spot"; people are mere adjuncts of the stones and wine. It is the scene that sticks in the memory. Places, buildings, all kinds of physical objects take up most of the available space in the Dickensian world. Later, when the revolutionary characters are introduced and made to come alive in their dazzling way, we discover that even in the delineation of character Dickens depends on the physical setting, the *mise-en-scène*, the concrete object, for his favorite effects. In the passage quoted it is the objects that have character, that exist "expressly to lame all living creatures that approached them"; in other passages the people derive much of their special kind of life from the things which invariably accompany them: Madame Defarge and her knitting, Doctor Manette and his cobbler's bench, Jerry Cruncher and his spiky hair, Gaspard[1] and his nightcap are typical examples. This insistence on the bits and pieces of physical reality has attracted the attention of most of Dickens' readers in one way or another.

[. . .]

[. . .] Once the scene has become a human one, the narrative continues to be organized around the bits and pieces of the physical context[2]. [. . .]

Here [. . .] the details of the setting seem to determine the movement of the narrator's eye: the wine is sipped and dipped, squeezed out and dammed up and cut off; mugs and handkerchiefs, mud and fragments of wood, figure more prominently than the people handling them. Even the dramatic feeling—the passion and despair of the characters, the meanness of their daily lives—is given through these vulgar objects and their uses.

It is worth pressing this point, for by just such means do we feel the pressure of atmosphere which is so powerful in Dickens, the impression that the world is thick with moods and presences, that will affect the course of events and drive the characters to their fate. The "unnecessary details" and "needless ramifications" fill up this world, and whether needless or not they constrain and determine action as the pebbles of a gravelly soil at once guide and hinder the searching roots.

---

1  Gaspard is the father of the child run over by the Marquis. He then murders the Marquis and is hanged for this crime.
2  Stoehr quotes the description of the people lapping up the wine in the street, Book I, Chapter 5.

[. . .]

When one first comes upon it in the novel, this passage[3] foreshadows little more than the explicit prophecy of the last sentence, but as we read further we find that the little details thrown out so lavishly, and as it were so casually, have their echoes throughout the story. We meet the same woodsawyer again, and we begin to connect him with the "Woodman Fate" of the opening chapter. We see and hear the stained feet again—the echoing footsteps in Lucie's life, the dancing feet of the Carmagnole, the cruel foot of Madame Defarge as she steadies the governor's head for her knife. The "tigerish smear about the mouth" is our first introduction to the "life-thirsting, cannibal-looking, bloody-minded juryman, the Jacques Three of St. Antoine." The tall citizen in the night-cap is Gaspard, who has in him still another note, also to be "scrawled," after the murder of the Marquis: "*Drive him fast to his tomb. This, from* JACQUES."

The whole narrative is webbed with such interconnections, based always on the foreshadowing or echoing detail. Such repetitions have the obvious function of promoting the unity and probability of the novels, but an even more important result is the creation of a density of atmosphere beyond the power of mere verisimilitude or circumstantiality to achieve: we are presented with a cosmos everywhere interdependent, so that even objects in the landscape contribute to the sense of an interlocking system. With their multiple linkages, the "unnecessary detail" and "needless ramifications" of Dickens' style and plot provide the very fiber and fabric of his tightly knit world. The notorious coincidences of his novels are not the weak expedients of melodrama, but have behind them this same cosmic rationale. [. . .]

There is much that will bear analysis in this passage, but for our present purposes what is interesting is the articulation of the narrative and descriptive materials by the use of the rhetorical device of *anaphora*, the repetition of the key word "Hunger" to introduce and mark off the successive items of the presented scene. This device, which may be seen at work very frequently in Dickens—for instance, in the Wine-Shop passages already quoted—epitomizes Dickens' method of ordering his imagined world. The details of the scene are not merely piled up, one upon another; rather, there is a kind of logic in their arrangement. Everything here is mentioned because it is a concomitant of hunger, because it is a familiar result or cause or symptom or contingency of that condition. Observation and report are controlled, selection is determined, by the key word. One cannot, however, argue the converse, that what is given in the scene necessitates the choice of the word "Hunger," for it is the word which tells the reader what to notice, how to take the descriptive elements. Substitution of another word—say, "Poverty" or "Misery"—would result in a different set of meanings for the same reported observations. Thus the principle of *relevance* in the passage seems to be determined by the choice of the anaphoric expression. But the principle of *order* in the passage seems to be differently derived. The reader is presented with a cinematic rendering of continuous space in continuous time, the narrator functioning as a camera-eye; details make their appearance according to their position in the imagined scene, one thing next to another, and still another next to that. We are invited to attend to the houses, to the clotheslines stretched from their windows, to the man sawing firewood in front of the houses, to the chimneys which show no sign of wood being burned inside, and back again to the street and its shops and shop signs, its chestnut stand, costermongers[4] and their wares. Although the selection of details is determined by the anaphora, the ordering seems to be given by the scene itself, by the mere contiguity of things. [. . .] The obligation to record everything is avoided by the use of anaphora, which acts as a delimiting device, a kind of lens and shutter marking off selected bits of the scene, moving the reader's attention from representative sample to representative sample, and thus building an impression of the whole from the enumerated parts. The rhetoric controls the time and space of perception and report by opening (and, at each new opening, also thereby closing) the windows of the linguistic medium, our access to the author's world.

## [The Death of the Marquis]

In the Marquis we have a perfect model, almost a prototype, for the well-known Dickens caricature, complete with social mask, hidden motives, and an exaggerated oddity—the nose—which provides the necessary key to the connection between the apparent and the real character. The cluster of information about the Marquis—his cold indifference (to the child's death), his heritage of cruelty (the riding-whips), his crafty hatred (of Darnay, his nephew)—circles persistently about the central image of his masklike face with its pinched and dinted nose. Everything comes back to that mask, that nose, and those dints, which finally take on more life than the Marquis himself.

[. . .]

[. . .] there is a special advantage to these circling yet fixed patterns of association, in that a single part of any cluster may be used synecdochically[5] to suggest the whole. Typically in Dickens there is some pivotal detail that serves in this way; the image of the stone mask with its pinched nose sets off the train of associations. Thus at the end of Chapter IX, where Dickens sums up all the Marquis' sins and their punishment, he returns to this dominant image:

> The Gorgon had surveyed the building again in the night, and had added the one stone face wanting; the stone face for which it had waited through about two hundred years.
>
> It lay back on the pillow of Monsieur the Marquis. It was like a fine mask, suddenly startled, made angry, and petrified.

The mask has usurped the field; nothing else of the cluster remains. The Marquis has been totally dehumanized, and exists only as a stone face. [. . .]

Dickens' iconography is in no sense unsophisticated or unpsychological. In the example of the Marquis' nose, the Marquis' defining quality is not ordinary anger but rage, habitually suppressed and therefore white-hot. In the stone mask with

---

4   Sellers of fruit from a barrow.
5   Synecdoche is a kind of metonymy in which the name of a part is used to signify the whole.

the pinched, pulsating dints in the nose, Dickens manages to express both the fury and its suppression. Moreover, while the Marquis' nose gives us the key to his character, other elements in the scene itself are used to elaborate this indirect presentation. When the Marquis leaves the town house of Monseigneur, furious because he is out of favor, the anger is allowed to show only in his pulsating nose. But for once the image is not adequate to the power of the feeling, which is actually expressed in the scene that follows, when the Marquis' *coach* runs down a helpless child—thus conveying, by a perfectly appropriate metonymy, the murderous rage that possesses him. In general, the Marquis cannot be allowed to have any direct contact with the fulfillment of his fiery desires, since it is his character to suppress his feelings. His ancestors wielded the riding whips, his coach acts out his fury, his nose betrays his hidden passion.

The extreme of his detachment is given in the vengeance he takes for his own murder, for now he exists *only* as a stone mask with a dinted nose:

> A rumour just lived in the village—had a faint and bare existence there, as its people had—that when the knife struck home, the faces changed, from faces of pride to faces of anger and pain; also, that when that dangling figure [of Gaspard] was hauled up forty feet above the fountain, they changed again, and bore a cruel look of being avenged, which they would henceforth bear for ever. In the stone face over the great window of the bedchamber where the murder was done, two fine dints were pointed out in the sculptured nose, which everybody recognised, and which nobody had seen of old. [. . .]

In Chapter XXIII of the second book, the Marquis' anger reaches its climax when the revolutionaries have seized power and are destroying his château. Appropriately enough, the Marquis is himself consumed in his own rage, symbolized in the scene by the holocaust:

> The château was left to itself to flame and burn. In the roaring and raging of the conflagration, a red-hot wind, driving straight from the infernal regions, seemed to be blowing the edifice away. With the rising and falling of the blaze, the stone faces showed as if they were in torment. When great masses of stone and timber fell, the face with the two dints in the nose became obscured: anon struggled out of the smoke again, as if it were the face of the cruel Marquis, burning at the stake and contending with the fire.

Dickens says "as if it were the face of the cruel Marquis," but indeed the Marquis' face has become stone, and we finally see him in his true aspect, concealed so long behind the mask: "burning at the stake and contending with the fire."

Stoehr goes on to argue that these clusters provide an interconnectedness that is spatial as well as temporal. Foreshadowing is worked out as in a dream sequence, where the meaning of the images is conveyed through their combination rather than just through narrative. He discusses the storm in Soho passage (see Key Passages, **pp. 128–31**) to demonstrate "synecdochic fore-shadowing, from which the lines of correspondence stretch out both forward and backward to encompass the whole novel."

## [The Storm in Soho Square]

In the first paragraph the still developing relations among the characters are sketched: Doctor Manette, his loyal daughter, her future husband, and, removed from them all, Carton, in a characteristic posture. The mention of "spectral wings" suggests that what follows may not be merely what it seems. And indeed almost every detail—even bits of the syntax—reaches outside the scene. The triad "large, heavy, and few," which Doctor Manette uses to describe the rain, gives place by the end of the scene to "fast, fierce, and furious," and this in turn looks forward to the phrase "headlong, mad, and dangerous," which later in the novel will be used to describe the outbreak of the revolutionary storm. In accord with the quickening tempo implied in this sequence, the tempest begins slowly, if surely, as Doctor Manette and Carton observe. Their remarks parallel those of Defarge and his wife, as they too await the "tempest" and its lightning, in Chapter XVI of the second book:

> "It is a long time," repeated his wife; "and when is it not a long time? Vengeance and retribution require a long time; it is the rule."
> "It does not take a long time to strike a man with Lightning," said Defarge.
> "How long," demanded madame, composedly, "does it take to make and store the lightning? Tell me."

But Defarge has not long to wait, nor does the little group in Soho. The footsteps that echo in the dark room are in a hurry, pounding into their lives. They are the footsteps of the wine-stained feet in St. Antoine, of the blood-stained feet yet to come. Ironically it is Darnay (through whom the others are all involved in the Revolution) who asks whether the footsteps are coming to them as a group or individually. In the end, of course, they are coming not for Lucie or Darnay, but for Carton, and his voluntary acceptance of whatever they may bring exactly forecasts his final acceptance of another's fate. Finally the tempest is upon them. The description looks forward, with its "rush and roar," its "thunder and lightning," to the Revolution scene:

> Saint Antoine had been, that morning, a vast dusky mass of scarecrows heaving to and fro, with frequent gleams of light above the billowy heads, where steel blades and bayonets shone in the sun. A tremendous roar arose from the throat of Saint Antoine, and a forest of naked arms struggled in the air like shrivelled branches of trees in a winter wind: all the fingers convulsively clutching at every weapon or semblance of a weapon that was thrown up from the depths below, no matter how far off.

Who gave them out, whence they last came, where they began, through what agency they crookedly quivered and jerked, scores at a time, over the heads of the crowd, like a kind of lightning, no eye in the throng could have told. [. . .]

The "crash, and fire, and rain" also match the three chapters that describe the Revolution: "Echoing Footsteps," "The Sea Still Rises," and "Fire Rises." But most precise of all is the foreshadowing "sweep of water" which, in its rush, "stopped" Carton. Compare his last moments on the scaffold:

The murmuring of many voices, the upturning of many faces, the pressing on of many footsteps in the outskirts of the crowd, so that it swells forward in a mass, *like one great heave of water*, all flashes away.[6] [. . .]

Even Carton's final resurrection is hinted in the rising of the moon which ends the storm. In fact, no major movement of the novel is without its reflection in this scene—the introduction of characters and of the relations between them; the awaiting of the tempest, the listening to approaching footsteps; the breaking of the storm; Carton's sacrifice, his death, his resurrection.

## From **Ana Laura Zambrano, "Charles Dickens and Sergei Eisenstein: The Emergence of Cinema,"** (1975) *Style*, 9, pp. 469–87

In this essay, Ana Laura Zambrano, an expert on Dickens's influence on the early filmmakers D.W. Griffith (1875–1948) and Sergei Eisenstein (1898–1948), argues that Eisenstein learned from Dickens how to structure his work through "interlocking movement, repetition, and variation in rhythm" to "create an organic whole, allowing images and tempo to affect emotion and allowing the dramatic theme to merge into both structure and symbol (Zambrano, p. 476)". In this passage, Zambrano calls attention to the rhythmic quality of the writing in the famous storming of the Bastille passage (see Key Passages, **pp. 139–43**). See also Carlyle's version of this scene (Contemporary Documents, **pp. 33–5**).

In the hands of Dickens and Eisenstein, montage[1] embodies more than rhythm and structure; it becomes the propelling force of the work, evolving through the clash and variations of its images a synthesis of elements to form an organic vision that is continually being defined and modified. Theme and symbols merge with the rhythm of montage, determining its structure as well as drawing their significance from the interaction of the whole. In *A Tale of Two Cities*, Dickens' portrayal of the murderous Parisian mob storming the Bastille creates a complex interplay of solitary figures and mass movement building up through metaphor,

6    Italics are Stoehr's.

1    The selection and ordering of scenes to create an overall effect.

repetition, and onomatopoeic phrases into a crescendo as powerful as the sea to which it is compared.

> As a whirlpool of boiling waters has a centre point,
> so, all this raging circled round Defarge's wine-shop,
> and every human drop in the caldron
> had a tendency to be sucked towards the vortex. . . .
> "Patriots and friends, we are ready! The Bastille!"
> With a roar that sounded as if all the breath in France had been shaped
>     into the detested word
> the living sea rose,
> wave on wave,
> depth on depth,
> and overflowed the city to that point.
> Alarm-bells ringing
> drums beating,
> the sea raging and thundering on its new beach,
> the attack begun.
>
> Deep ditches,
> double drawbridge,
> massive stonewalls,
> eight great towers,
> cannon,
> muskets,
> fire and smoke.
> Through the fire
> and through the smoke
> —in the fire
> and in the smoke,
> for the sea cast him up
> against a cannon, and on the instant he became a cannonier
> —Defarge of the wine-shop worked like a manful soldier,
> Two fierce hours. . . .

By breaking this scene into its component parts, as if each segment were a shot in a film, Dickens's artistry is revealed. The opening of the sequence is slow and rhythmic, but the phrases become progressively shorter as the movement of the mob is created through accelerated montage. The images recur throughout, but the emphasis shifts from the visual to the furious sound of battle.

> Shrieks,
> volleys,
> execrations,
> bravery without stint,
> boom,
> smash
> and rattle,

and the furious sounding of the living sea;
but, still the deep ditch,
and the single drawbridge,
and the massive stone walls,
and the eight great towers,
and still Defarge of the wine-shop at his gun,
grown doubly hot by the service of four fierce hours.

A white flag
from within the fortress,
and a parley—
this dimly perceptible through the raging storm,
nothing audible in it
—suddenly the sea rose immeasurably
wider
and higher,
and swept Defarge of the wine-shop
over the lowered drawbridge,
past the massive stone outer walls,
in among the eight great towers surrendered! [. . .]

The scene opens and closes with aerial views of the action, almost with an Olympian calm that contrasts with the furious imagery and rhythm which pulls us into the center of turmoil.

Dickens uses the unifying image of the living sea to construct an analogy which turns the peasants into an elemental force of nature as fundamentally necessary to the formation of society as was the sea to the creation of life, and yet as relentlessly powerful as a natural cataclysm. The swirling, at times rising, movement of the mob clashes with the obdurate, motionless repetition of the obstacles that must still be overcome. Defarge is but a part of this movement, as much controlled as controller. Defarge links the sea metaphor with the Bastille as he organizes the whirling mob about his shop, commands the "living sea" to rise, and is cast by the sea against the cannon which helps secure victory. Each of the movements in the passage produces a rolling sensation as the sea rises "wave on wave, depth on depth," while the obstacles, carefully dehumanized and faceted into massive units, remain obdurate as if they will never to destroyed—like waves cresting and breaking on rocks only to crest again. We see the image of Defarge surfacing again and again, and the noise of the battle becomes dominant in the latter sequence, rising into a crescendo of "shrieks, volleys, execrations, bravery without stint, boom, smash and rattle," only to be broken by the silent parley which is seen from a distance as Dickens momentarily withdraws from the battle, and finally the deluge of movement as victory is secured. Each phase of the action merges into the next as sounds, images, and characters clash only to emerge in new conjunctions.

From **John P. McWilliams, Jr., "Progress without Politics: *A Tale of Two Cities*,"** (1977) *Clio*, 7: 1, pp. 19–31

McWilliams, Jr., is one of many critics to examine *A Tale of Two Cities* as an historical novel. Seeking to explain the novel's well-recognized weaknesses of characterization, humor, and credibility, he argues that Dickens concentrated on the domestic plot in order to avoid political issues. McWilliams, Jr., discusses Dickens's response to the Chartist movement (see Contextual Overview, **p. 13**), noting that he favored nonviolent reform brought about by public pressure, a pressure that he realized is hard to sustain. Because Dickens had no confidence in the ruling classes and he feared violent, revolutionary action in response to Victorian England's social problems, the novel deliberately veers away from political questions by turning them, and their solution, into moral issues. Through the plot, "Dickens could still control the monster of revolution by devising a tale in which no political issue is finally pertinent either to the assumed certainty of social progress or to the conduct of the truly virtuous man."[1] For another reading that stresses Dickens as a moral rather than political writer (and praises rather than faults him for it) see Orwell (Modern Criticism, **pp. 68–70**).

Thus the novel was written at a time when Dickens, fearing French invasion, could discover no political outlet for his sense of social outrage.[2] The power of its French scenes, in turn, derives from Dickens' ability to build unrelieved fear and anger simultaneously in his reader. His descriptions of pre-Revolutionary France create a demand for political and social action. The hunger of the masses, oppressive feudal dues, *lettres de cachet*, the *droit du seigneur*, legalized torture, a treasure depleted by aristocratic graft[3] – all of these injustices induce the reader to sympathize, not with the Jacquerie as men, but with their cause. After Saint Antoine has risen to power, however, the persistence of mass hunger, the denial of legal rights to the accused, confiscation of property, and mob violence condoned by self-appointed tribunals are made to seem equally intolerable. One set of abuses simply replaces another, with sympathy extended to the victim, be he peasant or aristocrat. There seems to be no possibility for moderation, no way in which legalized abuses could find legal remedy. What Carlyle called "the whole *daemonic* nature of man"[4] surfaces in every segment of French Society – in Saint Antoine, in Monseigneur's salon, in revolutionary tribunals – and

---

1    McWilliams, Jr., "Progress without Politics," p. 30.
2    In May 1859 (Dickens began writing *A Tale of Two Cities* in February), the British Government agreed to the formation of a Volunteer Rifle Corps in response to a growing threat of war with France. In a speech on December 22 1859, Dickens praised the brave volunteers who were ready to defend their country from invasion. See K.J. Fielding (ed.), *The Speeches of Charles Dickens*, Hemel Hempstead: Harvester-Wheatsheaf, 1988, pp. 288–9.
3    Illicit profit by corrupt means. For a discussion of these evils of the *ancien régime* see Contextual Overview, **pp. 8–9**. The *droit de seigneur* was the right of the feudal lord to take the place of the groom on his wedding night. It is unlikely that this right was ever commonly practised but it became a popular legend in discussions of the *ancien régime* before and after the Revolution.
4    [McWilliams' note.] Carlyle, *The French Revolution*, I, 14. See also Contemporary Documents, pp. 31–7.

prevents the reader from approving any means, or even any possibility, of social betterment. Feudal law, popular rule and mob anarchy seem, in practice, but three faces of tyranny.

Dickens' portrayal of pre-Revolutionary France forces his reader to accept the need for investing sufficient power in the citizenry to guarantee individual rights. Dickens' portrayal of Revolutionary France, however, shows society's need for permanent laws to control the anarchy of the mob. Through his ability to dramatize injustice, Dickens convinces the reader that these conflicting needs are equally worthy, yet he refuses to confront the dilemma of resolving them. The emotional energies created by clashing political feelings are allowed no constructive outlet. Dickens can relieve the fears aroused by his novel's chain of tyrannies only by wishing its individual links out of existence. The narrator may denounce the principle of vengeance, but he exults in Gaspard's murder of the Marquis. Similarly, the rite of murder celebrated beside the grindstone elicits a response from the author which is as brutal as any act of the mob: "And as the frantic wielders of these weapons snatched them from the stream of sparks and tore away into the streets, the same red hue was red in their frenzied eyes – eyes which any unbrutalized beholder would have given twenty years of life to petrify with a well-directed gun".[5] Because no political means of controlling either the Marquis or the mob can be conceived, killing them has become disquietingly attractive.

Vengeful sentiments appear almost exclusively in the "picturesque" historical scenes of the novel, scenes in which the fictional plot is not advanced, time is momentarily frozen, and the major characters appear in real but subsidiary roles. This fact suggests Dickens' crucial, but possibly unintentional, fictive method. The complex, ingenious tale Dickens has devised for the Revolutionary era is his means of controlling his volatile political attitudes. His shaping of plot and deployment of characters permit him to maintain the viewpoint of a middle-class Englishman, a bystander who need not adopt a consistent political stance. Characters are imagined, a plot is invented, which allow Dickens to turn political issues into moral issues, to maintain an unchallengeable skepticism regarding political affairs, and ultimately to dismiss presumably insoluble political considerations altogether.

[. . .]

By control of plot, Dickens turns historical and political issues into familial and moral issues. Evrémonde uses the *droit du seigneur* and the *lettre de cachet* to hideous ends, but Dickens emphasizes the moral outrage these practices work upon the families of Dr. Manette and Madame Defarge (separating husband from wife, killing children) rather than the injustice of the law itself. Similarly, the reader's emotions during Darnay's two French trials are directed, not toward the lawlessness of the tribunal's judicial procedures, but toward the impending guillotining of an innocent man and his separation from his wife. Madame Defarge, who is offered to the reader as the implacable force underlying all actions of the Jacquerie, has no political opinions, ideas, or policies whatsoever. She is solely motivated by an insatiable craving to avenge the wrongs done her

---

5    See p. 149.

sister, brother, and father. By refusing to endow Madame Defarge with any sense of political principle, Dickens effectively discredits the Revolutionary cause. In all three instances, the reader's anger over the crime done to the family is aggravated at the expense of his protest against those legal abuses which permit the crime.

[. . .]

The extent to which Dickens shifts political issues into moral issues can most readily be seen in his omissions. Carlyle had held no great respect for the "Gospel of Jean Jacques," but he had recognized the importance of words in moving Frenchmen to action.[6] Among the figures at Monseigneur's salon, Dickens includes "unbelieving Philosophers who were remodelling the world with words" (II, 7). Nowhere else in the novel, however, does he intimate that the Revolution had an ideological basis. Carlyle had devoted many chapters to the Constitutional Monarchy, to the attempts of the National and Legislative Assemblies to make a constitution, and to the sincere if misguided attempts to widen the franchise, to disestablish the church, and to centralize governmental bureaucracy.[7] Dickens, however, singles out Carlyle's scenes of mass violence in history (the fall of the Bastille, the massacre of Foulon, the Terror, the guillotine), then reworks Carlyle's accounts into even more visual, and equally rhetorical, set pieces. All the attempts at reform, all the debates over various polities, in fact all the strictly political history of the Revolution, are wholly ignored. Dickens presumably believes that political developments had no more lasting importance in the 1790's than in the 1850's.

At this point we should remind ourselves that the political history of France between 1789 and 1792 comprises at least as dramatic, and almost as picturesque, a source of fictional material as its scenes of popular action. To include such materials, however, would blur Dickens' attack upon the evils of both the old and new orders. It would suggest that political reform might achieve something, that non-emigrating aristocrats helped to lead the Revolution, and that an achieved revolution is not necessarily synonymous with the Terror. In 1860 these are possibilities Dickens does not wish to emphasize. All he will say for Darnay's "glorious vision of doing good" upon returning to France in 1792, for example, is that it represents "the sanguine mirage of many good minds." All the more unfortunate, Dickens reflects, because Darnay knew in his heart "that bad aims were being worked out in his own unhappy land by bad instruments" (II, 24).

It is the plot which frees Dickens from the complexities of Carlyle's history and enables him to picture a revolution made inevitable by aristocracy, but instigated by mobs of the lowest classes. While the political implications of revolution are thereby avoided, its class implications are steadily confronted. The reader's anger against feudalism is repeatedly aroused, not by the wrongs done to the poor in Saint Antoine, who remain caricatures of crazed vengeance, but by the imprisonment of Dr. Manette, a middle-class professional man. Dickens' nominal hero (the man who marries his heroine) is a liberal aristocrat who discards his feudal rights, but not his property. His reward and happiness is to become an untitled wage earner without sacrificing either his gentlemanly bearing or his feelings

---

6    [McWilliams' note.] Carlyle, I, 282. [Jean-Jacques is Jean-Jacques Rousseau. See Contemporary Documents, **pp. 30–1**].

7    See Contextual Overview, **pp. 9–11**.

of noblesse oblige. Darnay knows that he is simply "better" than the ruling Jacquerie (II, 4). His superior character is often confirmed by Dickens, who insists, for example, that the Revolutionary Tribunals[8] were made up of "the lowest, cruelest and worst" people of Paris (III, 6). [. . .]

Carlyle had explicitly recognized that the Revolution had been supported, and in considerable measure led, by lawyers and by merchants who sought a freer marketplace. In Dickens' France there seem to be only the dehumanized, vengeful masses and the luxury loving, cruel aristocracy. Dickens' Jacobins are not lawyers but the starving urban poor. The job-holding, middle-class figures in the novel – Stryver, Carton, Charles Darnay, Mr. Lorry, and Dr. Manette – are all either Englishmen or French emigrés living in England. Neither the French aristocracy nor the peasantry seem human. The Jacquerie are caricatures, the mob is consistently compared to animals, and the aristocracy are characterized by images of stone and statuary. Dickens, of course, seeks to discredit the Revolution by depriving it of any support from liberal gentlemen or the middle class. The intended contemporary relevance of Dickens' misinterpretation, however, is less clear. Dickens may be implying that, because England still has middle and genteel classes, a revolution at home is not likely. Or, in accord with his darkening temper, he may be convinced that the English middle class, now truly a mere "fringe" on the aristocracy, has become so small in number, so selfish in motive, that it no longer acts as a buffer or supports social reform.

[. . .]

The concluding scene of *A Tale of Two Cities*, and the public's reaction to it, reveal that the coming of a French Revolution to England was a prophecy which neither Dickens nor his contemporaries could easily bear. The Christlike death of Sydney Carton washes away the dire political threat of the Terror. The reader is offered an individual resurrection to atone for the patent failure of a political resurrection. Carton dies, not to save Charles Darnay for the future good of England, but to save Lucie Manette's family from destruction. The false religion of Revolution, subtly portrayed in the patterned ecstasies of the Carmagnole, the sacramental blood markings beside the grindstone, and the worship of the Goddess of Liberty, are thus replaced by an exemplum of the highest Christian conduct. It is little wonder that, in late nineteenth-century dramatic versions, *A Tale of Two Cities* became in great measure the story of Sydney Carton. By holding up Carton's death to the reader, Dickens reassures him that the insanity and bloodletting of revolution, even if it should come again, will not ultimately matter. Personal sacrifice is a sufficient recompense for the evils of history.

A closer reading of Dickens' ending, however, reveals how reluctant he was to give up the treasured nineteenth-century ideal of social progress. Like Carlyle, Dickens wished to offer at least a possibility that society as well as the individual could be redeemed. After Carton dies contemplating the words "I am the Resurrection and the Life," Dickens re-creates for us Carton's last prophetic thoughts: "I see a beautiful city and a beautiful people arising from this abyss, and in their struggles to be truly free, in their triumphs and defeats, through long years

---

8    On March 11, 1793, a Revolutionary Tribunal was established in Paris to try people accused of anti-Revolutionary activities or sentiments. In September the Tribunal was expanded to four courts so that cases could be heard day and night.

to come, I see the evil of this time, and of the previous time of which this is the natural birth, gradually making expiation for itself and wearing out" (III, 15). These are, truly, mere words which are unconfirmed by anything Dickens has shown us in revolutionary history or by his observations of man as a political animal. A hope phrased as a certainty, these words depend on the pathos of the fictional situation for whatever plausibility they possess. It is as if the death of Sydney Carton somehow can atone for revolutionary insanity; as if, by his death, Carton had made possible the social progress for which Dickens could find no adequate political means.

## From **Albert Hutter, "Nation and Generation in *A Tale of Two Cities*,"** (1978) *PMLA*, 93, pp. 448–62

This essay is the most influential and far-reaching of the Freudian studies of the novel. Whereas many readers have complained that the private love story of Lucie Manette and Charles Darnay is artificially projected onto the backdrop of the French Revolution and that Madame Defarge's revenge has no political meaning (see McWilliams, Jr., for example, **pp. 80–1**), Hutter argues that the novel dramatizes the interplay between family dynamics and political or economic events that brings about social change. He takes his title from Bruce Mazlish's *James and John Stuart Mill: Father and Son in the Nineteenth Century*,[1] in which Mazlish identifies nineteenth-century generational conflict between fathers and sons as deriving from the industrial, scientific, and political revolutions of the time. He argues that this generational conflict gave rise to social change just as surely as did class conflict. Hutter finds this relationship between generational and political conflict played out in *A Tale of Two Cities*. The story depicts the revolution that was occurring in both family and public life in the England of 1859, centering on father–son conflict. The French Revolution and the resulting reform movement in England "inevitably changed Victorian father–son relations. But the changing Victorian family, in turn, reshaped society."[2] Hutter centers his reading around the psychoanalytic implications of the father–son conflict, found in the "primal scene"[3] that begins the action (although hidden until nearly the end of the novel): a young Doctor Manette is "forced to witness the aftermath of a violent sexual assault" perpetrated by an authority (or father) figure, Charles Darnay's uncle the Marquis.

[. . .] As much as any other work of 1859, *A Tale of Two Cities* demonstrates the correlation between family and nation, and it uses the language of psychological conflict and psychological identification to portray social upheaval and the restoration of social order.

1  New York: Basic Books, 1975.
2  Hutter, p. 448, paraphrasing Mazlish, pp. 7–8.
3  Psychoanalysts have for years recognized the importance of the "primal scene," the child's first observation of parental sex. For Freud, this observation is always traumatic and can lead to neurosis.

Nation and generation converge in the earliest chronological event of *A Tale of Two Cities*, Doctor Manette's story of the Evrémondes' brutality (III, 10 [. . .]). [. . .] The events Manette describes, a microcosm of the larger narrative, trigger the major actions and reversals of the double plot. The rape itself implies social exploitation, a class-wide droit du seigneur. Conversely, one peasant's attack on his master anticipates the nation's reply to such abuse. The Evrémonde who raped the girl and murdered her brother will later run down a small child from the Paris slums, and as a result will be "driven fast to his tomb." The retaliation denied one peasant, a generation earlier, is carried out by the revolutionary "Jacques." Even the Paris tribunal at which Manette's story is read reflects a struggle between parents and children: Manette has condemned his son-in-law to death.

[. . .]

Manette's story is the narrative equivalent of a trauma: it recalls an event that precedes all the other action of the novel and organizes that action, although it is not "recovered" until quite late in the novel. Modern psychoanalytic theory recognizes the retrospective quality of trauma, the way in which the individual reconstructs his past life to conform with present conflicts and thereby invests a past event with significance—some of it real, often some of it imagined. Manette's document stands in a similar relationship to the larger novel: within the structure of the *Tale* it acts like a traumatic memory, reliving the significant antecedent events of the entire plot at the climax of Darnay's second trial. The document reveals the combination of public and private acts that informs the narrative; it records the "primal scene" of the text itself.

[. . .]

Spying, like virtually everything else in this novel, has two meanings—one public, the other private. The official spies, like Barsad, are instruments of repression and representatives of the "fathers," the men in power. But in other contexts, like the Cruncher scenes, children spy on their parents. In both cases spying expresses the *Tale*'s dominant conflicts. Thus the Gorgon's Head witnesses much more than the murder of the Marquis: it sees the deadly struggle between two generations, which is climaxed by implicit filicide and patricide. Dickens anticipates the public murders of the Revolution while suggesting the private conflict of Charles Darnay through the subtle mixture of two plot lines. [. . .]

The Marquis has desired the death of his nephew, and Charles, more covertly, has imagined the sudden death of his father's twin. There is the suggestion, but never the realization, of both filicide and patricide. But the exchange between the Marquis and his nephew is framed by the murder of a child and the murder of the Marquis himself. The former symbolizes the Marquis's murderous impulses toward his brother's child, as well as the cruelty of the French ruling classes toward their dependents, like the abuse witnessed by Doctor Manette eighteen years earlier. At the same time, the revenge that follows is both an actualization of Charles's revenge against his father's surrogate and a gesture that shows the French peasantry rising up to murder its rulers, as they will ultimately murder the father of their country in the revolutionary act of regicide. [. . .]

That Darnay should flee such a country is hardly surprising, but the political reasons for flight are intensified by his personal desire to avoid the retribution prophesied by his mother for the sins of his fathers. And the futility of that flight becomes apparent with his return to France after the Revolution. Darnay's fate is to be forced, against his conscious desire, into a deadly struggle with his fathers: his own father, his father's identical twin, his father-in-law. Although Darnay and Manette learn to respect and love each other, their goodwill is repeatedly subverted by events. Charles's marriage to Lucie nearly kills Manette, and Manette's document in turn condemns Darnay to the guillotine. The characters seem to be moved by something larger than their individual desires, by the sins of a nation, which inevitably lead only to more sin, to an orgy of murder and retribution. The political meaning of these acts is intensified by a deep and persistent psychological theme, at times so perfectly merged with the political that one and the same act may be construed as personal revenge, patricide, and regicide.

If the murderer of Evrémonde symbolically enacts Darnay's violence and vengeance, then Sydney Carton enacts another side of Darnay's character and pays for the hero's aggression. Carton's sacrifice is a convenient, if implausible, device to free Charles from the Bastille; it is also an attempt to solve an insoluble political dilemma. The revolutionaries justifiably overthrow their rulers, but their hatred leads to excesses that turn despised oppressor into sympathetic victim. The sins of the fathers are endlessly repeated, from generation to generation, and Dickens' unrealistic solution creates a character who, Christlike, will sacrifice himself for the sins of all mankind. But Carton's transformation from guilty scoundrel to hero also indicates a deeper, psychological transformation. This paragon of irreverence, having mocked and antagonized Mr. Lorry, now achieves a sudden closeness to the old banker. [. . .] He[4] transforms his life by internalizing his father's image, using Lorry as a surrogate: his earlier aimlessness dissolves and a new mission identifies him with the most famous—and self-sacrificing—of sons. Carton begins to achieve a sense of historical and personal identity, and the novel ends with Carton reborn through his namesakes, Lucie's son and grandson. And with Carton's newfound strength and purpose, Darnay becomes "like a young child in [Carton's] hands." Unconscious, Darnay is delivered to old Manette and Lucie and carried out of France like a sleeping baby (III, xiii). This sequence suggests that, as the hero's double internalizes paternal authority and willingly sacrifices himself to it, the innocent hero may be reborn.

In the next section, omitted here, Hutter compares the father–son conflict as it played out in England and France in the nineteenth century. He argues that in England, and particularly in the world of business (represented in the novel by Mr. Lorry and Tellson's bank), sons turn external authority into internal self-control and become authority figures in their turn. In Dickens's France, this accommodation is impossible, and the result is anarchy and mob violence. Even in Jerry Cruncher's "business" the father–son relationship comments on the dominant theme. Jerry's son witnesses another "primal scene," both violent and sexual, "at once psychological and social, suggesting both a child's vision of his parents' sexuality and the historical nightmare of the French Revolution."

---

4  Carton.

Dickens' familial and political revolutions are expressed by his varied use of splitting throughout the novel, so that the theme of the work becomes as well its characteristic mode of expression. From the title through the rhetorically balanced opening paragraphs,[5] Dickens establishes the "twoness" of everything to follow: characters are twinned and doubled and paired; the setting is doubled; the women, as we shall see, are split; the historical perspective is divided between an eighteenth-century event and its nineteenth-century apprehension. "Splitting" thus describes a variety of stylistic devices, particularly related to character development and plot. But "splitting" also has two important psychoanalytic meanings: a splitting of the individual (specifically, the ego) and a splitting of the object. That is, an individual may deal with a specific problem, relationship, or trauma either by dividing himself or by dividing the problematic "other" (parent, loved one). Splitting is a fundamental mode of psychological defense and a key concept in the development of psychoanalytic theory. It originated in a description of schizophrenia and is now recognized as a central mechanism of multiple personality; but it may also be part of a normal adaptive strategy for coping with any intense relationship.

Dickens manipulates both emotional conflict and its solution by "splitting" in the technical, psychoanalytic sense: his characters distance their emotions from an immediate, and disturbing, reality (thus Lorry's remark to Lucie about his lack of feeling or Carton's apparent ability to separate himself from everything except the "higher" emotions at the close); he divides a single ego into two (Carton/Darnay); and he splits the "object," allowing one person (Charles's uncle) to bear the brunt of the hero's hatred or aggression toward Charles's father. Conversely, Dickens' use of doubles may suggest, not splitting, but reunifying something once divided or divisible: the comic identification of Jerry, Jr., with his father or the larger movement between London and Paris, which connects seemingly disparate incidents and persons and ultimately unites the two plots. Even in the famous rhetoric of the opening, the balanced opposites suggest their own ultimate fusion. The use of splitting in a work this long is too varied and extensive to justify simple praise or blame—splitting is primarily a descriptive term—but it should clarify the understandably divided critical assessment of the novel.

[. . .] I have suggested that the failed comedy of the Crunchers derives, in part, from a failure to control, or sufficiently disguise, the primal-scene material implicit throughout the text. Dickens' historical oversimplification reflects, as we have seen, a merging of family and class struggles that was both characteristic and particularly problematic in the nineteenth century. Carton's role, both as a "double" to the hero and as a melodramatic scapegoat at the close, develops the dual conflicts of the novel; indeed, much of the sentimentality of Carton-as-Christ is derived from his conversion, via Lorry, into the good son and the good conservative. Carton's solution is that of any son—or class—that willingly accepts the pain or injustice inflicted upon it by parents or rulers, and such a solution is not particularly satisfying to most readers. In his peculiarly calm and heroic way, Carton stands for the ideals of conservative belief, in the family and the nation, but he finally assumes too many meanings and is required to connect too many

---

threads of the novel. He suffers chronically from meaning too much in relation to too many other characters and themes and, like Manette's document, unites too many incidents; he becomes more strained as he becomes more important.

Other kinds of splitting in *A Tale of Two Cities* far more successfully project the text's central conflicts, precisely because they require no resolution. Dickens' caricature of the lion and the jackal, for example, exploits an inherent, unresolvable tension in his social subject. The division of labor between Carton and Stryver powerfully suggests not only Carton's divided self but the divided goals and morals of Victorian business. Divided imagery, like split objects, also contributes to the intense passages describing the Terror. [. . .]

## From **Garrett Stewart, "Traversing the Interval,"** (1984) in *Death Sentences: Styles of Dying in British Fiction* (Cambridge, Mass. and London: Harvard University Press, 1984), pp. 53–97

In his discussion of "traversing the interval," American interdisciplinary scholar Garrett Stewart examines the grammar and rhetoric of the prose that takes a literary character from life to death: "Death stands as a pivotal moment for language on the edge of silence, for evocation on the verge of the invisible, for narratability on the brink of closure."[1] In an earlier chapter, Stewart notes the popularity of drowning deaths for literature because they allow for the return of the dying person to nature and the instant recall of an entire lifetime at the moment of death. Sydney Carton's death (figuratively a drowning) redeems the iniquitous stone-heartedness of the aristocracy, symbolized by the Marquis's stony death (see Stoehr, **pp. 73–4**). That death scene "is channeled directly into, and filtered clean by, the sacrificial (and literal) decapitation of the hero, Carton, where the apocalyptic images of flood that follow from the marquis's murder are internalized as the private mind's 'drowning' vision. It is a vision compressed and, in the hero's access to narrative grace, prophetic."[2] In the following passages, Stewart draws attention to the "verbal rhythm" of Dickens's prose at the end of the novel that separates the human figures – Carton and the seamstress – from the mechanical mob watching them. He concludes that the reader shares in Darnay's rescue when we are a part of the group fleeing Paris for London (Key Passages, **pp. 155–7**). Stewart's is the most complete defence of both Carton's prophetic vision and his final lines (Key Passages, **pp. 162–3**), which Stewart relates to the antitheses of the opening chapter. The novel has moved from "the superlative degree of comparison only" to a "far, far better" comparison, in which Carton's sacrifice vindicates the sins of a whole epoch.

[. . .] One of the first full-scale renderings of the Parisian scene under the Reign of Terror comes to us filtered through its horrific revelation to the mind of

1    Stewart, "Traversing the Interval," p. 51.
2    Stewart, "Traversing the Interval," p. 85.

Jarvis Lorry: "All this was seen in a moment, as the vision of a drowning man, or any human creature at any very great pass, could see a world if it were there" (III, ch. 3). Drowning is Dickens's definitive metaphor for this rite of perceptual passage, with the noun "vision" suspended in the periodic sentence long enough to stand for both effect and cause, vista and empowered eyesight. Fortified by countless later analogies to the Terror as a bloody Flood come again, this simile foresees the visionary acuity that the hero himself achieves when he drowns symbolically in the tidal heave of revolutionary violence.

[. . .]

Lazarus-like, making good on the first person of the Lord's annunciation,[3] Carton ascends not through but to his death scene, from the stilled "deep" of his humanity into that public storm where "fifty-two were to roll that afternoon on the life-tide of the city to the boundless everlasting sea" (III, ch. 13). Even the figurative verb there is a threefold pun compounding the oceanic metaphor of death with its literal cause and effect in the remorseless roll of the condemned and the consequent roll of their heads under the guillotine. For the man whose mother had died in his infancy, his goal, shared with the seamstress whom he has befriended in his last hours, will be to rejoin the "Universal Mother" across the untraversable distance of death's "dark highway." It is a distance implicated in the interval of a nearby play on words, Carton and the girl hoping "to repair home together, to rest in her bosom" (III, ch. 15), where the imagined journey to their long home overtakes and includes the sense of a "reparation" for all earthly losses.

There, as throughout the death scene, the violent revolutionary sea changes seem to set in motion a compensatory verbal rhythm of wavering and restitution. As Carton nears his and the book's end, the Dickensian rhetoric detaches crucial phrases from within, releases words to each other in new ways, submits the burden of the unsayable to the ebb and turn of surprising allusions, nuances, and ambiguities. Here is the death of the seamstress just before Carton: "She goes next before him—is gone; the knitting-women count Twenty-Two" (III, ch. 15). A semicolon keeps separate the ledger of vendetta—ticking off its corpses with mindless metronomic precision—from the empathetic prose of the dying, clocked to a more humane rhythm. Across the dash of the scaffold's inflexible continuity in numeration and its fatal hiatus, the verb of motion, "goes," becomes the past participle of absence in "is gone," a phrase inserted above the line in Dickens's manuscript as a masterly afterthought. Similarly the adverb "next" and the preposition "before," each not only spatial but temporal, are evaporated with temporality itself into the paradoxical present tense of instant-aneous removal, "is gone," predicating still what in the same interval it eradi-cates. Imagine the phrase otherwise and you hear what Dickensian tact has managed with the grammatical parataxis,[4] "She goes next before him and is gone." With the refusal of ordinary conjunction in the world's terms, the suspended tense

---

3    Christ brought Lazarus, brother of Mary and Martha, back to life, fulfilling the promise of the annunciation (announcement to Mary that her baby, Jesus, would be the Son of God). In the Lazarus story Christ says the words reiterated several times by Sydney Carton in the novel: "I am the resurrection, and the life: he that believeth in me, though he were dead, yet shall he live; and whosoever liveth and believeth in me shall never die." See John 11:25–6.

4    The arrangement of clauses without connectives (Dickens removes "and" from the sentence).

of "is" lingers across the split second of recorded absence as a softening consecration of the girl's impress, if not still her presence, for the man who came out of himself to care.

That phrase "next before him" is the last direct reference, even by pronoun, to the hero. After a paragraph reiterating the text of "I am the Resurrection and the Life," we pass to another elided interval: "The murmuring of many voices, the upturning of many faces, the pressing on of many footsteps in the outskirts of the crowd, so that it swells forward in a mass like one great heave of water, all flashes away. Twenty-Three." In that long periodic building toward recapitulated subject and burst verb for the death sentence, the final predication of the hostile mob at its falling away from the hero, his from it, compresses its gerundive forms,[5] the named actions of the inimical world in all its otherness, weight, and forward thrust, lets its grammar heap forward even into a suspensive independent clause ("so that it swells"), and then, at the pivotal instant of similitude (the monosyllabic massing at "like one great heave of water") undercuts the whole cumulative grammar of the world's inertial resistance with a dismissive idiom. The phrase "flashes away" is not only a formulaic description of drowning quite common in literary treatments [. . .] but it is also an echo of that earlier murder of Madame Defarge and the sacrificial impairment of Miss Pross:[6] " 'I feel,' said Miss Pross, 'as if there had been a flash and a crash, and that crash was the last thing I should ever hear in this life' " (III, ch. 14). [. . .] For what Miss Pross, clinging to Madame Defarge "with more than the hold of a drowning woman," saw and heard, the murderousness of the world turned against itself, is what Carton will no longer be made to suffer, having taken the violence unto himself as his own liberating fate. The canceling "crash" that follows the earlier gunpowder "flash" has become the guillotine's twice-repeated "Crash!" by which the whole scene of terror, in a chiastic inversion[7] of the earlier death scene and its rhetoric, is finally "flashed" away for Carton, at the moment when the ferocious ocean of hate both overtakes and cleanses him.

> Here Stewart analyzes Carton's prophetic statement – a series of "I see's" that rewrite Doctor Manette's Bastille prophecy that his family would not remember him.

Enunciated in the unvoiced cadences of sublime confidence, style thus humanizes into visionary view the last interval of a death scene. [. . .] Degenerated history, exploded toward revolution and apocalypse by the death of Marquis St. Evrémonde, is returned after the flood of bitter judgment into the flow of temporal history again, regenerate now, imaginable by narrative even in its

---

5  "Murmuring," "upturning," and "pressing" are gerunds, or present participles (verb forms) used as nouns.
6  Miss Pross is left permanently deaf by the explosion of Madame Defarge's gun.
7  In chiasmus, two parts of a phrase are reversed in the next phrase, so Miss Pross's "flash and a crash" becomes for Carton the unmentioned "crash" of the guillotine followed by the flashing away of the hostile crowd. There was no "flash" for Miss Pross because she is deafened.

merely eventual shapes. [. . .] First, Carton does not see into and through the grave of his own fate to some intimation of immortality, or at least not until the novel's last clause. From the edge of eternity he peers back into the world of time, and forward there, as if through eternity's sanction as an incomparable vantage on time, into confident earthly prefiguration. Second, it is the final decorum of the novel as record, however fictional, that the generations availed and so evoked by Carton's sacrifice do not outdistance the time elapsed between the Revolution and Dickens's writing of the novel in the middle of the next century. Even within the myth of clairvoyance the authority of fiction, like the authority of deathbed revelation, is held to the precincts of retrospect.

[. . .] In the vanishing interval of final consciousness, Carton's metaphorically drowning mind does indeed look back on the story of his soul's dark night told over as conscious tragic narrative, a story of course transfigured by the death that offers it up as completed and transmissible tale. No novel could fasten more surely the always tacit bond between mortality and communicable narration. Carton's dramatized and consummating death scene is displaced into an articu-late exemplum discovered at the very moment of his death to be recoverable in the telling, time out of mind. And so the tale recounted by Lucie's son becomes, in short—and of course in its shortened form—the title scene of *The Tale* that earns its closure by foreseeing it.

From **Chris Brooks, " 'Recalled to Life': The Christian Myth of *A Tale of Two Cities*"** (1984), in *Signs for the Times: Symbolic Realism in the Mid-Victorian World* (London: George Allen & Unwin), pp. 84–95

The renowned cultural historian and Victorian scholar Chris Brooks provides the most comprehensive Christian reading of *A Tale of Two Cities*. Arguing that Dickens adopted Carlyle's "transcendental reading of history and his sub-sequent typological method[1]" [in *The French Revolution*, see Contemporary Documents, **pp. 31–7**]. Brooks finds the novel a sustained allegory of Christian redemption, based on the writings of the fourth-century theologian Saint Augustine (354–430). In *The City of God* (413–27) Augustine describes the material world, or the City of Man, as a sinful place that was separated from God by Adam and Eve's "original sin" in the Garden of Eden (known in Christian terms as the "Fall" or "lapse" of man; prelapsarian refers to the time in the Garden of Eden; postlapsarian is after the Fall). Christ came into the world to redeem fallen mankind and to bring the faithful to the City of God and everlasting life. Brooks begins by identifying both London and Paris in *A Tale of Two Cities* as Augustine's fallen City of Man. The shadow of the gallows hangs over both cities, and order is maintained by force, leading to anarchy, "an

1   Typology here refers to the foreshadowing of events in the New Testament by events in the Old Testament. The notion of the "fortunate Fall" (that Adam and Eve's sin brought about the coming of Christ) is such an event.

indiscriminate and institutionalised destructiveness".[2] Sydney Carton "carries the spiritual burden of the City of Man"[3] and only by taking on the divinity of Christ can he redeem not just Charles Darnay and his family but also the whole City of Man, as revealed in his prophetic words.

Condemned to physical and spiritual death in the City of Man, man cannot forge his own salvation. The hope represented by Lucie can only exist as long as the past can be ignored;[4] the Revolution is bound to the past and destroys all hope of the future. In the eschatological frame of the novel,[5] [. . .] the past event as a result of which man is condemned, and the consequences of which he cannot escape, is the Fall. Lapsarian[6] man is alienated from his fellow: that 'every human creature is constituted to be that profound secret and mystery to every other' is 'his natural and not to be alienated inheritance' (I, 3 [. . .]). Paralleling this, and inherent in it, man's separation from God [. . .] is announced through the physical, phenomenal world.

> And so, under a short grove of feebler and feebler over-swinging lamps, out under the great grove of stars.
>    Beneath that arch of unmoved and eternal lights . . . the shadows of the night were broad and black. (I, 6 [. . .])

The semantics of the passage become clear in the context both of the rest of the novel and of earlier novels. As the fireflies mimic the stars and man imitates a 'better order of beings' in *Little Dorrit*,[7] so here the 'unmoved and eternal' lights of heaven find echo in the 'feebler and feebler' lamps of the City of Man, contending inadequately with the 'broad and black' shadows of 'the darkness of this world'. Trapped in the City of Destruction,[8] man's separation from the stars is fixed and, for anything he can do to help himself, final. When Darnay as Evrémonde is finally condemned, Carton's statement, ' "He will perish: there is no real hope" ' (III, 11 [. . .]), has a suggestiveness far greater than its immediate function as part of the machinery of dramatic tension. Carton is right: the 'real' world of the novel is, quite literally, hopeless. The conclusion towards which so much of Dickens's imaginative development had been leading is, in Carton's statement, reached. In the 'real' world, man is inescapably doomed. [. . .]

2  Chris Brooks, "Recalled to Life," p. 85.
3  Chris Brooks, "Recalled to Life," p. 92.
4  Brooks has argued that Lucie brings hope to her father, Doctor Manette, and her husband, Charles Darnay, but both men fail to acknowledge their past lives in France so Lucie cannot save them.
5  Eschatalogy in Christian thought refers to the Last Judgment, when Christ returns to judge the living and the dead, and the life after death of individual souls.
6  More commonly known as postlapsarian; see headnote.
7  The novel which preceded *A Tale of Two Cities*, published in monthly parts from December 1855 to June 1857.
8  The Puritan writer John Bunyan refers to Augustine's City of Man as the City of Destruction in his allegory of the Christian life, *The Pilgrim's Progress* (1678). Carton dies for "Evrémonde", or Everyman.

Hemmed in by the darkness of the City of Man, the final stage of Carton's journey towards his spiritual identity, the journey 'of a tired man, who had wandered and struggled and got lost, but who at length struck into his road and saw its end' (II, 9 [. . .]), begins with the formal announcement of the Christian doctrine of resurrection.[9] [. . .] During the night, with the words of the covenant of resurrection 'in the echoes of his feet, and . . . in the air', Carton walks contemplating 'the whole life and death of the city' which, 'dominated by the axe', has 'travelled that length of self-destruction' to the denial of Christian hope. The procession of victims is endless and futile; the graveyards promise only 'Eternal Sleep'. Finally, Carton arrives at the river.[10] [. . .] The passage builds through two parallel semantic movements, from death to rebirth that simultaneously figure shifts of existential level from the mundane to the transcendental. The first of these movements is cosmic, universal. The day of Thanatos[11] comes, 'looking like a dead face out of the sky'; Sydney watches the created world die, the City of Man become a City of the Dead. But the triumph of Thanatos lasts only 'for a little while'. The brevity of 'Death's dominion' has specific biblical reference and authority: 'Christ being raised from the dead dieth no more; death hath no more dominion over him.'[12] The rising of 'the glorious sun' is, via traditional religious punning, the rising of the Son, in glory, over the kingdom of Death. [. . .] Dickens makes the connection between the sunrise of the risen Christ and Carton quite explicit. The 'long bright rays' not only realise the resurrection for Carton, but also bridge the gulf between the inner self and the sun/Son, between man and the Godhead. Nor is the bridge only a seeming reality: verbally and semantically bivalent, the 'bridge of light' both appears in the sense of 'seems', and appears in the sense of 'is made manifest'. The bridge exists both subjectively, in Sydney's perception, and objectively, a fact of the phenomenal [sic] world. In a single movement at once actual and symbolic, Carton's spiritual self, 'the light within him', disguised by mortality, imprisoned by the mundane world, is liberated through direct mystical communion with the transcendental non-self, the light of the risen sun, and becomes one with it. With the sudden immanence of the transcendental, Sydney Carton is ready to assume his spiritual identity.

The second half of the passage must be read in the context of the death and resurrection pattern of the first half, a pattern which it echoes and completes. Carton considers his mortal condition as it is imaged in the external world through the habitual Dickensian emblem of transience, the flowing river, 'so swift, so deep, and certain'. But 'the strong tide' that carries the assurance of mortality is 'like a congenial friend', for, in the Christian paradox of man's two states, death is the precondition to life. Carton's reading of the meaning of the river is not only an acceptance of inevitable mortality, but also, through the image of the eddy, a nihilistic renunciation of his life as 'purposeless'. In the parallelism set up by the paragraph divisions, and in the transcendental context of the preceding part of the passage, Carton's renunciation, the dismissal of his own life, may

9  Carton recalls the words read at his father's funeral, from Christ's resurrection of Lazarus. See note 3, p. 88.
10  See Key Passages, pp. 150–1 for the passage that Brooks analyzes in the next two paragraphs.
11  In Greek mythology, the personification of death.
12  [Brooks' note.] Romans, 6:9.

be seen as a symbolic death, a resignation of the ' "me" ' that is the mortal self to 'Death's dominion'. As before, that dominion does not last long. Straight-forwardly, but with potent effect, the figurative meaning of the eddy is, at the beginning of the next paragraph, imaginatively transferred to the trading-boat, with its sail, evocatively, 'the softened colour of a dead leaf'. With the passing of the boat, Sydney prays for forgiveness, his prayers ending coincidentally with the disappearance of the boat's 'silent track'. This juxtaposition of processes effects a symbolic transmission: the dying-away of the boat and the fading of its wash signal the relinquishing of mortal life and its attendant 'blindnesses and errors'. 'For he that is dead is freed from sin.'[13] What is left is the statement of resurrec-tion. The movement through death to rebirth in the first half of the passage is re-enacted in the personal microcosm of the second half. The liberation of Carton's spiritual inner self that concludes the first two paragraphs is completed by the relinquishment of the mortal and its attributes in the second two para-graphs. Overall, a cumulative process releases the transcendental from the mundane and climaxes in a final prayer that is also an affirmation: ' "I am the resurrection and the life." ' The speaker is Carton and, with the shock that comes from a suddenly apparent switch of focus, one realises that the supplicant has become the author of the prayer.[14]

## From **Cates Baldridge, "Alternatives to Bourgeois Individualism in *A Tale of Two Cities*"** (1990), *Studies in English Literature*, 30, pp. 633–54

Most readers find in *A Tale of Two Cities* a clear condemnation of collective thought and action, typified by the mob behavior of the Jacquerie and answered by the personal sacrifice of Sydney Carton. In this essay, American scholar Cates Baldridge argues that while, on the surface, Dickens espoused the middle-class, capitalist approval of individualism (the growing belief in "self help" and free enterprise made possible by the Industrial Revolution), a close reading of the novel uncovers a distinctly hostile attitude to individualism and a surprising sympathy with the Revolutionaries and their cry of "fraternity." While Baldridge explains that his argument involves a neo-Marxist interpretation of the novel, he is not arguing that Dickens was a Marxist, positing class conflict as the road to social progress. Rather, he is suggesting that Dickens, perhaps unconsciously, undermined his blatant attack on the Revolutionary collective through his depiction of the businessman Mr. Lorry and Sydney Carton's identification with Charles Darnay. Mr. Lorry, he argues, shares in the Revolutionary idea of the collectivity through his association with Tellson's Bank. Baldridge concludes by finding in the closing passages' insistence on Carton's individuality the proof that Dickens recognized his own subversive text and took pains to return the text to classical liberalism. Central to Baldridge's argument is the "night shadows" passage at the beginning of Book I, Chapter 3 (See Key Passages, **p. 122**).

---

13  [Brooks' note.] Romans, 6.7.
14  Carton, the supplicant asking for redemption, has been transformed into Christ, the provider of redemption.

[. . .] Middle-class orthodoxy posits the discrete human subject as primary and inviolable, a move which Harvey declares to be the indispensable core of Classical Liberalism, that ideology which he credits both with nurturing the infant genre of the novel in the eighteenth century and assuring its triumph in the nineteenth. Broadly defined, Liberalism is, says Harvey, a "state of mind [which] has as its controlling centre an acknowledgment of the plenitude, diversity and individuality of human beings in society, together with the belief that such characteristics are good as ends in themselves," and he goes on to assert that "tolerance, skepticism, [and] respect for the autonomy of others are its watchwords" while "fanaticism and the monolithic creed [are] its abhorrence."[1] Harvey's phrasing may strike some as overly laudatory, but it does help to underscore why the chronically permeable barriers of the self in *A Tale of Two Cities* constitute such a politically dangerous issue: in depicting the Revolution, the text takes pains to portray—and to roundly denounce—a counter-ideology to Classical Liberalism, in which the claims of the individual are assumed to be secondary to those of the collectivity, and in which the individual is seen as anything but sacrosanct. It should come as little surprise, then, that Dickens's most forceful statement of subversive sympathy for the Revolution's attack upon the idea of the discrete subject, his most anguished confession of ambivalence concerning the bourgeois notion of an inviolable individual, comprises what has long been considered merely an "anomalous" or "digressive" portion of the text—I refer specifically to the "Night Shadows" passage, a striking meditation upon the impenetrable barriers separating man from man which has proved perennially troublesome to readers.

[. . .] What clearly comes across is a deeply felt sadness and frustration before the impermeableness of the barriers between self and self—a despairing desire to merge the discrete and opaque personalities dictated by *Gesellschaft*[2] and to enter a state of communal knowledge and even communal being. Reflecting upon the iron-clad separation of souls within the "great city" may indeed provoke wonder and awe—but it also clearly elicits a wish that things might be otherwise.

The imagery employed in the passage is also pertinent if we remember that the working title of *A Tale* was "Buried Alive," for the passage continually attempts to blur the distinction between life and death, presenting a portrait of urban existence as a kind of living entombment. Not only does the incommunicability of souls have "something of the awfulness, even of Death itself . . . referable" to it, but the narrator, in his quest for closer communion with his fellow beings, speaks of himself as looking into "depths" for "glimpses of buried treasure." Furthermore, the deaths of his friend, neighbor, and love are described as "the inexorable consolidation and perpetuation" of their isolated, living states—as if these people are most true to their nature only after they have ceased to breathe. The final sentence, in which the corpses in actual graveyards are declared to be "sleepers" no more "inscrutable" than the town's "busy inhabitants," completes the equation of the living community with that of the dead. What the narrator has accomplished here is graphically to portray the "great city" as a metropolis in which

1  [Baldridge's note.] W.J. Harvey, *Character and the Novel* (Ithaca: Cornell Univ. Press, 1968), p. 24.
2  German for "society."

everyone is virtually "buried alive": to depict a condition of society in which each citizen goes about his everyday offices—and even endures his supposedly most intimate moments—enclosed in a sarcophagus of impenetrable individuality. As we shall see, this damning critique of the way we live now inaugurates the subversive subtext which runs beside and beneath the narrator's subsequent denigration of the French Revolution's insistence that collectivities must supersede the individual as the fundamental unit of social life; it is here that we can apprehend the first movement of that counter-current which dares to consider the ideology of the Jacquerie as a possible escape from the "solitary confinement" mandated by bourgeois individualism.

In the next section, Baldridge looks at the overtly anticollective rhetoric of the novel (in the mob scenes, for example) to argue that its very obviousness calls it into question.

I will now turn from *A Tale of Two Cities*' explicit rhetoric to its countervailing subtext and examine those passages in which the novel's repressed desire to escape the constraints of its own prevailing ideology can best be discerned. My argument is that the sentiments voiced in the "anomalous" Night Shadows passage do in fact recur throughout the text, but that Dickens's sincere allegiance to the commonplaces of Classical Liberalism forces him to displace them in two directions: toward the comic and toward the private. The former movement is expressed through Jarvis Lorry's at best intermittently successful suppression of his own personal claims in the interest of Tellson's Bank, a process which is rendered yet more innocuous by that institution's exaggerated traditionalism and firm allegiance to bourgeois social practices.[3] (This despite the fact that even the musty "House" is shot through with reminders of the darker results of collectivist modes of thought brewing across the Channel.) The latter—and more important—movement manifests itself in the trajectory of Sydney Carton's career. As we shall see, Carton's progress through the text first underscores the pernicious effects of bourgeois-capitalist conceptions of individualism, then affirms the heroic potential unleashed by abandoning them, only to turn back upon itself and to reaffirm the tenets of Classical Liberalism in its last hours. Furthermore, Carton is allowed to escape the culturally dictated bounds of the self only in a manner which obfuscates the process's ideological import: for a few crucial moments he and Darnay genuinely transcend those traditional barriers which wall off the inviolable individual from all his fellow beings, but this merging of a *single* discrete self with *one* other deflects a broad social goal of the Revolution into the realm of private psychology—and then too, it is performed as part of an attempt to *thwart* the very revolutionary practices it imitates in miniature.

[. . .]

The central irony which emerges from Carton's successful commingling with Darnay in prison is that Sydney's "cure" is effected in the shadow of the novel's

---

3   Mr. Lorry prides himself on keeping his relationship with Tellson's clients businesslike, with no friendly feeling or sentiment exchanged.

explicit condemnation of the very practice which heals him, for while he partici-
pates in a process whereby one man is able to transcend the suffocating barriers of
the bourgeois self, the Revolution's insistence that the same is to be done for *all*
men meets with nothing but scorn. And here one can anticipate an objection:
the obvious fact that Sydney and the Jacquerie see the annihilation of the con-
ventional barriers between individuals as the means to ends which are diametric-
ally opposed does not weaken this irony to the extent that one might initially
suppose. Yes, Carton abandons his personal claims for the protection of bourgeois domesticity (one might even say for the Victorian hearth, since Sydney's
figurative descendents are to recount his story for generations) while the Paris
Tribunal[4] demands that the individual subsume himself into the polity in order to
speed the flourishing of, as the narrator puts it, the Republic One and Indivisible
of Liberty, Equality, Fraternity, or Death. But my point is that the former cause
rests upon the foundation stone of bourgeois individualism while the latter is
committed to its destruction, and that Carton can only ensure the safety of Liberal
society (in the form of the Darnays, Manette, Lorry, and Pross) by temporarily
violating one of its fundamental tenets. To put it another way, Carton can only
make the world safe for discrete subjects by temporarily ceasing to be one himself
and thereby blocking the plans of a regime bent on abolishing the entire concept
of the discrete subject forevermore.

> Baldridge notes here that on his midnight walk, Sydney sees himself as drifting
> into the sea, the dominant image of the Revolutionary mob.

[. . .] On the evening after Darnay has been condemned, Carton urges Manette to
try his influence with the judges one final time. Lorry, watching the doctor depart,
opines that he has "no hope" that the old man will succeed. Carton agrees, and
explains why he has sent him on what must be a futile mission. What is striking
about this passage is that since Sydney has already made up his mind to replace
Darnay upon the guillotine, but has not told the banker of his plan, he and Lorry
have two different individuals in mind when they employ the pronouns "his" and
"he":

> "Don't despond," said Carton, very gently; "don't grieve. I encouraged
> Doctor Manette in this idea, because I felt that it might one day be
> consolatory to her. Otherwise, she might think 'his life was wantonly
> thrown away or wasted,' and that might trouble her."
> "Yes, yes, yes," returned Mr. Lorry, drying his eyes, "you are right.
> But he will perish; there is no real hope."
> "Yes, He will perish: there is no real hope," echoed Carton. And
> walked with a settled step, down-stairs. [. . .]

This sharing of pronouns, causing momentary confusion about who is being
referred to, is reminiscent of nothing so much as those passages in which Jacques

speaks to Jacques. It is as if Carton had already ceased to be a discrete subject, his personality commingling with that of Darnay's as he approaches his salvational moment. This process of merging reaches its climax during the scene in Charles's cell,[5] where the two, having already exchanged boots, cravats, coats, and ribbons, write what amounts to a joint letter to Lucy [sic], Carton dictating as Darnay holds the pen. As the latter scribbles, Sydney gradually applies his hidden narcotic, so that we see Charles's individuality diffusing itself too, his consciousness drifting beyond its normal boundaries as he attempts to record Carton's sentiments. [. . .]

As any reader will attest, it is nearly impossible to read this passage without backtracking, for Dickens makes it especially difficult to keep the speakers straight for any length of time. And it is not only we who are confused as to who is being referred to, for soon afterwards Barsad finds Sydney's unorthodox use of pronouns disconcerting:

> "Have no fear! I shall soon be out of the way of harming you, and the rest will soon be far from here, please God! Now, get assistance and take me to the coach."
> "You?" said the Spy nervously.
> "Him, man, with whom I have exchanged." [. . .]

Although Carton exchanges literal freedom for imprisonment in this scene, he simultaneously effects his escape from Dickens's solipsistic City of Dreadful Night,[6] for the entombing barriers surrounding the discrete subject of Liberal society have momentarily been shattered. Furthermore, the imagery and wordplay here associate Sydney with the self-subsuming Jacquerie at the very moment when he prevents the Tribunal from executing the man Madame Defarge defines as the last of the "race" of Evrémondes.

## From **Lisa Robson, "The 'Angels' in Dickens's House: Representation of Women in *A Tale of Two Cities*"** (1992), *Dalhousie Review* 72:3, pp. 311–33

Lisa Robson's title comes from a popular Victorian phrase for women as guardians of morality through their role as wives and mothers. The term was coined by the poet Coventry Patmore in his series of poems of that name (1854–63), and he intended it as a compliment. Many women at the time and since have seen the phrase as condescending, relegating women to the domestic or private sphere of home and family and denying them a voice and place in the public spheres of politics and work. Robson, a Canadian professor, is

5   See Key Passages, **pp. 151–5**.
6   This phrase for despair was popularized in a poem of that name by the Scottish poet James Thomson in 1874. It derives from Dante's *Inferno*, in which the inscription over the Gate of Hell reads "Through me is the way into the doleful city." Baldridge is recalling his discussion of the "Night Shadows" passage, in which Dickens describes the isolation of the citizens of a city at night. Solipsistic means intensely self-absorbed.

the first critic to examine in detail the female characters and female symbols in the novel. She places Dickens's account of Revolutionary women (Madame Defarge and her followers) in the context of the historical women of the French Revolution to argue that Dickens cannot prevent his patriarchal attitudes from stifling the potential for liberation in his female characters. Robson begins by arguing that while Lucie and Miss Pross (despite her superficial masculinity) are traditional "angels in the house," they are actually prevented from acting as saviors in a patriarchal society that maintains the superiority of the male.

Such a depiction of severe male violence against women[1] pointedly questions the novel's advocacy of feminine self-sacrifice as a means of redemption and the proposed importance of women's endless love, forgiveness and submission. Certain critics (such as Albert D. Hutter, who examines the relations between father and sons in "Nation and Generation in *A Tale of Two Cities*"[2]), suggest that Dickens indicts the patriarchal system in *Tale*, and it is true that Dickens levels much criticism against the hierarchical social and political world of his novel. However, any criticism of the patriarchy concerns women only in a narrow sense. Although Dickens's representation of women's exploitation indicates his recognition of some of the difficulties women face and his interest in their plight, his investigation goes no further. In fact, Dickens may expose some of the ambiguities in his feminine ideal and acknowledge some of the dangers of women's subordination within a patriarchal system, but his text offers no relinquishment of its sentimentalized perception of women; rather, the novel continues to affirm and cherish a feminine ideal according to which women continue to be victims. Dickens may emphasize the angel's redemptive powers, thereby allowing for the possibility of her effective agency, but because she cannot meet the contradictory demands placed on her within a patriarchal system, she is rendered passive and silent.

In the next section, Robson discusses the historical role of women in the French Revolution, noting that Dickens gives his Revolutionary women an active political role in the novel, which accords with current views of their influence. Carlyle took a more conservative and repressive view.

As the main representative of the French women in this rebellion, Dickens presents Thérèse Defarge, valued and trusted confidante of her husband, Ernest, and his circle of lower-class conspirators. Dickens removes Madame Defarge from a typical, domestic feminine realm to place her in the midst of the turbulent Revolution. Thus, because of her combative posture, she seems to renegotiate or redefine Dickens's feminine contradiction; as a dynamic revolutionary, she is

---

1   Doctor Manette's account of the rape of Madame Defarge's sister, for example.
2   See Modern Criticism, pp. 83–7.

neither submissive victim nor saintly savior. Madame Defarge demonstrates her capacity as a politically active woman responding to class suppression, for example, in the storming of the Bastille episode, when she stands out as a leader of women, forcefully declaring female equality in her sadistic cry, "We can kill as well as the men when the place is taken!" [. . .].[3] Such determination, near-perfect self-control and consistency of purpose render her hateful yet admirable. Although Dickens makes no attempt to indicate Madame Defarge's political awareness, instead rendering women's involvement in the Revolution a result of hunger or a sense of personal wrong, his acknowledgement, through Madame Defarge, of women's participation and what appears to be their often powerful influence, seems to recognize the progressive nature of their role. As a politically determined and apparently determining being, Madame Defarge appears to avoid some of the restrictions placed on other women in the novel.

[. . .], Dickens singles out Madame Defarge as a magnified representation of the unnatural horror of revolutionary violence;[4] he also pointedly connects her with Lucie Manette. He begins by suggesting that Madame Defarge, like the other women of the Revolution, is disfigured by the "time." This statement implies that Madame Defarge is negatively distorted by her environment, that, had she been exposed to different circumstances, she might have turned out quite differently, perhaps even like Lucie herself. But the years leading to the Revolution turn her into a ruthless, strong, fearless, shrewd woman. Her readiness and determination render her wholly unfeminine, and the reference to her "beauty" secures her position as the fair, angelic Lucie's dark-haired antithesis. She substitutes her knitting needles of revenge, which she uses to denounce traitors, for Lucie's golden thread of harmony, and in lieu of the compassionate emotions to which Lucie often succumbs, Madame Defarge is utterly devoid of the "virtue" of pity. Certainly, she derives motivation from fidelity to her natural sister, but she distorts that devotion in order to seek vengeance and death rather than forgiveness and life. While Lucie gives birth to angelic creatures like herself and tends them with love and concern, Madame Defarge has no children, an absence which ironically connects her with the aristocratic women whom Dickens also criticizes for lacking maternal affection. (He suggests that, although upper class ladies give birth, peasant women raise the children and are, thus, more deserving of the exalted title of "Mother," [. . .]). In short, Dickens depicts Madame Defarge as a woman of distorted potential, a woman of powerful feelings who, as the result of a lifetime of pain and oppression, turns to destruction. Because he connects her so obviously with Lucie, Madame Defarge represents a perversion of Dickens's feminine-savior figure.

[. . .] Depicting her persistent and insatiable brutality, Dickens portrays Madame Defarge as a force of nature as well as an animal, identifying her as an elemental, and hence unconquerable presence; she says to her husband, "tell Wind and Fire where to stop . . . but don't tell me" [. . .]. Such appeals to nature dehistoricize Madame Defarge, removing her from her culture and from the Revolution in order to render her effectively non-feminine and non-human, a mythic Fury.

---

3   See Key Passages, p. 141.
4   This is due to her relentless desire for the death of Charles Darnay and his family.

Here Robson likens Madame Defarge to some of the legendary women associated with the Revolution, such as Charlotte Corday, who murdered the journalist Jean-Paul Marat, and notes that the French Government severely restricted
women's political rights in the years following the Revolution.

By dismissing the unfeminine Madame Defarge as other than human and por-
traying women revolutionaries as beasts, Dickens apparently endorses this type of
denial of women's moral and intellectual suitability for public affairs. Dickens
impedes women's access to power in his representation of the Revolution by focus-
sing on a disfigured monster whose influence is more primal than political. He
thereby contains female subversion and denies women access to effective political
agency by characterizing their social activities as aberrant rather than "natural"
behavior. Furthermore, by endorsing only those women, such as Lucie, who do not
disturb the patriarchal agenda or threaten men's supremacy, Dickens reconfirms
women's subordinate status. As a half-French woman, Lucie serves as an example
for her French "sisters" because she embodies Rousseau's ideal,[5] constantly
remaining a politically submissive complement to the patriarchy represented in her
husband and father. Through this acceptance of Lucie and rejection of Madame
Defarge, Dickens affirms the exclusion of women from political life and reveals a
patriarchal fear of women becoming equal partners in the Revolution. [. . .]

In fact, Dickens seems to break down sexual barriers[6] only to re-create a
negative image of the Revolution itself as feminine. L. M. Findlay suggests
that Carlyle defines femininity in *The French Revolution* in part by means of
Maenadic reference, a depiction which helps to perpetuate patriarchal domination [. . .].[7] Here is a point where Dickens's and Carlyle's women begin to
meet, since Dickens emulates this type of representation in his historical novel.
Greek mythology characterizes Maenads, or the women worshippers of the god
Dionysus, largely by their shared capacity for irrationality, for their uncontrollable, emotional, senseless, and therefore feminine, dancing and singing, and
Dickens's portrait of the feminine figures in the Carmagnole echoes this description. Additionally, unreasonable and passionate French women such as Madame
Defarge and La Vengeance tend to characterize most revolutionary scenes [. . .],[8]
exceeding men in their savagery and strength, and dominating Dickens's representation of insurrection. It is important to note, however, that, despite their
energy and fervor, and like the Maenads who depend upon their relationship to
Dionysus to define their identity,[9] Dickens's women rely on men, or the circle of
Jacques, to direct their activities. Therefore, while women are marginalized

5  For Jean-Jacques Rousseau, see Contemporary Documents, **pp. 30–1**. Rousseau was vocal in
   advocating breast-feeding at home (as opposed to sending the child out to a wet-nurse).
6  In the androgyny of the Carmagnole, for example.
7  " 'Maternity must forth': The Poetics and Politics of Gender in Carlyle's *French Revolution*,"
   *Dalhousie Review* 66. 1/2 (1986), pp. 135–40.
8  Albert D. Hutter, "Nation and Generation in *A Tale of Two Cities*," PMLA, 93 (1978) p. 457. For
   Hutter, see Modern Criticism, **pp. 83–7**.
9  Findlay, "Maternity must forth," p. 138.

through denial of their independence, excessive revolutionary activity and its agents are negatively represented by reference to the feminine.[10]

[. . .] Just as his extreme portrayal and rejection of Madame Defarge and his exaggerated depiction of Lucie as a desired feminine form demonstrates patriarchal anxiety about powerful women, so Dickens's use of feminine and female symbols to represent the French Revolution, its causes and effects, underscores a need for containment of such convulsion and a fear of revolution itself.

10  These references are the personification of the guillotine as female (a common attribution during the Revolution) and Dickens's description of the Marquis's château (and by implication the Marquis himself) having been turned to stone by Medusa, the gorgon of Greek mythology. Robson argues that Medusa "represents the stone-like, upper class indifference to the poor" (p. 329).

# The Novel in Performance

Dickens began his writing career as a playwright, and all his life he was a keen amateur actor, stage manager, and theatregoer. For many years he toured Great Britain and even the USA giving wildly popular dramatized readings from his works. Much has been written about the influence of the contemporary theatre on Dickens's novels, an influence which is particularly strong in *A Tale of Two Cities* because the idea for it came out of Dickens's experience acting the part of Richard Wardour in the play he helped to write and stage, Wilkie Collins's *The Frozen Deep* (see Contemporary Documents, **pp. 44–5**). He later wrote that if he had been able to act Sydney Carton as he did Richard Wardour he "could have done something with his life and death."[1] Anxious to see *A Tale of Two Cities* transferred to the stage, Dickens sent advance proof-sheets to his friend François Régnier (1807–85), a French actor and producer, in the hopes that it could be dramatized in Paris, but Régnier advised against it.[2] Dickens did help with the first London stage production of the novel, however, attending the rehearsals and advising the cast.

From the beginning, Sydney Carton became the central interest, as he has remained in the many stage and film versions of the novel. The first famous Carton was Sir John Martin-Harvey, who starred in a stage version entitled *The Only Way* that ran for three decades from 1899. A silent film version of the play appeared in 1926 and a television production in 1948. Other famous Cartons include Ronald Colman, who starred in David O. Selznick's 1935 MGM version, and Dirk Bogarde, who was Carton in the 1958 J. Arthur Rank version, produced by Betty Box. Colman has become identified with the part in the same way that *A Christmas Carol* belongs to Alastair Sim, despite the many Scrooges who have succeeded him.

The difficulty for producers of the novel is that, unlike most heroes, the enigmatic Sydney Carton does not dominate the work; in fact he does not appear until the second chapter of Book II, and even then his presence is characterized by

---

1   Letter to Mary Boyle, in G. Storey (ed.), *The Letters of Charles Dickens*, Vol. IX, Oxford: Clarendon Press, 1997, p. 177.
2   Napoleon Bonaparte's nephew (Napoleon III) had established the Second French Empire in 1852. Until 1860 he ruled France as a dictator and would have prohibited a play that sympathized with republicanism, however ambivalent Dickens's sympathies may have been in *A Tale of Two Cities*.

reticence and a nonchalant absence of mind until almost the end. To centre attention on Carton from the beginning, the film versions have generally focused the plot around the love story (the central interest in *The Frozen Deep*); the 1958 version introduces the relationship between Carton and Lucie in the opening shots by putting a drunken Carton on the coach to Dover with Lucie and Mr. Lorry. The film versions also increase the role of the seamstress in order to make the most of the handsome hero's romantic appeal in the closing scenes of the novel. In any complex role, however, a good actor can hold the audience's interest even when he is just lounging in the background, as Carton so often is.

The first stage version, produced by Tom Taylor at the Lyceum Theatre in London on January 30, 1860, opened with Doctor Manette's visit to the Evrémonde château, a revelation of the secret that in the novel is not disclosed until Manette's letter is read to the court that condemns Charles Darnay to the guillotine. While writing the novel, Dickens had rejected this early disclosure when his friend and fellow novelist Wilkie Collins had suggested that it would have been preferable. Dickens replied that if Doctor Manette's trauma had been revealed at the beginning "it would have been overdone in that manner—too elaborately trapped, baited, and prepared—in the main, anticipated and its interest wasted."[3] Later film versions have also opened with the château scene, but none has adopted the radical rewriting undertaken by one of the early stage adaptations. In F. Fox Cooper's play, produced in July 1860, a cowardly Carton saves himself from the guillotine by drugging Barsad and leaving him to be executed. The film versions have adapted the plot less dramatically, in order to overcome the coincidences that some readers find objectionable. In the 1958 version, for instance, Manette asks his servant, Ernest Defarge, to seek out the surviving sister of the wronged peasant family, thus accounting for Defarge marrying Thérèse. Barsad is seldom Miss Pross's brother, and in some versions he is in the employ of the Marquis.

The 1935 film, starring Ronald Colman, places a subtle emphasis on the Christian themes of the novel that have been deliberately avoided in more recent versions. Christmas carols form a part of the background music, and although Carton does not speak the words "I am the resurrection and the life," they appear in text at the end. He accompanies Miss Pross and Lucie to a Christmas church service after Darnay has given his regrets; when Miss Pross lights a candle for Carton, a closeup of his haunted face suggests the underlying seriousness of his character that has been evident in Dickens's text but is harder to convey on screen. Colman studied his role in the novel and altered the script to conform with the character as envisaged by Dickens (see The Novel in Performance, pp. 105–6).

Problematic for twentieth-century filmmakers are the melodramatic scenes in the novel, such as Lucie's first meeting with her father and Doctor Manette's description of Madame Defarge's dying sister and brother at the château. David O. Selznick regretted the lack of interesting characters in *A Tale of Two Cities* compared to *David Copperfield*, which he had just filmed, and he feared that the novel would not transfer to the screen so successfully without Dickens's text.

3   Letter to Wilkie Collins, in Storey, *Letters*, p. 127.

He considered the novel to be "sheer melodrama and when the scenes are put on the screen, minus Dickens' brilliant narrative passages, the mechanics of melodramatic construction are inclined to be more than apparent, and in fact, to creak."[4] Film versions have also excluded some of the sentimental scenes, such as the death of Lucie's little son (see The Novel in Performance, **p. 107**). Reviews of the 1989 movie faulted Dickens for his failure to write a love story without resorting to the sentimental and melodramatic, but Selznick is closer to the truth in laying the blame on the screen's inability to include the "brilliant narrative passages" of the original novel. The film versions' emphasis on the love story also takes away from Dickens's portrayal of the French Revolution and his blending of the private story of the Manettes and Defarges with the public event. Madame Defarge's personal desire for revenge becomes the central focus, rather than the wider issues of hunger and deprivation contained in the narrative.[5] Even the set pieces (such as the breaking of the wine cask) that are highly cinematic in Dickens's rendering of them often seem oddly flat on film. (For an analysis of Dickens's cinematic techniques see Zambrano, Modern Criticism, **pp. 76–8**.) None of the famous film versions include Carton's closing prophetic thoughts, a loss that one television reviewer lamented in his highly critical review of the 1989 film.[6]

Dickens prepared a reading version of Book I of the novel, condensed into three scenes, but he never performed it. Entitled "The Bastille Prisoner," it tells the story of Lucie's and Mr. Lorry's recovery of Doctor Manette from the room above the wine-shop but without any reference to the coming Revolution. The reading would no doubt have been very effective (Dickens was a brilliant actor who could have made much of Doctor Manette's gradual recognition of his lost daughter) but, as with his rejected title for the novel, "Buried Alive," perhaps Dickens felt that the reading, too, would be "too grim."

The next section contains commentary on two films of A Tale of Two Cities, the acclaimed 1935 version that starred Ronald Colman and a controversial television/video version from 1989.

From **Juliet Benita Colman, *Ronald Colman: A Very Private Person***
(1975), (London: W. H. Allen), pp. 178–84

In this biography, Ronald Colman's daughter describes her father's intense identification with the role of Sydney Carton in the 1935 MGM film version, and she includes an interview with David O. Selznick, the producer. The distinguished cast included Elizabeth Allan as Lucie, Blanche Yurka as Madame Defarge, Reginald Owen as Stryver, and Basil Rathbone as the Marquis. This film remains one of the classics of the 1930s and a highlight of Colman's career.

---

4    Quoted in James Robert Parish and Gregory W. Mank, *The Best of MGM: The Golden Years*, Westport, Conn.: Arlington House, 1981, p. 204.
5    For comment on the novel's emphasis on the personal story rather than politics see McWilliams, Jr., pp. 80–3.
6    Peter Lennon, "A Tale of Two Dummies," *The Listener*, June 1, 1989, p. 38.

MGM had had an enormous success the previous year with *David Copperfield* (1934) and were quick to follow in its wake with another Dickens spectacular, including some of the same cast. [. . .] Both films were produced by the same man:

*David Selznick:* "In adapting *Copperfield*, the problem was principally one of eliminating a sufficient number of characters and story tangents to bring this work within the limits of a single photoplay, and still give an impression of preserving the original intact. In adapting *A Tale of Two Cities*, there was no such problem, because the story itself was not too long for picturization. Different problems, however, confronted us. For instance, there are long stretches in the book in which the character does not appear.[1] As we worked on the script, it became obvious that, granting an interesting portrayal, the audience would become intrigued by the character of Carton and would expect to follow him, the more so because of casting Colman in the role. The cure for this lay in a rearrangement of the sequences.

"Intensifying the romantic interest between Carton and Lucie, played by Elizabeth Allan, was another major problem. Dickens left this attachment almost entirely to the imagination of his readers. On the screen, it is given more stress. Transferring the vivid scenes, working in the important characters— the De Farges [*sic*], La Vengeance, the Woodcutter, Gaspard—without lessening the focal interest in the major characters, was still another problem of no small consequence.

[. . .]

Ronnie knew Dickens's novel virtually by heart and had longed to play the role of Carton for many years. Seven years before he was finally cast for the film, in an interview with a magazine writer, he said: "In Sidney Carton, he [Dickens] conceived a character that only a genius would know; a whimsical, sardonic, bitterly disillusioned fellow who successfully—or almost so—masks his emotions beneath an unmoved exterior. Dickens wrote of this man with a glorious power. He has lived for me since the first instant I discovered him in the pages of the novel. . . . It has a charm that is greater than magnificence, the charm of intimacy in the midst of spectacle."

He considered Carton to be literature's prime example of the man who truly believes in Be Yourself. "He was never anything else than entirely natural. It was impossible for Carton to make compromises with others, with himself or with the problems of life. He was the most unheroic of heroes, but he had the fundamental fortitude to walk to the guillotine with a grin on his face, because he was strong enough to be himself. He lacked utterly any desire to court popularity although he was a man of brilliant talents. Indeed, he lived his life without a thought for the impression he was making on those around him. And it was this trait of character that, in my opinion, has made him live vividly for almost a century."[2]

At the end of each day's filming Ronnie took home his script and compared passages with the book, often making alterations to the former.

1  Sydney Carton.
2  [Colman's note.] *Picturegoers Weekly Supplement*. [For Dickens's view of Sydney Carton, see Contemporary Documents, pp. 42–3 and Contextual Overview, pp. 14–6.]

He became so interested in the filming that he broke one of his professional habits—that of never visiting the set unless he was actually working. During *Two Cities* he was there virtually the entire time. [. . .]

Carton/Colman first appears after the film has been running for almost half an hour, and is on the screen for relatively little of the film's two hours. However, one might only realize this in retrospect. During the film one is totally involved with this powerful character, who quietly, steadily dominates every scene he is in. One's thoughts are with him during most of the story, whether he is on camera or not. It is a subtle and complete character portrayal: pensive, drunk, sardonic, morose, finally happy, ever shrewd. The actor gives a rare insight into this unusual hero with triumphant strength of character.

[. . .]

*A Tale of Two Cities* took five months to film. Luckily for MGM, Dickens was prone to detailed description, which was invaluable to the producers. The styles of furniture, tablewear, clothing were carefully examined in the pages by various departments. This, plus all the information gathered by cameramen dispatched to France and England to photograph everything from 200-year-old buildings to wallpaper, was entered in lengthy reports that resulted in the sets and costumes.

From **Arthur Hopcraft, "The Spirit of Revolution"** (1989) *Listener,* 18 May, pp. 10–11

In this article, English screenwriter Arthur Hopcraft (1933–2004) discusses his dramatization of the novel for Granada Television in 1989. It was shown on Masterpiece Theatre and is now available on video. Intended to commemorate the bicentenary of the French Revolution, this production (directed by French writer Philippe Monnier) was an Anglo-French coproduction with French and English actors, filmed in Bordeaux, France, and Manchester, England. The production has been criticized for the artificiality of the French actors' talking to each other in heavily accented English for the version shown in England. In the French version, the passages spoken in English were dubbed into French.

I suppose it will disappoint some Dickens buffs, and outrage as many more, that my dramatisation of *A Tale of Two Cities* does not begin with the Dover mail coach struggling through the mud up Shooters Hill, Jerry Cruncher galloping after it in the night with his message to stalwart old Mr Lorry, and Lorry delivering the marvellous line, at once baffling and beckoning, "Jerry, say that my answer was, 'Recalled to life' ".[1]

It cannot be denied that this opening sequence of the novel is enticingly filmic. [. . .] The sense of mystery, menace, of something frightful on the way, is grippingly realised in these passages. Why, then, reject them?

The trouble is that the coach takes us to the Royal George Hotel, its Concord bedchamber, its coffee-room, a good bottle of claret after dinner for Mr Lorry,

---

1   See *A Tale of Two Cities*, Book 1, Chapter 2, and Key Passages, pp. 120–4.

and *then* the arrival on the scene of Lucie Manette. [. . .] On the screen we have to move a little faster than that; at least, in my view.

So, although episode one starts with a carriage labouring up a muddy hill, the road leads to Paris, not Dover, the only passengers are Lorry and Lucie, their faces plain to the eye. [. . .]

I fretted about how to begin the series because [. . .] the story of *A Tale of Two Cities* is not told in a slow unravelling of intricate threads. It is for the most part taut and direct. One could almost call it plain-speaking, except that even unembellished Dickens cannot suppress the invention of that least plain of minds. [. . .]

It is the marvel of Dickens, of course, that he can handle this mix of gory drama and high romance with such control as to lead us, so unresisting, to those final words. [. . .]

Dickens insists on a sublime heroism. But then he was not dealing in what is normally meant by 'reality'—it wasn't real enough for him. *His* Sydney Carton never dies. Instead he goes thankfully to 'a far, far better rest . . . than I have ever known'. Dickens understood the world of the senses—the reality of feelings. [. . .]

He suffered to our great gain. A random selection of set-pieces offers some dazzling imagery: the starved populace of Saint Antoine scrambling in the gutters to scavenge the spilled wine from a broken cask, [. . .] Evremonde's carriage [. . .] hurtling through the narrow streets [. . .] until it stops with a child crushed dead under a wheel; [. . .]

I hope the Dickens buffs will find all this and more to their satisfaction. I warn them to prepare for one particular absence. They will not see Lucie's little son, who dies with a radiant smile [. . .] I do not apologise for this omission. I think Dickens would be grateful.

# 3

# Key Passages

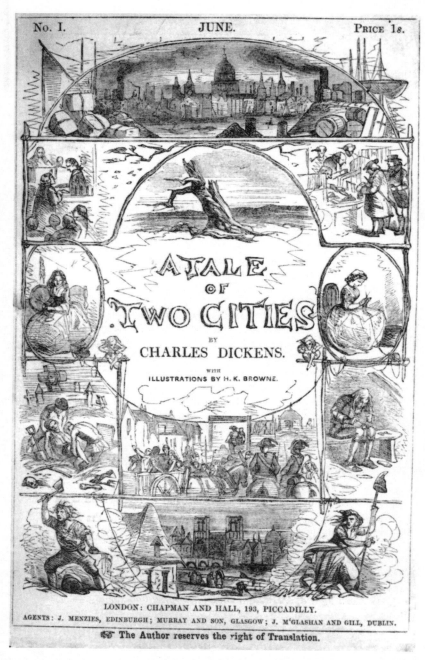

*Figure 2* From the original cover of the Monthly Parts by Hablot
   Knight Browne

# Introduction

## Note on the Key Passages

*A Tale of Two Cities* is famous for several graphic scenes that for many readers have become a part of their impressions of the French Revolution. These include the breaking of the wine cask outside the Defarges' shop, the storming of the Bastille, the murder of the Marquis, the grindstone, Madame Defarge's encounter with Miss Pross, and Sydney Carton's death. Other passages are less well known but indicate the power of the novel as it is written rather than filtered through the lens of a camera. The variety and complexity of Dickens's language is evident in many of the following extracts, some of which are analyzed in the critical essays contained in this sourcebook. Other passages are selected for their importance to the plot or to the threads of imagery (footsteps, shadows, echoes, seas) that bring coherence, atmosphere, and foreshadowing to a plot that unfolds in two places and over several years. Headnotes point out the significance of each extract for the novel as a whole and refer the reader to other commentary in this sourcebook. Annotations clarify historical and other references.

## A Note on the Text

The Key Passages are taken from the first edition of the novel as it appeared in *All the Year Round* (see Introduction, p. 2). The idiosyncratic punctuation (especially the frequency of commas) was typical of nineteenth-century literature.

## Synopsis of the Plot

*A Tale of Two Cities* is divided into three parts, or "books" as Dickens called them. The story opens in 1775, when Mr. Lorry, an English banker, and Lucie Manette travel to Paris to take Lucie's father, recently released after eighteen years in the Bastille Prison, to England. The two meet at Dover on the south coast of England before crossing the channel, leaving Miss Pross, Lucie's faithful servant, behind. They find Doctor Manette, deranged from his long imprisonment, in the care of Ernest Defarge, former servant of Doctor Manette and now the owner of a wine-shop in the Saint Antoine district of Paris. Doctor Manette believes himself still in the Bastille, working as a shoemaker; he does not remember Lucie but instinctively responds to her voice.

The second book moves ahead to 1780. A young Frenchman, Charles Darnay, is on trial for treason, accused of revealing England's military plans in America to the French king. Lucie and Doctor Manette (restored to health) are called to testify against him, having seen him on the boat returning from France in 1775. More damning evidence is discounted when an eyewitness's identification of Darnay is shaken by the observation that the defense counsel's assistant, Sydney Carton, could be mistaken for Darnay. Two of the witnesses, John Barsad and Roger Cly, are shown to be lying scoundrels by Mr. Stryver, the defense counsel. Darnay is acquitted. As a result of seeing her at the trial, Darnay, Carton, and Stryver all become would-be suitors of Lucie.

Back in Paris, the Marquis Saint Evrémonde has attended a reception at the house of a superior aristocrat and has been snubbed by him. Driving away recklessly, he runs over a child. At the Marquis's country home that evening Charles Darnay arrives and unsuccessfully tries to convince the Marquis, his uncle, to make amends for the family's appalling history of cruelty and abuse. During the night, the dead child's father, Gaspard, sneaks in and stabs the Marquis to death.

In London, Darnay asks Doctor Manette for Lucie's hand, and Carton tells Lucie that he would make any sacrifice for her or anyone she loved. Jerry Cruncher, the messenger for Tellson's Bank, attends the funeral of Roger Cly, one of the witnesses at Darnay's trial. That night he goes to exhume the body (intending to sell it for medical research), secretly watched by his son, and returns home, where he beats his long-suffering wife.

Gaspard has been hanged for the murder of the Marquis. John Barsad arrives at the Defarges' wine shop, which is now the center of the revolutionary movement in Paris. Madame Defarge keeps a register of possible enemies of the movement by adding their names as a pattern in her knitting. She adds Barsad's name to her register, recognizing him as a spy. He tells the Defarges that Lucie is to be married to Charles Darnay, formerly Evrémonde. Ernest tries to plead with his wife on Darnay's behalf as the son-in-law of their old friend Doctor Manette, but she knits his name into the register anyway as an aristocrat and therefore an enemy of the republican movement.

On the morning of the wedding, Charles Darnay reveals his real name to Doctor Manette, as promised. After the young couple has left, Doctor Manette obsessively takes up his shoemaking again until, nine days later, Mr. Lorry speaks to him about it. Mr. Lorry and Miss Pross destroy the bench and bury the tools in the garden, hoping to free him from his memories. Carton befriends the Darnay family, whose peaceful life is disturbed only by the death of Lucie and Charles's young son.

It is now 1789 and Revolution breaks out in Paris with the storming of the Bastille and the murder of its governor, De Launay. Defarge finds his way to Doctor Manette's old cell and searches it closely, looking for documents that Doctor Manette might have written and secreted. Foulon, Louis XVI's Counselor of State, is murdered by Madame Defarge and the mob. The Evrémonde château is burnt to the ground, and Gabelle, Charles Darnay's old servant, is threatened by the rioters despite having treated the peasantry very fairly.

The action moves ahead to 1792, and Tellson's Bank in England has become a refuge for French émigrés (aristocrats fleeing for their lives). Darnay receives a letter from Gabelle, who has been imprisoned in Paris for remaining loyal to Darnay and acting as his agent at the château. Only Darnay can verify that Gabelle has been acting in the interest of the villagers.

The third book opens with Darnay's return to France, where he is arrested and imprisoned in Paris. Mr. Lorry is also in Paris with Jerry Cruncher on bank business. Lucie arrives with her father, her daughter, and Miss Pross during the four days of the September Massacres (see Contextual Overview, p. 11). Lucie pleads unsuccessfully with Madame Defarge to help release Charles. For the next few months, Doctor Manette works in the prisons, a hero as a former inmate of the Bastille. Lucie stands outside La Force, Charles' prison, every day in November 1793 in case Charles can see her from a high window; she is observed by a woodcutter, a former road mender from the Marquis's village. When Darnay comes to trial in December, he is released on the testimony of Doctor Manette and Gabelle, but within hours he is rearrested, denounced by the Defarges and "one other," unnamed. Running into John Barsad in the street, Miss Pross recognizes him as her errant brother, Solomon Pross, and Jerry Cruncher knows him as the spy who testified falsely at Darnay's London trial. Sydney Carton suddenly appears and identifies Barsad as a spy for Republican France. Knowing he can blackmail Barsad with his proof that Barsad once acted for the English crown, Carton enlists his aid. He finds another ace up his sleeve when Jerry Cruncher reveals that Barsad's fellow spy in Paris is Roger Cly, whose death and burial Jerry knows to have been faked.

After a thoughtful talk with Mr. Lorry, Sydney Carton spends the night roaming the streets of Paris. The next day, Darnay comes before the Revolutionary Tribunal, where he is denounced by Doctor Manette through a letter the Doctor wrote during his imprisonment and hid in the chimney of his cell. The letter, written in 1767, reveals that in 1757 Doctor Manette was hired by the Evrémonde brothers to tend a young woman and her brother at their château. An appalling story of abuse and violence pours from the young man before he dies; the Evrémondes were responsible for the rape of the girl and the death of her husband and (indirectly) her father. While Doctor Manette is there, she and her brother die in considerable agony. Doctor Manette is allowed to go home, where he prepares a letter of complaint. He has just finished it when a woman and her young son arrive, the wife and son of one of the Evrémondes. Mme. Evrémonde deplores the behavior of her husband and brother-in-law and expresses her desire to help a younger sister of the victimized family. She fears that otherwise her son will be required to atone for his father's and uncle's crimes. The boy is Charles Darnay. The letter ends with a condemnation of the Evrémonde family, "to the last of their race." So condemned, Darnay is sentenced to the guillotine.

When Ernest Defarge urges his wife to stop with the death of Darnay and not to pursue Lucie and her child, Madame Defarge reveals to the other Revolutionaries that she is the younger sister of the victimized family, and that she will enact vengeance on the whole Darnay family. Knowing this danger, Sydney Carton arranges with Mr. Lorry that they will flee Paris with Lucie, her daughter, and Doctor Manette, who has relapsed into his Bastille days again. With Barsad's help, Carton gains access to Darnay's cell where he has him write a letter to Lucie.

Carton drugs Darnay, exchanges clothes with him, and has him taken out to the waiting coach. Carton befriends a young seamstress in the prison while the coach hurries through the French countryside.

Madame Defarge goes in search of Lucie and her daughter but encounters only Miss Pross. In the ensuing struggle, Madame Defarge's gun goes off, killing her and leaving Miss Pross deaf. Jerry Cruncher and Miss Pross leave Paris together, Jerry having undergone a change of heart. The novel ends with the seamstress and Sydney Carton going to the guillotine. Carton's unspoken thoughts of what the future will hold are given before his last words.

# Chronology of the Novel and of the French Revolution

Events from history appear in italics. For the history of the Revolution see also Contextual Overview, **pp. 7–11**.

December 22, 1757: The Evrémonde brothers hire the services of Doctor Manette. Madame Defarge's brother dies.
December 29, 1757: Madame Defarge's sister dies.
December 31, 1757: Doctor Manette is taken to the Bastille Prison.
December 1767: Doctor Manette begins to write his memoir.
November 1775: Doctor Manette is released from the Bastille.
March 1780: Charles Darnay is tried for treason at the Old Bailey.
July 1780: Darnay's uncle, the Marquis, attends a salon, runs over Gaspard's child, and is murdered.
Summer 1781: Lucie and Darnay marry; the Defarges meet the mender of roads.
1783: The Darnays' daughter is born.
July 14, 1789: *The storming of the Bastille.*
July–August 1789: *French aristocrats begin to leave France (émigrés); the Great Fear (provincial unrest)*; Evrémonde château burned down.
June 21, 1792: Gabelle writes to Darnay.
August 13, 1792: *French royal family is imprisoned.*
August 14, 1792: Darnay leaves for Paris.
August 15–18, 1792: Darnay is arrested and imprisoned in Paris.
September 2–6, 1792: *The September Massacres.* Lucie and Doctor Manette arrive in Paris.
September 1792–December 1793: Darnay is held in prison; Lucie, her father, and her daughter live in Paris.
September 20, 1792: *France is declared a republic. From September 21, 1792 to September 20, 1793 is known as The Year One of Liberty.*
January 21, 1793: *Louis XVI is executed.*
April 1793–July 1794: *The Reign of Terror.*
October 16, 1793: *Marie-Antoinette (wife of Louis XVI) is executed.*
November 9, 1793: *Madame Roland is executed* (see Key Passages, **p. 162**).
December 1793: Darnay's first trial. Carton arrives in Paris.
December 1793–January 1794: Darnay's second trial and death sentence.

# Key Passages

## The Preface

Dickens published the following Preface in the first edition of *A Tale of Two Cities* in book form in December 1859, at the conclusion of its appearance in simultaneous weekly and monthly parts. Here, Dickens lays out what he sees as the two main influences on his book: Wilkie Collins's play *The Frozen Deep* and Thomas Carlyle's *The French Revolution*. For an account of these two sources for the novel see the Contextual Overview, **pp. 12, 14–16**. Extracts from Carlyle's "wonderful book" can be found on **pp. 31–7**. For a contemporary review that took issue with almost every statement of the Preface see the anonymous review from *The Observer*, **pp. 61–2**.

When I was acting, with my children and friends, in Mr WILKIE COLLINS's drama of The Frozen Deep, I first conceived the main idea of this story. A strong desire was upon me then, to embody it in my own person; and I traced out in my fancy, the state of mind of which it would necessitate the presentation to an observant spectator, with particular care and interest.

As the idea became familiar to me, it gradually shaped itself into its present form. Throughout its execution, it has had complete possession of me; I have so far verified what is done and suffered in these pages, as that I have certainly done and suffered it all myself.

Whenever any reference (however slight) is made here to the condition of the French people before or during the Revolution, it is truly made, on the faith of trustworthy witnesses. It has been one of my hopes to add something to the popular and picturesque means of understanding that terrible time, though no one can hope to add anything to the philosophy of Mr CARLYLE's wonderful book.

# From Book I, Chapter I: "The Period"

In this somewhat uncharacteristic opening chapter, Dickens establishes the historical setting of the novel. No characters are introduced and no plot, it seems, is set in motion. But the chapter strikes several keynotes that will resonate throughout this well-integrated novel.

The famous opening paragraph, actually just a single sentence, moves through a series of antithetical statements that appear to relate only to the past – it "was" the best and worst of times – but the sentence closes with the unexpected revelation that this time past is like nothing so much as the present time in which the narrator is writing. This connection, mentioned again only obliquely in the novel, has led many readers to see *A Tale of Two Cities* as Dickens's warning to Victorian England that revolution could happen there if the abuses of the time are not addressed. (For a discussion of England in 1859 see the Contextual Overview, **pp. 13–14**. For Dickens's attitude to revolution see Orwell, Modern Criticism, **pp. 68–70** and McWilliams, Jr., Modern Criticism, **pp. 79–83**.)

The movement of the opening long sentence through a series of balanced contrasting statements serves as an introduction to the central method of the novel, contained also in the title, *A Tale of Two Cities*. Contrasts, parallels, and doublings of character, incident, place, time, and theme enact the dualisms established in these statements. (For the psychoanalytic significance of doubling or "splitting" see Hutter, Modern Criticism, **pp. 83–7**.) Pre-Revolutionary France was the best time and the worst, depending on whether one was aristocrat or peasant; the Revolution itself was fraught with ambiguities – was it darkness or light, hope or despair, wisdom or foolishness? Was it all of these? Victorian England was also fraught with inconsistencies. In 1851 the Great Exhibition had boasted to the world of England's achievements in scientific inventions, trade, and manufacturing. But Dickens and other commentators were unimpressed, remembering the living conditions of thousands of city dwellers in London and the other industrial cities of Victorian England. The opening antitheses also draw attention to the spiritual center of the novel in their pairings of belief and incredulity, light and darkness, Heaven and Hell. The year 1859 was equally torn, the publication of *A Tale of Two Cities* coinciding with Darwin's *The Origin of Species*, a book that was to shake fundamental Christian belief to its foundations. (For a Christian reading of the novel see Brooks, **pp. 90–3**.)

Dickens goes on to catalogue the evils inherent in both French and English society in 1775, reiterating his often-expressed impatience with those who romanticized the "good old days" and yearned for a return to them. He begins with a characteristic attack on the English attraction to spiritualism and super-stition, popularly substituted for true religious belief in both 1775 and 1859. Moving to France, he provides a single, horrifying example of the cruelty and intolerance of the established church before the Revolution. Although he will come to condemn the atheism of the Revolution (see Key Passages, **p. 150**), here his target is the brutality that was carried on under the guise of

Christianity. The boy whose gruesome sentence Dickens accurately describes here was the Chevalier de la Barre, found guilty in 1766 of sacrileges that included failing to remove his hat when a religious procession passed by. Although his sentence was partly commuted (to torture and beheading), the injustices of his trial were typical of the day. The novel will later condemn the equally unjust tribunals that were to operate during the Revolution, condemning Charles Darnay and many others to death. (See also Dickens's condemnation of pre-Revolutionary France in "Judicial Special Pleading," Contemporary Documents, **pp. 39–41**.)

In describing the abuses of eighteenth-century England, Dickens adopts a less critical tone. But in England, too, the ordinary citizen cannot depend upon the justice system to protect him. This comparison between the two countries will be elaborated and the differences heightened as the novel progresses into the Revolution and beyond. (See, for example, Key Passages, **pp. 148–9**, which contrasts the tranquil Parisian office of Tellson's Bank with the preparation for massacre taking place outside its windows. In Key Passages, **pp. 158–60** the Englishwoman Miss Pross defeats the Frenchwoman Madame Defarge.)

Central to the opening comparison is the reminder that underlying the two societies, where in France the power of the Church and aristocratic privilege were seemingly inviolable, and in England lawlessness and arbitrary punishment were the norm, was an historical process that would shake to their foundations the "lords of the State" who believed that "things in general were settled for ever." (For another view of this complacency see Percy Fitzgerald, Contemporary Documents, **pp. 45–8**.) In the forest, trees are growing that will be built in their time into the deadly guillotine. Here Dickens is echoing Carlyle (see Contemporary Documents, **pp. 31–7**) who, in Book II, Chapter 1 of *The French Revolution* describes the coming of the Revolution in the same metaphor: "The oak grows silently, in the forest, a thousand years; only in the thousandth year, when the woodman arrives with his axe, is there heard an echoing through the solitudes; and the oak announces itself when, with far-sounding crash, it *falls*." However blindly the aristocracy and their royal families, carrying "their divine rights with a high hand," may be pursuing their arrogant and luxurious lives, all around them not just the oppressed servant class, but nature itself, is secretly, silently preparing to bring them down.

The chapter ends with the metaphor of the journey, one that will reverberate throughout the novel in the form of footsteps, carriages, and the tumbrils that roll to the guillotine as the novel moves inexorably from 1775 to 1794.

It was the best of times, it was the worst of times, it was the age of wisdom, it was the age of foolishness, it was the epoch of belief, it was the epoch of incredulity, it was the season of Light, it was the season of Darkness, it was the spring of hope, it was the winter of despair, we had everything before us, we had nothing before us, we were all going direct to Heaven, we were all going direct the other way – in short, the period was so far like the present period, that some of its noisiest authorities insisted on its being received, for good or for evil, in the superlative degree of comparison only.

There were a king with a large jaw and a queen with a plain face, on the throne of England; there were a king with a large jaw and a queen with a fair face, on the throne of France.[1] In both countries it was clearer than crystal to the lords of the State preserves of loaves and fishes, that things in general were settled for ever.

It was the year of Our Lord one thousand seven hundred and seventy-five. Spiritual revelations were conceded to England at that favoured period, as at this. Mrs. Southcott[2] had recently attained her five-and-twentieth blessed birthday, of whom a prophetic private in the Life Guards had heralded the sublime appearance by announcing that arrangements were made for the swallowing up of London and Westminster. Even the Cock-lane ghost had been laid only a round dozen of years, after rapping out its messages, as the spirits of this very year last past (supernaturally deficient in originality) rapped out theirs. Mere messages in the earthly order of events had lately come to the English Crown and People, from a congress of British subjects in America:[3] which, strange to relate, have proved more important to the human race than any communications yet received through any of the chickens of the Cock-lane brood.

France, less favoured on the whole as to matters spiritual than her sister of the shield and trident,[4] rolled with exceeding smoothness down hill, making paper money and spending it.[5] Under the guidance of her Christian pastors, she entertained herself, besides, with such humane achievements as sentencing a youth to have his hands cut off, his tongue torn out with pincers, and his body burned alive, because he had not kneeled down in the rain to do honour to a dirty procession of monks which passed within his view, at a distance of some fifty or sixty yards. It is likely enough that, rooted in the woods of France and Norway, there were growing trees, when that sufferer was put to death, already marked by the Woodman, Fate, to come down and be sawn into boards, to make a certain movable framework with a sack and a knife in it, terrible in history. It is likely enough that in the rough outhouses of some tillers of the heavy lands adjacent to Paris, there were sheltered from the weather that very day, rude carts, bespattered with rustic mire, snuffed about by pigs, and roosted in by poultry, which the Farmer, Death, had already set apart to be his tumbrils of the Revolution. But, that Woodman and that Farmer, though they work unceasingly, work silently, and no one heard them as they went about with muffled tread: the rather, forasmuch as to entertain any suspicion that they were awake, was to be atheistical and traitorous.

---

1   George III and his wife Charlotte Sophia in England, and Louise XVI and his wife Marie-Antoinette in France.
2   Joanna Southcott (1750–1814) was a prolific writer of religious prophecies. Dickens was always hostile to any kind of sham spiritualism that he considered gave genuine Christianity a bad name. Private in the Life Guards: soldier in one of two horse regiments, formed in 1660. Westminster: seat of the British government. The Cock-lane ghost was supposedly the ghost of a murdered woman that appeared in 1762 in a house in Cock Lane, London, but it turned out to be a hoax. Spirit rapping refers to the belief that the dead can communicate to particular people (mediums) by knocking or rapping.
3   The first Continental Congress of the American colonies was held in September and October 1774.
4   Brittania, the female figure that has represented Britain since Roman times, is depicted as holding a shield and a trident, the three-pronged spear associated with Poseidon (Neptune), Greek (Roman) god of the sea and therefore a symbol of naval power.
5   France was seriously in debt prior to the Revolution because of its military spending. See Contextual Overview, pp. 7–9.

In England, there was scarcely an amount of order and protection to justify much national boasting. Daring burglaries by armed men, and highway robberies, took place in the capital itself every night; families were publicly cautioned not to go out of town without removing their furniture to upholsterers' warehouses for security; the highwayman in the dark was a City tradesman in the light, and, being recognized and challenged by his fellow-tradesman whom he stopped in his character of "the Captain",[6] gallantly shot him through the head and rode away; the mail was waylaid by seven robbers, and the guard shot three dead, and then got shot dead himself by the other four, "in consequence of the failure of his ammunition": after which the mail was robbed in peace; that magnificent potentate, the Lord Mayor of London, was made to stand and deliver on Turnham Green, by one highwayman, who despoiled the illustrious creature in sight of all his retinue;[7] prisoners in London gaols fought battles with their turnkeys, and the majesty of the law fired blunderbusses[8] in among them, loaded with rounds of shot and ball; thieves snipped off diamond crosses from the necks of noble lords at Court drawing-rooms; musketeers went into St. Giles's,[9] to search for contraband goods, and the mob fired on the musketeers, and the musketeers fired on the mob; and nobody thought any of these occurrences much out of the common way. In the midst of them, the hangman, ever busy and ever worse than useless, was in constant requisition; now, stringing up long rows of miscellaneous criminals; now, hanging a house-breaker on Saturday who had been taken on Tuesday; now, burning people in the hand at Newgate by the dozen, and now burning pamphlets at the door of Westminster Hall;[10] to-day, taking the life of an atrocious murderer, and to-morrow of a wretched pilferer who had robbed a farmer's boy of sixpence.

All these things, and a thousand like them, came to pass in and close upon the dear old year one thousand seven hundred and seventy-five. Environed by them, while the Woodman and the Farmer worked unheeded, those two of the large jaws, and those other two of the plain and the fair faces, trod with stir enough, and carried their divine rights with a high hand.[11] Thus did the year one thousand seven hundred and seventy-five conduct their Greatnesses, and myriads of small creatures – the creatures of this chronicle among the rest – along the roads that lay before them.

6 Colloquial title used by highwaymen in the eighteenth century. The City tradesman with a shady night-time job becomes Jerry Cruncher in the novel. See headnote to Book I, Chapter 2, p. 120.
7 According to Andrew Sanders, John Sawbridge, Lord Mayor of London, was held up at Turnham Green in west London in 1776, not 1775. See The Companion to A Tale of Two Cities, London: Unwin Hyman, 1988, p. 32.
8 A short hand-gun with a wide bore, to scatter shot at short range.
9 St. Giles was a poor area of London. Musketeers were soldiers armed with muskets, or small shoulder guns.
10 Newgate was a prison in London; Westminster Hall was the highest law court in England. Dickens's examples of lawlessness and inequitable treatment were taken from the Annual Register, a listing of all notable events for the year. Hand branding was a minor penalty handed out by the courts, who also ordered the burning of libelous publications.
11 The medieval belief that monarchs reigned by divine authority and were accountable only to God was rejected in England following the Glorious Revolution of 1688 and in France after the Revolution.

# From Book I, Chapter 2: "The Mail"

Chapter 2 acts as a companion piece to the opening chapter (one of the many paired chapters in the novel). The metaphorical road that closes Chapter 1 is now graphically realized as Shooter's Hill in south-east London, favorite haunt of the highwaymen that figure largely in Dickens's opening description of England in 1775. Jarvis Lorry, respected employee of Tellson's Bank in London, is laboring on foot with his fellow passengers in order to lighten the load of the mail coach and horses. The description of the mire and the mist swirling around them in the darkness, like "an unwholesome sea," recalls the famous fog passage that opens Dickens's 1853 novel, *Bleak House*. As in that novel, the poisonous mist is ambiguous, both separating the characters from each other (a separation reinforced by the heaviness of their garments), and joining them in an uneasy confederacy against the dark, cold and hostile world beyond the lamps on the coach. Suspicious of each other (because each passenger is hidden from view), they are suddenly threatened by a sound in the mist, a man on horseback. The rider turns out to be Jerry Cruncher, bringing a message to Mr. Lorry from Tellson's. Although not a highwayman, Jerry is going to resemble "the Captain" of the opening chapter, because he too lives a double life that is hinted at in the closing lines of Chapter 2. To Jerry's message "Wait at Dover for Ma'amselle," Mr. Lorry replies enigmatically "RECALLED TO LIFE." After the encounter, Jerry remarks to his horse that he would be in a "blazing bad way" if recalling to life were to become popular. Later we learn that Jerry's nocturnal occupation is that of "resurrection man," digging up corpses from graveyards to sell to the medical profession for experimentation. Because a law limited the number of corpses that could be made available to medical students and doctors, this trade was a very active and lucrative one in the late eighteenth century. It came to the attention of a horrified public in 1828 when William Burke and William Hare were found to have murdered at least sixteen people in order to sell their bodies to an Edinburgh surgeon.

Jerry's secret calling is just one of the mysteries that are hinted at in the mist and the mud of the opening journey. Mr. Lorry's odd message puzzles his fellow travelers, and the reader. And the suspicion with which the fellow travelers regard each other – each wrapped up and unidentifiable – points to a central motif of the novel (spying and surveillance) and the hidden relationships between the characters. It is developed in the next key passage. We learn later that one of those muffled passengers is Charles Darnay, whose life is going to be tragically linked to the people cryptically referred to in Jarvis Lorry's message and reply.

It was the Dover road that lay, on a Friday night late in November, before the first of the persons with whom this history has business. The Dover road lay, as to him, beyond the Dover mail, as it lumbered up Shooter's Hill. He walked up-hill in the mire by the side of the mail, as the rest of the passengers did; not because they had the least relish for walking exercise, under the circumstances, but because the hill, and the harness, and the mud, and the mail, were all so heavy, that the horses had three times already come to a stop, besides once drawing the coach across the road, with the mutinous intent of taking it back to Blackheath. Reins and whip and coachman and guard, however, in combination, had read that article of war which forbad a purpose otherwise strongly in favour of the argument, that some brute animals are endued with Reason; and the team had capitulated and returned to their duty.[1]

[. . .]

There was a steaming mist in all the hollows, and it had roamed in its forlornness up the hill, like an evil spirit, seeking rest and finding none. A clammy and intensely cold mist, it made its slow way through the air in ripples that visibly followed and overspread one another, as the waves of an unwholesome sea might do. It was dense enough to shut out everything from the light of the coach-lamps but these its own workings, and a few yards of road; and the reek of the labouring horses steamed into it, as if they had made it all.

Two other passengers, besides the one, were plodding up the hill by the side of the mail. All three were wrapped to the cheek-bones and over the ears, and wore jack-boots.[2] Not one of the three could have said, from anything he saw, what either of the other two was like; and each was hidden under almost as many wrappers from the eyes of the mind, as from the eyes of the body, of his two companions. In those days, travellers were very shy of being confidential on a short notice, for anybody on the road might be a robber or in league with robbers. As to the latter, when every posting-house and ale-house could produce somebody in "the Captain's" pay, ranging from the landlord to the lowest stable non-descript, it was the likeliest thing upon the cards. So the guard of the Dover mail thought to himself, that Friday night in November one thousand seven hundred and seventy-five, lumbering up Shooter's Hill, as he stood on his own particular perch behind the mail, beating his feet, and keeping an eye and a hand on the arm-chest before him, where a loaded blunderbuss lay at the top of six or eight loaded horse-pistols, deposited on a substratum of cutlass.

## From Book I, Chapter 3: "The Night Shadows"

The opening paragraph of Chapter 3 seems at first glance to be a bit of Dickensian longwindedness that some modern readers find unnecessary to the story. But this fine contemplation on the separateness of human beings follows on from the previous key passage. Cates Baldridge provides the most detailed analysis of this evocative passage as it is central to his thesis that the novel only nominally champions the individual (Carton) against the collective (the Revolutionaries). Baldridge draws attention to the tone of regret in the passage, the sense of sadness that we are as separated from each other in life as we are in death. (See Baldridge, Modern Criticism, **pp. 94–5**.)

---

1    Eighteenth-century Enlightenment philosophers emphasized mankind's possession of reason, which was worshiped as a goddess during the Revolution. Here Dickens's horses are clearly more reasonable than their human masters.

2    Stout military boots that extend above the knee.

The night shadows encompass not just the mists that surround the coach on its way to Dover but also the mind of Mr. Lorry as he ponders his place of work, Tellson's Bank, and the secrets contained in its vaults, and the parallel story of the man who has just been dug out of another vault, the Bastille. Mr. Lorry's hallucinatory thoughts are characteristic of Dickens's interest in the operation of the mind under stress, an interest which will soon focus on the man who has been "buried alive," Doctor Manette. Later in the book, Lucie will feel a shadow fall over her in the figure of Madame Defarge, and the substance of that shadow – first encountered here by Mr. Lorry – will emerge in Doctor Manette's buried letter, dug out of the Bastille in 1789. The imagery of this passage – Mr. Lorry's digging of the grave, and the crumbling of the "wretched creature" into dust – graphically and horrifyingly prefigure resurrection, the central theme of the novel. This chapter concluded the first weekly part.

A wonderful fact to reflect upon, that every human creature is constituted to be that profound secret and mystery to every other. A solemn consideration, when I enter a great city by night, that every one of those darkly clustered houses encloses its own secret; that every room in every one of them encloses its own secret; that every beating heart in the hundreds of thousands of breasts there, is, in some of its imaginings, a secret to the heart nearest it! Something of the awfulness, even of Death itself, is referable to this. No more can I turn the leaves of this dear book that I loved, and vainly hope in time to read it all. No more can I look into the depths of this unfathomable water, wherein, as momentary lights glanced into it, I have had glimpses of buried treasure and other things submerged. It was appointed that the book should shut with a spring, for ever and for ever, when I had read but a page. It was appointed that the water should be locked in an eternal frost, when the light was playing on its surface, and I stood in ignorance on the shore. My friend is dead, my neighbour is dead, my love, the darling of my soul, is dead; it is the inexorable consolation and perpetuation of the secret that was always in that individuality, and which I shall carry in mine to my life's end. In any of the burial-places of this city through which I pass, is there a sleeper more inscrutable than its busy inhabitants are, in their innermost personality, to me, or than I am to them?

As to this, his natural and not to be alienated inheritance, the messenger on horseback had exactly the same possessions as the King, the first Minister of State, or the richest merchant in London. So with the three passengers shut up in the narrow compass of one lumbering old mail-coach; they were mysteries to one another, as complete as if each had been in his own coach and six, or his own coach and sixty, with the breadth of a county between him and the next.

[. . .]

But, though the bank was almost always with [Jarvis Lorry], and though the coach (in a confused way, like the presence of pain under an opiate), was always with him, there was another current of impression that never ceased to run, all through the night. He was on his way to dig someone out of a grave.

Now, which of the multitude of faces that showed themselves before him was the true face of the buried person, the shadows of the night did not indicate; but they were all the faces of a man of five-and-forty by years, and they differed principally in the passions they expressed, and in the ghastliness of their worn and wasted state. Pride, contempt, defiance, stubbornness, submission, lamentation, succeeded one another; so did varieties of sunken cheek, cadaverous colour, emaciated hands and figures. But the face was in the main one face, and every head was prematurely white. A hundred times the dozing passenger inquired of this spectre:

'Buried how long?'
The answer was always the same: 'Almost eighteen years.'
'You had abandoned all hope of being dug out?'
'Long ago.'
'You know that you are recalled to life?'
'They tell me so.'
'I hope you care to live?'
'I can't say.'
'Shall I show her to you? Will you come and see her?'

The answers to this question were various and contradictory. Sometimes the broken reply was, 'Wait! It would kill me if I saw her too soon.' Sometimes, it was given in a tender rain of tears, and then it was, 'Take me to her.' Sometimes, it was staring and bewildered, and then it was, 'I don't know her. I don't understand.'

After such imaginary discourse, the passenger in his fancy would dig, and dig, dig – now, with a spade, now with a great key, now with his hands – to dig this wretched creature out. Got out at last, with earth hanging about his face and hair, he would suddenly fall away to dust. The passenger would then start to himself, and lower the window, to get the reality of mist and rain on his cheek.

Yet even when his eyes were opened on the mist and rain, on the moving patch of light from the lamps, and the hedge at the roadside retreating by jerks, the night shadows outside the coach would fall into the train of the night shadows within. The real Banking-house by Temple-bar,[1] the real business of the past day, the real strong-rooms, the real express sent after him, and the real message returned, would all be there. Out of the midst of them, the ghostly face would rise, and he would accost it again.

'Buried how long?'
'Almost eighteen years.'
'I hope you care to live?'
'I can't say.'

Dig – dig – dig – until an impatient movement from one of the two passengers would admonish him to pull up the window, draw his arm securely through the leathern strap, and speculate upon the two slumbering forms, until his mind lost its hold of them, and they again slid away into the bank and the grave.

1  Temple Bar was a stone gate that marked one of the entrances to the City of London. At one time the heads of executed criminals were exhibited on spikes on Temple Bar, just as the Revolutionaries held heads aloft on pikes at the storming of the Bastille (see Key Passages, p. 143).

'Buried how long?'
'Almost eighteen years.'
'You had abandoned all hope of being dug out?'
'Long ago.'

   The words were still in his hearing as just spoken – distinctly in his hearing as ever spoken words had been in his life – when the weary passenger started to the consciousness of daylight, and found that the shadows of the night were gone.
   He lowered the window, and looked out at the rising sun. There was a ridge of ploughed land, with a plough upon it where it had been left last night when the horses were unyoked; beyond, a quiet coppice-wood, in which many leaves of burning red and golden yellow still remained upon the trees. Though the earth was cold and wet, the sky was clear, and the sun rose bright, placid, and beautiful.
   "Eighteen years!" said the passenger, looking at the sun. "Gracious Creator of Day! To be buried alive for eighteen years!"

# From Book I, Chapter 5: "The Wine-Shop"

Chapter 5 moves the story to the suburb of Saint Antoine, a densely populated area of Paris that included the Bastille Prison. This introduction to the people who are poised for revolution already casts them as deformed out of human shape by suffering and deprivation. Dickens wrote a very similar scene in his first historical novel, *Barnaby Rudge* (1841), and in both accounts we see his interest in mob behavior, but the political comment that is central to the scene in *A Tale of Two Cities* does not play a role in the earlier novel. There, the wine drinkers have taken part in anti-Catholic riots, and their looting and burning culminates in their crazed (and fatal) drinking of burning liquor as it pours through the gutters from a torched vintner's house. In *A Tale of Two Cities*, the wine fills empty stomachs and there is a camaraderie in the "wine-game" while it lasts. Hunger was a major immediate cause of the French Revolution. A hailstorm in July 1788 destroyed the crops around Paris, causing a devastating famine that followed years of bad harvests. Dickens is correct in suggesting that the hunger of their families drew women into the Revolution (see Contextual Overview, **p. 10**).
   Soon, the wine begins to stain, and the correlation between wine and blood both suggests the resurrection theme of the novel (at the Last Supper, Christ told his disciples that the wine was his blood, shed for humankind) and takes on an ominous significance. When Gaspard writes "BLOOD" on the wall with wine, we may recall Percy Fitzgerald's comparison of the Paris aristocracy's reveling to "Belshazzar's feast over again, and the handwriting on the wall" (see Fitzgerald, Contemporary Documents, **p. 47**). In the biblical story, Belshazzar and his predecessor Nebuchadnezzar were kings who, like the French aristocracy, ruled in pride and luxury. God had punished Nebuchadnezzar by depriving him of reason and feeding him grass (as Joseph-François Foulon, Counsellor of State, will be similarly degraded by the Revolutionaries; see Key

Passages, **pp. 145–6**). During one of Belshazzar's parties, writing mysteriously appeared on the wall as a warning that the end of his reign was near. Clearly Gaspard's word is a warning to the French ruling classes; later, he will enact the first act of retribution when he kills the Marquis. The rhetoric of these passages is powerful. For a detailed discussion of point of view, atmosphere, and use of detail and repetition see Stoehr, Modern Criticism, **pp. 71–3**.

A large cask of wine had been dropped and broken, in the street. The accident had happened in getting it out of a cart; the cask had tumbled out with a run, the hoops had burst, and it lay on the stones just outside the door of the wine-shop, shattered like a walnut-shell.

All the people within reach had suspended their business, or their idleness, to run to the spot and drink the wine. The rough, irregular stones of the street, pointing every way, and designed, one might have thought, expressly to lame all living creatures that approached them, had dammed it into little pools; these were surrounded, each by its own jostling group or crowd, according to its size. Some men kneeled down, made scoops of their two hands joined, and sipped, or tried to help women, who bent over their shoulders, to sip, before the wine had all run out between their fingers. Others, men and women, dipped in the puddles with little mugs of mutilated earthenware, or even with handkerchiefs from women's heads, which were squeezed dry into infants' mouths; others made small mud-embankments, to stem the wine as it ran; others, directed by lookers-on up at high windows, darted here and there, to cut off little streams of wine that started away in new directions; others, devoted, themselves to the sodden and lee-dyed pieces of the cask, licking, and even champing the moister wine-rotted fragments with eager relish. There was no drainage to carry off the wine, and not only did it all get taken up, but so much mud got taken up along with it, that there might have been a scavenger in the street, if anybody acquainted with it could have believed in such a miraculous presence.

A shrill sound of laughter and of amused voices – voices of men, women, and children – resounded in the street while this wine-game lasted. There was little roughness in the sport, and much playfulness. There was a special companionship in it, an observable inclination on the part of every one to join some other one, which led, especially among the luckier or lighter-hearted, to frolicsome embraces, drinking of healths, shaking of hands, and even joining of hands and dancing, a dozen together. When the wine was gone, and the places where it had been most abundant were raked into a gridiron-pattern by fingers, these demonstrations ceased, as suddenly as they had broken out. The man who had left his saw sticking in the firewood he was cutting, set it in motion again; the woman who had left on a door-step the little pot of hot ashes, at which she had been trying to soften the pain in her own starved fingers and toes, or in those of her child, returned to it; men with bare arms, matted locks, and cadaverous faces, who had emerged into the winter light from cellars, moved away to descend again; and a gloom gathered on the scene that appeared more natural to it than sunshine.

The wine was red wine, and had stained the ground of the narrow street in the suburb of Saint Antoine, in Paris, where it was spilled. It had stained many hands, too, and many faces, and many naked feet, and many wooden shoes. The hands of the man who sawed the wood, left red marks on the billets; and the forehead of the woman who nursed her baby, was stained with the stain of the old rag she wound about her head again. Those who had been greedy with the staves of the cask, had acquired a tigerish[1] smear about the mouth; and one tall joker so besmirched, his head more out of a long squalid bag of a nightcap than in it, scrawled upon a wall with his finger dipped in muddy wine lees – BLOOD.

The time was to come, when that wine too would be spilled on the street-stones, and when the stain of it would be red upon many there.

And now that the cloud settled on Saint Antoine, which a momentary gleam had driven from his sacred countenance, the darkness of it was heavy – cold, dirt, sickness, ignorance, and want, were the lords in waiting on the saintly presence – nobles of great power all of them; but, most especially the last. Samples of a people that had undergone a terrible grinding and re-grinding in the mill, and certainly not in the fabulous mill which ground old people young,[2] shivered at every corner, passed in and out at every doorway, looked from every window, fluttered in every vestige of a garment that the wind shook. The mill which had worked them down, was the mill that grinds young people old; the children had ancient faces and grave voices; and upon them, and upon the grown faces, and ploughed into every furrow of age and coming up afresh, was the sign, Hunger. It was prevalent everywhere. Hunger was pushed out of the tall houses, in the wretched clothing that hung upon poles and lines; Hunger was patched into them with straw and rag and wood and paper; Hunger was repeated in every fragment of the small modicum of firewood that the man sawed off; Hunger stared down from the smokeless chimneys, and started up from the filthy street that had no offal,[3] among its refuse, of anything to eat. Hunger was the inscription on the baker's shelves, written in every small loaf of his scanty stock of bad bread; at the sausage-shop, in every dead-dog preparation that was offered for sale. Hunger rattled its dry bones among the roasting chestnuts in the turned cylinder; Hunger was shred into atomies in every farthing porringer[4] of husky chips of potato, fried with some reluctant drops of oil.

# From Book II, Chapter 3: "A Disappointment"

The second book opens with Charles Darnay's trial for treason at the Old Bailey. He is defended by Mr. Stryver, Sydney Carton's old school friend to whom Carton is a junior in their law practice (jackal to Stryver's lion) because he refuses to "strive" for anything (see Contemporary Documents, **p. 42**).

1   Madame Defarge will later be associated with the beautiful but dangerous tiger. See also Carlyle, p. 36.
2   Mills that ground old people into young ones were common in British folklore.
3   Offal is the normally rejected parts of a carcass.
4   The farthing, the smallest unit of British currency prior to decimalization, went out of circulation in 1956; a porringer is small dish for porridge or soup. Andrew Sanders points out that according to the *Oxford English Dictionary*, this is the first use of "chips" for fried potatoes in the English language. See Sanders, *Companion*, p. 44.

The reporting of the trial demonstrates Dickens's flexibility in reporting speech. In his stylistic analysis of the trial, critic Michael Gregory identifies narrative, narrative comment, direct, indirect, and free indirect speech at work in the following passage.[1] By reserving direct speech for Darnay's counsel and supporters (including Lucie and Alexandre Manette), Dickens subtly (and often humorously) suggests the duplicity of the prosecution and its witnesses. In this passage, the resemblance between Sydney Carton and Charles Darnay is first noted. It saves Darnay's life and will do so again at the end of the novel. The "disappointment" is reserved for the English onlookers, bloodthirstily hungry for a conviction and brutal punishment.

A singular circumstance then arose in the case. The object in hand, being, to show that the prisoner went down, with some fellow-plotter untracked, in the Dover mail on that Friday night in November five years ago, and got out of the mail in the night, as a blind, at a place where he did not remain, but from which he travelled back some dozen miles or more, to a garrison and dockyard, and there collected information; a witness was called to identify him as having been at the precise time required, in the coffee room of an hotel in that garrison – and – dockyard town, waiting for another person. The prisoner's counsel was cross-examining this witness with no result, except that he had never seen the prisoner on any other occasion, when the wigged gentleman who had all this time been looking at the ceiling of the court, wrote a word or two on a little piece of paper, screwed it up, and tossed it to him. Opening this piece of paper in the next pause, the counsel looked with great attention and curiosity at the prisoner.

'You say again you are quite sure that it *was* the prisoner?'
The witness was quite sure.
'Did you ever see anybody very like the prisoner?'
Not so like (the witness said), as that he could be mistaken.

'Look well upon that gentleman, my learned friend there,' pointing to him who had tossed the paper over, 'and then look well upon the prisoner. How say you? Are they very like each other?'
Allowing for my learned friend's appearance being careless and slovenly, if not debauched, they were sufficiently like each other to surprise, not only the witness, but everybody present, when they were thus brought into comparison. My Lord being prayed to bid my learned friend lay aside his wig, and giving no very gracious consent, the likeness became much more remarkable. My Lord inquired of Mr Stryver (the prisoner's counsel), whether they were next to try Mr Carton (name of my learned friend) for treason? But, Mr Stryver replied to my Lord, no; but he would ask the witness to tell him whether what happened once, might happen twice; whether he would have been so confident if he had seen this illustration of his rashness sooner; whether he would be so confident, having seen it;

1   "Old Bailey Speech in 'A Tale of Two Cities,' " *Review of English Literature*, 6 (1965), pp. 42–55.

and more. The upshot of which, was, to smash this witness like a crockery vessel, and shiver his part of the case to useless lumber.

## From Book II, Chapter 6: "Hundreds of People"

After appearing as unwilling witnesses for the prosecution in Charles Darnay's trial for treason, Lucie and her father befriend Darnay and are kind to the disagreeable malcontent, Sydney Carton. Their home in Soho, London, is a peaceful retreat that will serve as a contrast with the maelstrom that is building around the Defarges' wine-shop in Saint Antoine, Paris. Lucie, whose name means "light," is the "golden thread" of the novel (the title of Book II). Derived from Ariadne's thread that led Theseus safely out of King Minos' labyrinth in Greek mythology, the golden thread suggests the center of truth underlying the world's deceptions.

In this passage, a link emerges between the two households, although as yet Dickens does not reveal his hand. The recurring images of footsteps and rain foreshadow a "crowd" coming to shatter their peaceful lives, and the discord will be let loose by whatever in Darnay's story of hidden writing in a prison has troubled Doctor Manette. Sydney Carton speaks prophetically when he tells Lucie that he will take the threatening footsteps into his own life, and the imagery at the end of the chapter – "a memorable storm of thunder and lightning broke with that sweep of water, and there was not a moment's interval in crash, and fire, and rain" – will be repeated in Carton's sacrificial death at the end of the novel. (See Key Passages, **pp. 160–3** as well as Stoehr, Modern Criticism, **p. 76**, and Stewart, Modern Criticism, **pp. 87–90**.) The footsteps, which recall the feet of the Saint Antoine people, stained red by the spilling of the wine cask, are an excellent example of Dickens's characteristic use of synecdoche – where a part represents the whole. Here, the footsteps ominously and powerfully indicate the Paris mob, unstoppable and dangerous. Allied to the raindrops, however, there is also a sense that the Revolution was the natural outcome of the oppression that preceded it.

It was an oppressive day, and, after dinner, Lucie proposed that the wine should be carried out under the plane-tree, and they should sit there in the air. As everything turned upon her and revolved about her, they went out under the plane-tree, and she carried the wine down for the special benefit of Mr Lorry. [. . .]

He had been talking,[1] all day, on many subjects and with unusual vivacity. "Pray, Doctor Manette," said Mr Darnay, as they sat under the plane-tree – and he said it in the natural pursuit of the topic in hand, which happened to be the old buildings of London – "have you seen much of the Tower?"

"Lucie and I have been there; but only casually. We have seen enough of it, to know that it teems with interest; little more."

1   Doctor Manette.

*Figure 3* **Frontispiece from the original edition; Under the Plane Tree.**

"*I* have been there, as you remember," said Darnay, with a smile, though reddening a little angrily, "in another character, and not in a character that gives facilities for seeing much of it. They told me a curious thing when I was there."

"What was that?" Lucie asked.

"In making some alterations, the workmen came upon an old dungeon, which had been, for many years, built up and forgotten. Every stone of its inner wall was covered with inscriptions which had been carved by prisoners – dates, names, complaints, and prayers. Upon a corner stone in an angle of the wall, one prisoner who seemed to have gone to execution, had cut, as his last work, three letters.

They were done with some very poor instrument, and hurriedly, with an unsteady hand. At first, they were read as D. I. C.; but, on being more carefully examined, the last letter was found to be G. There was no record or legend of any prisoner with those initials, and many fruitless guesses were made what the name could have been. At length, it was suggested that the letters were not initials, but the complete word, DIG. The floor was examined very carefully under the inscription, and, in the earth beneath a stone, or tile, or some fragment of paving, were found the ashes of a paper, mingled with the ashes of a small leathern case or bag. What the unknown prisoner had written will never be read, but he had written something, and hidden it away to keep it from the gaoler."

"My father!" exclaimed Lucie, "you are ill!"

He had suddenly started up, with his hand to his head. His manner and his look quite terrified them all.

"No, my dear, not ill. There are large drops of rain falling, and they made me start. We had better go in."

He recovered himself almost instantly. Rain was really falling in large drops, and he showed the back of his hand with rain-drops on it. But, he said not a single word in reference to the discovery that had been told of, and, as they went into the house, the business eye of Mr Lorry either detected, or fancied it detected, on his face, as it turned towards Charles Darnay, the same singular look that had been upon it when it turned towards him in the passages of the Court House.

He recovered himself so quickly, however, that Mr Lorry had doubts of his business eye. The arm of the golden giant in the hall[2] was not more steady than he was, when he stopped under it to remark to them that he was not yet proof against slight surprises (if he ever would be), and that the rain had startled him.

Tea-time, and Miss Pross making tea, with another fit of the jerks upon her, and yet no Hundreds of people. Mr Carton had lounged in, but he made only Two.

The night was so very sultry, that although they sat with doors and windows open, they were overpowered by heat. When the tea-table was done with, they all moved to one of the windows, and looked out into the heavy twilight. Lucie sat by her father; Darnay sat beside her; Carton leaned against a window. The curtains were long and white, and some of the thunder-gusts that whirled into the corner, caught them up to the ceiling, and waved them like spectral wings.

"The rain-drops are still falling, large, heavy, and few," said Doctor Manette. "It comes slowly."

"It comes surely," said Carton.

They spoke low, as people watching and waiting mostly do; as people in a dark room, watching and waiting for Lightning, always do.

There was a great hurry in the streets, of people speeding away to get shelter before the storm broke; the wonderful corner for echoes resounded with the echoes of footsteps coming and going, yet not a footstep was there.

"A multitude of people, and yet a solitude!" said Darnay, when they had listened for a while.

"Is it not impressive, Mr Darnay?" asked Lucie. "Sometimes, I have sat here of

---

2    Earlier in the chapter, Dickens has referred to the Darnays' house as having a golden arm on the wall. It would originally have hung over a gold-beater's shop.

an evening, until I have fancied – but even the shade of a foolish fancy makes me shudder to-night, when all is so black and solemn—"

"Let us shudder too. We may know what it is?"

"It will seem nothing to you. Such whims are only impressive as we originate them, I think; they are not to be communicated. I have sometimes sat alone here of an evening, listening, until I have made the echoes out to be the echoes of all the footsteps that are coming by-and-by into our lives."

"There is a great crowd coming one day into our lives, if that be so," Sydney Carton struck in, in his moody way.

The footsteps were incessant, and the hurry of them became more and more rapid. The corner echoed and re-echoed with the tread of feet; some, as it seemed, under the windows; some, as it seemed, in the room; some coming, some going, some breaking off, some stopping altogether; all in the distant streets, and not one within sight.

"Are all these footsteps destined to come to all of us, Miss Manette, or are we to divide them among us?"

"I don't know, Mr Darnay; I told you it was a foolish fancy, but you asked for it. When I have yielded myself to it, I have been alone, and then I have imagined them the footsteps of the people who are to come into my life, and my father's."

"I take them into mine!" said Carton. "*I* ask no questions and make no stipulations. There is a great crowd bearing down upon us, Miss Manette, and I see them!—by the Lightning." He added the last words, after there had been a vivid flash which had shown him lounging in the window.

"And I hear them!" he added again, after a peal of thunder. "Here they come, fast, fierce, and furious!"

It was the rush and roar of rain that he typified, and it stopped him, for no voice could be heard in it. A memorable storm of thunder and lightning broke with that sweep of water, and there was not a moment's interval in crash, and fire, and rain, until after the moon rose at midnight.

# From Book II, Chapter 7: "Monsieur the Marquis in Town"[1]

Although Dickens is often accused of stereotyping the French aristocracy, (see Stephen, Early Critical Reception **pp. 62–4**, for example), there are many legitimate sources for his portrayal of the Marquis's high-handed and callous killing of Gaspard's child. Aggressive drivers are as old as the Roman chariots, and according to one of Dickens's sources, Louis-Sébastien Mercier, they were a menace in pre-Revolutionary France. (See Percy Fitzgerald's similar account,

---

1   Only the *All the Year Round* version of *A Tale of Two Cities* used this title; in the manuscript and all subsequent editions Dickens used "Monseigneur in Town," which could ambiguously refer either to the great lord who has hosted the reception, or to Charles Darnay's uncle, who is snubbed at the reception. "Monseigneur" was usually reserved for more exalted aristocrats than the Evrémondes.

Contemporary Documents, **p. 47**.) It has been suggested that Dickens may also have read the memoirs of Hermann Ludwig Heinrich, Prince von Pueckler-Muskau (published in England in 1832), in which he describes running over a child with his carriage (see Andrew Sanders, **p. 119**, n. 7). For Dickens's other comments on the French aristocracy, see Contemporary Documents, **pp. 39–41**.

The Marquis, Charles Darnay's uncle, has just come from the salon of a Monseigneur, where he was snubbed by the great man. His pride hurt by his own class, the Marquis typically takes out his anger on the class beneath him. The scene is important because the child's death leads to Gaspard's murder of the Marquis. Dickens clearly sympathizes with the crowd's rejection of the Marquis's coins. In trying to pay for the dead child, the Marquis is exploiting what Thomas Carlyle[2] deplored as the cash-nexus, the replacing of human contact with money. Dickens and Carlyle both saw the cash-nexus operating increasingly in the relationship between masters –the new aristocracy –and their workers in Victorian Britain. In killing Gaspard's child, the Marquis is once again epitomizing the bad father (who is already responsible for a rape and a murder). As the aristocrat, he stands in the position of father to his tenants, so ironically Gaspard's murder of him is parricide. (For the relationship between family and class see Hutter, Modern Criticism, **pp. 83–7**.)

With a wild rattle and clatter, and an inhuman abandonment of consideration not easy to be understood in these days, the carriage dashed through streets and swept round corners, with women screaming before it, and men clutching each other and clutching children out of its way. At last, swooping at a street corner by a fountain, one of its wheels came to a sickening little jolt, and there was a loud cry from a number of voices, and the horses reared and plunged.

But for the latter inconvenience, the carriage probably would not have stopped; carriages were often known to drive on, and leave their wounded behind, and why not? But the frightened valet had got down in a hurry, and there were twenty hands at the horses' bridles.

"What has gone wrong?" said Monsieur, calmly looking out.

A tall man in a nightcap had caught up a bundle from among the feet of the horses, and had laid it on the basement of the fountain, and was down in the mud and wet, howling over it like a wild animal.

"Pardon, Monsieur the Marquis!" said a ragged and submissive man, "it is a child."

"Why does he make that abominable noise? Is it his child?"

"Excuse me, Monsieur the Marquis –it is a pity –yes."

The fountain was a little removed; for the street opened, where it was, into a space some ten or twelve yards square. As the tall man suddenly got up from the ground, and came running at the carriage, Monsieur the Marquis clapped his hand for an instant on his sword-hilt.

"Killed!" shrieked the man, in wild desperation, extending both arms at their length above his head, and staring at him. "Dead!"

The people closed round, and looked at Monsieur the Marquis. There was nothing revealed by the many eyes that looked at him but watchfulness and eagerness; there was no visible menacing or anger. Neither did the people say anything; after the first cry, they had been silent, and they remained so. The voice of the submissive man who had spoken, was flat and tame in its extreme submission. Monsieur the Marquis ran his eyes over them all, as if they had been mere rats come out of their holes.

He took out his purse.

"It is extraordinary to me," said he, "that you people cannot take care of yourselves and your children. One or the other of you is for ever in the way. How do I know what injury you have done my horses. See! Give him that."

He threw out a gold coin for the valet to pick up, and all the heads craned forward that all the eyes might look down at it as it fell. The tall man called out again with a most unearthly cry, "Dead!"

He was arrested by the quick arrival of another man, for whom the rest made way. On seeing him, the miserable creature fell upon his shoulder, sobbing and crying, and pointing to the fountain, where some women were stooping over the motionless bundle, and moving gently about it. They were as silent, however, as the men.

"I know all, I know all," said the last comer. "Be a brave man, my Gaspard! It is better for the poor little plaything to die so, than to live. It has died in a moment without pain. Could it have lived an hour as happily?"

"You are a philosopher, you there," said the Marquis, smiling. "How do they call you?"

"They call me Defarge."

"Of what trade?"

"Monsieur the Marquis, vendor of wine."

"Pick up that, philosopher and vendor of wine," said the Marquis, throwing him another gold coin, "and spend it as you will. The horses there; are they right?"

Without deigning to look at the assemblage a second time, Monsieur the Marquis leaned back in his seat, and was just being driven away with the air of a gentleman who had accidentally broken some common thing, and had paid for it, and could afford to pay for it; when his ease was suddenly disturbed by a coin flying into his carriage and ringing on its floor.

"Hold!" said Monsieur the Marquis. "Hold the horses! Who threw that?"

He looked to the spot where Defarge the vendor of wine had stood, a moment before; but the wretched father was groveling on his face on the pavement in that spot, and the figure that stood beside him was the figure of a dark stout woman, knitting.

"You dogs!" said the Marquis, but smoothly, and with an unchanged front, except as to the spots on his nose: "I would ride over any of you very willingly, and exterminate you from the earth. If I knew which rascal threw at the carriage, and if that brigand were sufficiently near it, he should be crushed under the wheels."

So cowed was their condition, and so long and so hard their experience of what such a man could do to them, within the law and beyond it, that not a voice, or a hand, or even an eye, was raised. Among the men, not one. But, the woman who stood knitting looked up steadily, and looked the Marquis in the face. It was not for his dignity to notice it; his contemptuous eyes passed over her, and over all the other rats; and he leaned back in his seat again, and gave the word "Go on!" [. . .]

[. . .] The father had long ago taken up his bundle and hidden himself away with it, when the women who had tended the bundle while it lay on the base of the fountain, sat there watching the running of the water and the rolling of the Fancy Ball[3] – when the one woman who had stood conspicuous, knitting, still knitted on with the steadfastness of Fate.[4] The water of the fountain ran, the swift river ran, the day ran into evening, so much life in the city ran into death according to rule, time and tide waited for no man, the rats were sleeping close together in their dark holes again, the Fancy Ball was lighted up at supper, all things ran their course.

## From Book II, Chapter 9: "The Gorgon's Head"[1]

After the Marquis kills Gaspard's child, he returns to his village, where he cruelly rejects the heartfelt plea of a woman asking to have her husband's grave marked. Charles Darnay arrives at the château and engages in an argument with his uncle, denouncing the family's history of cruelty and regretting that he has not yet fulfilled his mother's dying wish that he redress the wrongs that his family has committed. The argument is heated on Charles's side; his uncle remains as unmoved (on the surface) as in his previous encounters with Gaspard and the poor woman:

Every fine straight line in the clear whiteness of his face, was cruelly, craftily, and closely compressed, while he stood looking quietly at his nephew, with his snuff-box in his hand. Once again he touched him on the breast, as though his finger were the fine point of a small sword, with which, in delicate finesse, he ran him through the body, and said,

"My friend, I will die, perpetuating the system under which I have lived."

With these prophetic words, the Marquis goes to bed, and the chapter ends with his death, performed stealthily and in the dark by Gaspard, who has been seen by a road mender hanging on below the Marquis's coach as it approached the village. This passage exemplifies Dickens's artistry in depicting a violent act entirely through association. The passage of time from bedtime to morning is

---

3   Earlier in the passage Dickens had referred to the passing carriages of the aristocracy as the "whole Fancy Ball," a reference to the fairy tale of Cinderella, the poor girl who is magically whisked away to a grand party hosted by a prince.
4   Dickens frequently makes a connection between Madame Defarge and the figure of Fate because of her relentless pursuit of the Darnay family. In Greek mythology, Fate was depicted as three women spinning the yarn that represented an individual human life. They decided when that life would end.

---

1   In Greek mythology, the Gorgon (Medusa) was a female monster with snakes for hair. She turned to stone anyone who looked directly at her.

conveyed through the château and its inhabitants, in an unfolding of action reminiscent of the story of Sleeping Beauty (Dickens's style is frequently influenced by fairy-tales). The passage also reiterates many of the motifs of the novel. As the sun stains the château red, we recall the staining of the hungry wine-drinkers (see Key Passages, **p. 126**), and Gaspard's writing "BLOOD" on the wall in wine. Here, Gaspard's desire for the blood of his child's murderer is fulfilled. Another link is the fountain, a symbol present at the death of Gaspard's child in Paris, again at the château, and finally in the village, when Gaspard is hanged for the murder of the Marquis. The central image of the Marquis – his stone heart – culminates in his transformation to a stone face on the façade of the stone house that has concealed the brutal acts perpetrated by the Evrémonde brothers. For an analysis of the cluster of images surrounding the Marquis, see Stoehr, Modern Criticism, **pp. 73–5**. For comment on the generational conflict between the Marquis and Charles Darnay see Hutter, Modern Criticism, **pp. 84–5**, and Dickens, Contemporary Documents, **p. 48**.

So, leaving only one light burning on the large hearth, he let his thin gauze curtains fall around him, and heard the night break its silence with a long sigh as he composed himself to sleep.

The stone faces on the outer walls stared blindly at the black night for three heavy hours; for three heavy hours, the horses in the stables rattled at their racks, the dogs barked, and the owl made a noise with very little resemblance in it to the noise conventionally assigned to the owl by men-poets. [. . .]

For three heavy hours, the stone faces of the château, lion and human, stared blindly at the night. Dead darkness lay on all the landscape, dead darkness added its own hush to the hushing dust on all the roads. The burial-place had got to the pass that its little heaps of poor grass were undistinguishable from one another; the figure on the Cross might have come down, for anything that could be seen of it. In the village, taxers and taxed[2] were fast asleep. Dreaming, perhaps, of banquets, as the starved usually do, and of ease and rest, as the driven slave and the yoked ox may, its lean inhabitants slept soundly, and were fed and freed.

The fountain in the village flowed unseen and unheard, and the fountain at the château dropped unseen and unheard – both melting away, like the minutes that were falling from the spring of Time – through three dark hours. Then, the grey water of both began to be ghostly in the light, and the eyes of the stone faces of the château were opened.

It grew lighter and lighter, until at last the sun touched the tops of the still trees, and poured its radiance over the hill. In the glow, the water of the château fountain seemed to turn to blood, and the stone faces crimsoned. The carol of the birds was loud and high, and, on the weather-beaten sill of the great window of the bedchamber of Monsieur the Marquis, one little bird sang its sweetest song with all its might. At this, the nearest stone face seemed to stare amazed, and, with open mouth and dropped under-jaw, looked awe-stricken.

2   See Contextual Overview, pp. 8–9.

Now, the sun was full up, and movement began in the village. Casement windows opened, crazy doors were unbarred, and people came forth shivering – chilled, as yet, by the new sweet air. Then began the rarely lightened toil of the day among the village population. Some, to the fountain; some, to the fields; men and women here, to dig and delve; men and women there, to see to the poor live stock, and lead the bony cows out, to such pasture as could be found by the roadside. In the church and at the Cross, a kneeling figure or two; attendant on the latter prayers, the led cow, trying for a breakfast among the weeds at the Cross-foot.

The château awoke later, as became its quality, but awoke gradually and surely. First, the lonely boar-spears and knives of the chase had been reddened as of old; then, had gleamed trenchant in the morning sunshine; now, doors and windows were thrown open, horses in the stables looked round over their shoulders at the light and freshness pouring in at doorways, leaves sparkled and rustled at iron-grated windows, dogs pulled hard at their chains, and reared impatient to be loosed.

All these trivial incidents belonged to the routine of life, and the return of morning. Surely, not so the ringing of the great bell of the château, nor the running up and down the stairs, nor the hurried figures on the terrace, nor the booting and tramping here and there and everywhere, nor the quick saddling of horses and riding away?

What winds conveyed this hurry to the grizzled mender of roads, already at work on the hill-top beyond the village, with his day's dinner (not much to carry) lying in a bundle that it was worth no crow's while to peck at, on a heap of stones? Had the birds, carrying some grains of it to a distance, dropped one over him as they sow chance seeds? Whether or no, the mender of roads ran, on the sultry morning, as if for his life, down the hill, knee-high in dust, and never stopped till he got to the fountain.

All the people of the village were at the fountain, standing about in their depressed manner, and whispering softly, but showing no other emotions than grim curiosity and surprise. [. . .] What did all this portend, and what portended the swift hoisting-up of Monsieur Gabelle[3] behind a servant on horseback, and the conveying away of the said Gabelle (double-laden though the horse was), at a gallop, like a new version of the German ballad of Leonora?[4]

It portended that there was one stone face too many, up at the château.

The Gorgon had surveyed the building again in the night, and had added the one stone face wanting; the stone face for which it had waited through about two hundred years.

It lay back on the pillow of Monsieur the Marquis. It was like a fine mask, suddenly startled, made angry, and petrified. Driven home into the heart of the stone figure attached to it, was a knife. Round its hilt was a frill of paper, on which was scrawled:

"*Drive him fast to his tomb. This, from* JACQUES."

3   Gabelle is named for the unpopular salt tax, see Contextual Overview, p. 8. In *The French Revolution*, Carlyle writes that the tax-gatherer "long hunting as a biped of prey, may now find himself hunted as one" (I, 238). See Contemporary Documents, p. 31.
4   A ballad written by Gottfried August Burger in 1773. When Leonora is visited by the ghost of her lover, she rides away with him.

# From Book II, Chapter 19, "An Opinion"

When Charles Darnay asks Doctor Manette for his daughter's hand in marriage, he insists on telling Doctor Manette his real name. They agree that he will do so on the wedding morning. As feminist critic Hilary M. Schor points out,[1] the relationship between Darnay and Doctor Manette takes precedence over that of Darnay and Lucie in the novel; we do not even hear his proposal to her because what passes secretly between Darnay and Manette is going to be of much greater importance. In Chapter 18, "Nine Days," the planned exchange between Doctor Manette and Darnay occurs, leaving the Doctor "deadly pale." After the young couple has left on their honeymoon, Mr. Lorry discovers Doctor Manette back at work on the shoemaking bench that occupied his time during his eighteen-year imprisonment in the Bastille. Days go by, and Mr. Lorry "could not fail to observe that the shoemaker, whose hand had been a little out at first, was growing dreadfully skilful, and that he had never been so intent on his work, and that his hands had never been so nimble and expert, as in the dusk of the ninth evening." Darnay's revelation has cast Doctor Manette's always-fragile mind back into his cell, 105 North Tower, in the Bastille. Dickens's portrait of Doctor Manette is in part derived from his observation of prisoners held in solitary confinement at the Eastern Penitentiary in Philadelphia (see Contemporary Documents, **pp. 37–9** and the Contextual Overview, **pp. 18–20**). Troubled by the relapse, kind Mr. Lorry wonders how best to help his old friend, and he decides to speak to him of it as though speaking about someone else. The following exchange demonstrates Dickens's understanding of trauma and the delicate role of the therapist in drawing out the sufferer. Doctor Manette gratefully accepts the fiction that they are talking about a third person. Richard Maxwell suggests that the splitting of Doctor Manette into two people here is another example of the many doublings in the novel.[2] The closing scene in which Mr. Lorry and Miss Pross, "accomplices in a horrible crime," bury Doctor Manette's tools, is typical of Dickens's humorous rendering of serious events. In burying the physical representations of Doctor Manette's buried secret, Dickens plays upon the many manifestations of death and resurrection in the novel. The tools may be physically buried, but the secrets of that Bastille cell are waiting to be brought up into the light at a later date. The scene is connected also to Mr. Lorry's guilt-ridden dreams on his way to Paris to dig Doctor Manette out of his grave (see Key Passages, **pp. 122–4**).

"[. . .] But, unfortunately, there has been," he paused and took a deep breath – "a slight relapse."

The Doctor, in a low voice, asked, "Of how long duration?"

"Nine days and nights."

---

1    *Dickens and the Daughter of the House*, Cambridge: Cambridge University Press, 1999, p. 91.
2    *A Tale of Two Cities*, ed. Richard Maxwell, Harmondsworth: Penguin, p. 462.

"How did it show itself? I infer," glancing at his hands again, "in the resumption of some old pursuit connected with the shock?"

"That is the fact."

"Now, did you ever see him," asked the Doctor, distinctly and collectedly, though in the same low voice, "engaged in that pursuit originally?"

"Once."

"And when the relapse fell on him, was he in most respects – or in all respects – as he was then?"

"I think, in all respects."

"You spoke of his daughter. Does his daughter know of the relapse?"

"No. It has been kept from her, and I hope will always be kept from her. It is known only to myself, and to one other who may be trusted."

The Doctor grasped his hand, and murmured, "That was very kind. That was very thoughtful!" Mr Lorry grasped his hand in return, and neither of the two spoke for a little while.

"Now, my dear Manette," said Mr Lorry, at length, in his most considerate and most affectionate way, "I am a mere man of business, and unfit to cope with such intricate and difficult matters. I do not possess the kind of information necessary; I do not possess the kind of intelligence; I want guiding. There is no man in this world on whom I could so rely for right guidance, as on you. Tell me, how does this relapse come about? Is there danger of another? Could a repetition of it be prevented? How should a repetition of it be treated? How does it come about at all? What can I do for my friend? No man ever can have been more desirous in his heart to serve a friend, than I am to serve mine, if I knew how. But I don't know how to originate, in such a case. If your sagacity, knowledge, and experience, could put me on the right track, I might be able to do so much; unenlightened and undirected, I can do so little. Pray discuss it with me; pray enable me to see it a little more clearly, and teach me how to be a little more useful."

Doctor Manette sat meditating after these earnest words were spoken, and Mr Lorry did not press him.

"I think it probable," said the Doctor, breaking silence with an effort, "that the relapse you have described, my dear friend, was not quite unforeseen by its subject."

"Was it dreaded by him?" Mr Lorry ventured to ask.

"Very much." He said it with an involuntary shudder. "You have no idea how such an apprehension weighs on the sufferer's mind, and how difficult – how almost impossible – it is, for him to force himself to utter a word upon the topic that oppresses him."

"Would he," asked Mr Lorry, "be sensibly relieved if he could prevail upon himself to impart that secret brooding to any one, when it is on him?"

"I think so. But it is, as I have told you, next to impossible. I even believe it – in some cases – to be quite impossible."

"Now," said Mr Lorry, gently laying his hand on the Doctor's arm again, after a short silence on both sides, "to what would you refer this attack?"

"I believe," returned Doctor Manette, "that there had been a strong and extraordinary revival of the train of thought and remembrance that was the first cause of the malady. Some intense associations of a most distressing nature were vividly recalled, I think. It is probable that there had long been a dread lurking in his mind, that those associations would be recalled – say, under certain circumstances – say, on a particular occasion. He tried to prepare himself, in vain; perhaps the effort to prepare himself, made him less able to bear it."

"Would he remember what took place in the relapse?" asked Mr Lorry, with natural hesitation.

The Doctor looked desolately round the room, shook his head, and answered, in a low voice, "Not at all."

"Now, as to the future," hinted Mr. Lorry.

"As to the future," said the Doctor, recovering firmness, "I should have great hope. As it pleased Heaven in its mercy to restore him so soon, I should have great hope. He, yielding under the pressure of a complicated something, long dreaded and long vaguely foreseen and contended against, and recovering after the cloud had burst and passed, I should hope that the worst was over."

"Well, well! That's good comfort. I am thankful!" said Mr Lorry.

"I am thankful!" repeated the Doctor, bending his head with reverence.

[. . .]

On the night of the day on which he left the house, Mr Lorry went into his room with a chopper, saw, chisel, and hammer, attended by Miss Pross carrying a light. There, with closed doors, and in a mysterious and guilty manner, Mr Lorry hacked the shoemaker's bench to pieces, while Miss Pross held the candle as if she were assisting at a murder – for which, indeed, in her grimness, she was no unsuitable figure. The burning of the body (previously reduced to pieces convenient for the purpose), was commenced without delay in the kitchen fire; and the tools, shoes, and leather, were buried in the garden. So wicked do destruction and secrecy appear to honest minds, that Mr Lorry and Miss Pross, while engaged in the commission of their deed and in the removal of its traces, almost felt, and almost looked, like accomplices in a horrible crime.

## From Book II, Chapter 21: "Echoing Footsteps"

In Chapter 21, the echoing footsteps of Saint Antoine are heard in Soho, where the Darnay family have lost a baby boy but have a little Lucie, aged six. The following description of the fall of the Bastille on July 14, 1789 is heavily influenced by Carlyle's account in *The French Revolution* (see Contemporary Documents, **pp. 33–7**). See also the Contextual Overview, **p. 10**. Central to the plot is Ernest Defarge's discovery of Doctor Manette's letter, buried for over twenty years in the Bastille, which will condemn his son-in-law to death. For an analysis of the cinematic techniques in Dickens's style see Zambrano, Modern Criticism, **pp. 76–8**.

Headlong, mad, and dangerous footsteps to force their way into anybody's life, footsteps not easily made clean again if once stained red, the footsteps raging in Saint Antoine afar off, as the little circle sat in the dark London window.

Saint Antoine had been, that morning, a vast dusky mass of scarecrows heaving to and fro, with frequent gleams of light above the billowy heads, where steel blades and bayonets shone in the sun. A tremendous roar arose from the throat of Saint Antoine, and a forest of naked arms struggled in the air like shrivelled branches of trees in a winter wind: all the fingers convulsively clutching at every weapon or semblance of a weapon that was thrown up from the depths below, no matter how far off.

Who gave them out, whence they last came, where they began, through what agency they crookedly quivered and jerked, scores at a time, over the heads of the crowd, like a kind of lightning, no eye in the throng could have told; but, muskets were being distributed – so were cartridges, powder, and ball, bars of iron and wood, knives, axes, pikes, every weapon that distracted ingenuity could discover or devise. People who could lay hold of nothing else, set themselves with bleeding hands to force stones and bricks out of their places in walls. Every pulse and heart in Saint Antoine was on high-fever strain and at high-fever heat. Every living creature there, held life as of no account, and was demented with a passionate readiness to sacrifice it.

As a whirlpool of boiling waters has a centre point, so, all this raging circled round Defarge's wine-shop, and every human drop in the cauldron had a tendency to be sucked towards the vortex where Defarge himself, already begrimed with gunpowder and sweat, issued orders, issued arms, thrust this man back, dragged this man forward, disarmed one to arm another, laboured and strove in the thickest of the uproar.

"Keep near to me, Jacques Three," cried Defarge; "and do you, Jacques One and Two,[1] separate and put yourselves at the head of as many of these patriots as you can. Where is my wife?"

"Eh, well! Here you see me!" said madame, composed as ever, but not knitting to-day. Madame's resolute right hand was occupied with an axe, in place of the usual softer implements, and in her girdle were a pistol and a cruel knife.

"Where do you go, my wife?"

"I go," said madame, "with you, at present. You shall see me at the head of women, by-and-by."

"Come then!" cried Defarge, in a resounding voice. "Patriots and friends, we are ready! The Bastille!"

With a roar that sounded as if all the breath in France had been shaped into the detested word, the living sea rose, wave on wave, depth on depth, and overflowed the city to that point. Alarm-bells ringing, drums beating, the sea raging and thundering on its new beach, the attack begun.

Deep ditches, double draw-bridge, massive stone walls, eight great towers, cannon, muskets, fire and smoke. Through the fire and through the smoke – in the fire and in the smoke, for the sea cast him up against a cannon, and on the instant he became a cannonier – Defarge of the wine-shop worked like a manful soldier, Two fierce hours.

Deep ditch, single drawbridge, massive stone walls, eight great towers, cannon, muskets, fire and smoke. One drawbridge down! "Work, comrades all, work! Work, Jacques One, Jacques Two, Jacques One Thousand, Jacques Two

---

1    Part of the collective spirit of the Revolution was not to differentiate people by name but rather to refer to each other as "Citizen" or "Jacques".

Thousand, Jacques Five-and-Twenty Thousand; in the name of all the Angels or the Devils – which you prefer – work!" Thus Defarge of the wine-shop, still at his gun, which had long grown hot.

"To me, women!" cried madame his wife. "What! We can kill as well as the men when the place is taken!" And to her, with a shrill thirsty cry, trooping women variously armed, but all armed alike in hunger and revenge.

Cannon, muskets, fire and smoke; but, still the deep ditch, the single drawbridge, the massive stone walls, and the eight great towers. Slight displacements of the raging sea, made by the falling wounded. Flashing weapons, blazing torches, smoking waggon-loads of wet straw, hard work at neighbouring barricades in all directions, shrieks, volleys, execrations, bravery without stint, boom smash and rattle, and the furious sounding of the living sea; but, still the deep ditch, and the single drawbridge, and the massive stone walls, and the eight great towers, and still Defarge of the wine-shop at his gun, grown doubly hot by the service of Four fierce hours.

A white flag from within the fortress, and a parley – this dimly perceptible through the raging storm, nothing audible in it – suddenly the sea rose immeasurably wider and higher, and swept Defarge of the wine-shop over the lowered drawbridge, past the massive stone outer walls, in among the eight great towers surrendered!

So resistless was the force of the ocean bearing him on, that even to draw his breath or turn his head was as impracticable as if he had been struggling in the surf at the South Sea, until he was landed in the outer court-yard of the Bastille. There, against an angle of a wall, he made a struggle to look about him. Jacques Three was nearly at his side; Madame Defarge, still heading some of her women, was visible in the inner distance, and her knife was in her hand. Everywhere was tumult, exultation, deafening and maniacal bewilderment, astounding noise, yet furious dumb-show.

"The Prisoners!"

"The Records!"

"The secret cells!"

"The instruments of torture!"

"The Prisoners!"

Of all these cries, and ten thousand incoherencies, "The Prisoners!" was the cry most taken up by the sea that rushed in, as if there were an eternity of people, as well as of time and space. When the foremost billows rolled past, bearing the prison officers with them, and threatening them all with instant death if any secret nook remained undisclosed, Defarge laid his strong hand on the breast of one of these men – a man with a grey head who had a lighted torch in his hand – separated him from the rest, and got him between himself and the wall.

"Show me the North Tower!" said Defarge. "Quick!"

"I will faithfully," replied the man, "if you will come with me. But there is no one there."

"What is the meaning of One Hundred and Five, North Tower?" asked Defarge. "Quick!"

"The meaning, monsieur?"

"Does it mean a captive, or a place of captivity? Or do you mean that I shall strike you dead?"

"Kill him!" croaked Jacques Three, who had come close up.

"Monsieur, it is a cell."

"Show it me!"

"Pass this way then."

Jacques Three, with his usual craving on him, and evidently disappointed by the dialogue taking a turn that did not seem to promise bloodshed, held by Defarge's arm as he held by the turnkey's. Their three heads had been close together during this brief discourse, and it had been as much as they could do to hear one another, even then: so tremendous was the noise of the living ocean, in its irruption into the Fortress, and its inundation of the courts and passages and staircases. All around outside, too, it beat the walls with a deep, hoarse roar, from which, occasionally, some partial shouts of tumult broke and leaped into the air like spray.

Through gloomy vaults where the light of day had never shone, past hideous doors of dark dens and cages, down cavernous flights of steps, and again up steep rugged ascents of stone and brick, more like dry waterfalls than staircases, Defarge, the turnkey, and Jacques Three, linked hand and arm, went, with all the speed they could make. Here and there, especially at first, the inundation started on them and swept by; but, when they had done descending, and were winding and climbing up a tower, they were alone. Hemmed in here by the massive thickness of walls and arches, the storm within the fortress and without was only audible to them in a dull, subdued way, as if the noise out of which they had come had almost destroyed their sense of hearing.

The turnkey stopped at a low door, put a key in a clashing lock, swung the door slowly open, and said, as they all bent their heads and passed in:

"One hundred and five, North Tower!"

There was a small, heavily-grated, unglazed window high in the wall, with a stone screen before it, so that the sky could be only seen by stooping low and looking up. There was a small chimney, heavily barred across, a few feet within. There was a heap of old feathery wood ashes on the hearth. There were a stool, and table, and a straw bed. There were the four blackened walls, and a rusted iron ring in one of them.

"Pass that torch slowly along these walls, that I may see them," said Defarge to the turnkey.

The man obeyed, and Defarge followed the light closely with his eyes.

"Stop! – Look here, Jacques!"

"A. M.!" croaked Jacques Three, as he read greedily.

[. . .]

In the howling universe of passion and contention that seemed to encompass this grim old officer conspicuous in his grey coat and red decoration,[2] there was but one quite steady figure, and that was a woman's. "See, there is my husband!"

---

2    The officer is Bernard-René de Launay, Governor of the Bastille. The storming of the Bastille was not to release the seven prisoners, but to gain control of the gunpowder stored there and to have the guns on the roof taken down. When a deputation went to negotiate with de Launay they were well received, but various misunderstandings between the crowd outside and de Launay inside resulted in the attack on the prison. De Launay was promised safe passage to the Hôtel de Ville (the city government office), but he was murdered and beheaded on the way by Desnot a cook. Dickens merges historical fact and fiction in having Madame Defarge decapitate de Launay.

she cried, pointing him out. "See Defarge!" She stood immovable close to the grim old officer, and remained immovable close to him; remained immovable close to him through the streets, as Defarge and the rest bore him along; remained immovable close to him when he was got near his destination, and began to be struck at from behind; remained immovable close to him when the long-gathering rain of stabs and blows fell heavy; was so close to him when he dropped dead under it, that, suddenly animated, she put her foot upon his neck, and with her cruel knife – long ready – hewed off his head.

The hour was come, when Saint Antoine was to execute his horrible idea of hoisting up men for lamps to show what he could be and do. Saint Antoine's blood was up, and the blood of tyranny and domination by the iron hand was down – down on the steps of the Hôtel de Ville where the governor's body lay – down on the sole of the shoe of Madame Defarge where she had trodden on the body to steady it for mutilation. "Lower the lamp yonder?" cried Saint Antoine, after glaring round for a new means of death; "here is one of his soldiers to be left on guard!" The swinging sentinel was posted, and the sea rushed on.[3]

The sea of black and threatening waters, and of destructive upheavings of wave against wave, whose depths were yet unfathomed and whose forces were yet unknown. The remorseless sea of turbulently swaying shapes, voices of vengeance, and faces hardened in the furnaces of suffering until the touch of pity could make no mark on them.

But, in the ocean of faces where every fierce and furious expression was in vivid life, there were two groups of faces – each seven in number – so fixedly contrasting with the rest, that never did sea roll which bore more memorable wrecks with it. Seven faces of prisoners, suddenly released by the storm that had burst their tomb, were carried high over head: all scared, all lost, all wondering and amazed, as if the Last Day were come, and those who rejoiced around them were lost spirits. Other seven faces there were, carried higher,[4] seven dead faces, whose drooping eyelids and half-seen eyes awaited the Last Day. Impassive faces, yet with a suspended – not an abolished – expression on them; faces, rather, in a fearful pause, as having yet to raise the dropped lids of the eyes, and bear witness with the bloodless lips, "THOU DIDST IT!"

Seven prisoners released, seven gory heads on pikes, the keys of the accursed fortress of the eight strong towers, some discovered letters and other memorials of prisoners of old time, long dead of broken hearts, – such, and such-like, the loudly echoing footsteps of Saint Antoine escort through the Paris streets in mid-July, one thousand seven hundred and eighty-nine. Now, Heaven defeat the fancy of Lucie Darnay, and keep these feet far out of her life! For, they are headlong, mad, and dangerous; and in the years so long after the breaking of the cask at Defarge's wine-shop door, they are not easily purified when once stained red.

---

3  Lampposts were used for hanging victims of the riots.
4  The heads of de Launay and several other officials were held aloft on pikes, replacing artificial heads (made of wax) of heroes that the Revolutionaries had carried at the beginning of their riot.

# From Book II, Chapter 22: "The Sea Still Rises"

As well as the famous storming of the Bastille, Dickens chose to include the death of Foulon (which occurred a week later) in the novel because it was another variation of his "buried alive" theme. The details he derived from Carlyle, (see Contemporary Documents, pp. 31–2), although Carlyle may have invented Foulon's remark that the poor may eat grass. Joseph-François Foulon (1715–89) was Counsellor of State to King Louis XVI, and he did fake his death and mount a lavish funeral (the body belonging to a servant) so that he could escape to the country. Foulon was suspected of helping to create food shortages, so Dickens's emphasis on hunger as a motive in the Revolution makes him a prime target for the people's anger. When they stuff grass into his dead mouth, Dickens is recalling the Nebuchadnezzar story which underlies Gaspard's writing on the wall (see Key Passages, p. 126). After driving out the proud ruler and turning his mind into that of a beast, God feeds him grass.

Dickens does show some sympathy for old Foulon in this passage, when a ray of sunlight strikes "a kindly ray as of hope or protection" on his head. This is the first hint that Dickens is tempering his sympathy with the Revolutionaries, however much he may appreciate their suffering at the hands of people such as Foulon. His emphasis on the role of the women points to his horror at the growing violence and brutality of the Revolution. According to George Rudé, there were actually very few women participants in the fall of the Bastille and later events.[1] See also Lisa Robson (Modern Criticism, pp. 97–101) for an account of the women Revolutionaries. In the following passage, Ernest Defarge has just returned with the news that Foulon is alive.

"Not dead! He feared us so much – and with reason – that he caused himself to be represented as dead, and had a grand mock-funeral. But they have found him alive, hiding in the country, and have brought him in. I have seen him but now, on his way to the Hôtel de Ville, a prisoner. I have said that he had reason to fear us. Say all! *Had* he reason?"

Wretched old sinner of more than threescore years and ten, if he had never known it yet, he would have known it in his heart of hearts if he could have heard the answering cry.

A moment of profound silence followed. Defarge and his wife looked steadfastly at one another. The Vengeance[2] stooped, and the jar of a drum was heard as she moved it at her feet behind the counter.

"Patriots!" said Defarge, in a determined voice, "are we ready?"

Instantly Madame Defarge's knife was in her girdle; the drum was beating in the streets, as if it and a drummer had flown together by magic; and The Vengeance, uttering terrific shrieks, and flinging her arms about her head like

---

1   *The Crowd in the French Revolution*, New York: Oxford University Press, 1978, p. 58.
2   Madame Defarge's friend is known only as The Vengeance. It was common for the Revolutionaries to be given allegorical names.

all the forty Furies[3] at once, was tearing from house to house, rousing the women.

The men were terrible, in the bloody-minded anger with which they looked from windows, caught up what arms they had, and came pouring down into the streets; but, the women were a sight to chill the boldest. From such household occupations as their bare poverty yielded, from their children, from their aged and their sick crouching on the bare ground famished and naked, they ran out with streaming hair, urging one another, and themselves, to madness with the wildest cries and actions. Villain Foulon taken, my sister! Old Foulon taken, my mother! Miscreant Foulon taken, my daughter! Then, a score of others ran into the midst of these, beating their breasts, tearing their hair, and screaming, Foulon alive! Foulon who told the starving people they might eat grass! Foulon who told my old father that he might eat grass, when I had no bread to give him! Foulon who told my baby it might suck grass, when these breasts were dry with want! O mother of God, this Foulon! O Heaven, our suffering! Hear me, my dead baby and my withered father: I swear on my knees, on these stones, to avenge you on Foulon! Husbands, and brothers, and young men, Give us the blood of Foulon, Give us the head of Foulon, Give us the heart of Foulon, Give us the body and soul of Foulon, Rend Foulon to pieces, and dig him into the ground, that grass may grow from him! With these cries, numbers of the women, lashed into blind frenzy, whirled about, striking and tearing at their own friends until they dropped in a passionate swoon, and were only saved by the men belonging to them from being trampled under foot.

Nevertheless, not a moment was lost; not a moment! This Foulon was at the Hôtel de Ville, and might be loosed. Never, if Saint Antoine knew his own sufferings, insults, and wrongs! Armed men and women flocked out of the Quarter so fast, and drew even these last dregs after them with such a force of suction, that within a quarter of an hour there was not a human creature in Saint Antoine's bosom but a few old crones and the wailing children.

No. They were all by that time choking the Hall of examination[4] where this old man, ugly and wicked, was, and overflowing into the adjacent open space and streets. The Defarges, husband and wife, The Vengeance, and Jacques Three, were in the first press, and at no great distance from him in the Hall.

"See!" cried madame, pointing with her knife. "See the old villain bound with ropes. That was well done to tie a bunch of grass upon his back. Ha, ha! That was well done. Let him eat it now!" Madame put her knife under her arm, and clapped her hands as at a play.

The people immediately behind Madame Defarge, explaining the cause of her satisfaction to those behind them, and those again explaining to others, and those to others, the neighbouring streets resounded with the clapping of hands. Similarly, during two or three hours of drawl, and the winnowing of many bushels of words,[5] Madame Defarge's frequent expressions of impatience were taken up,

---

3  In Greek and Roman mythology, the Furies were winged women (usually only three), sometimes surrounded by snakes, whose role was to avenge crimes, especially crimes against family and kinship.
4  The Hôtel de Ville, residence of the chief magistrate of Paris. See note 13, p. 54.
5  Normally grain would be winnowed, or sorted into the wheat and the chaff. Dickens is once again using a metaphor associated with bread to reinforce the image of starving people.

with marvellous quickness, at a distance: the more readily, because certain men who had by some wonderful exercise of agility climbed up the external architecture to look in from the windows, knew Madame Defarge well, and acted as a telegraph between her and the crowd outside the building.

At length, the sun rose so high that it struck a kindly ray, as of hope or protection, directly down upon the old prisoner's head. The favour was too much to bear; in an instant the barrier of dust and chaff that had stood surprisingly long, went to the winds, and Saint Antoine had got him!

## From Book II, Chapter 23: "Fire Rises"

The burning of country châteaux in the wake of events in Paris was widespread in the so-called "Great Fear" of 1789 (see Contextual Overview, **p. 7**). In this chapter, Dickens suggests that mysterious, almost mythical beings appeared regularly – the mender of roads "would see [. . .] in these times" strange creatures, almost more animal than human, dressed in "homespun stuff and hairy skins of beasts." It is as though the Revolution has opened a Pandora's box of anarchy and unreason; the man's "benighted mind" knows only violence and destruction. Dickens's description is probably derived from Carlyle's *The French Revolution*:

Fancy, then, some Five full-grown Millions of such gaunt figures, with their haggard faces [. . .] starting up to ask, as in forest-roarings, their washed Upper-Classes, after long unreviewed centuries, virtually this question: How have ye treated us; how have ye taught us, fed us, and led us, while we toiled for you? The answer can be read in flames, over the nightly summer-sky. *This* is the feeding and leading we have had of you; EMPTINESS, – of pocket, of stomach, of head and of heart (Vol. I, Book 6, p. 237)

In this chapter, the Marquis's château is the target, and, as Taylor Stoehr points out (Modern Criticism, **pp. 73–4**), the Marquis himself is finally extinguished with his house.

[. . .]Far and wide, lay a ruined country, yielding nothing but desolation. Every green leaf, every blade of grass and blade of grain, was as shrivelled and poor as the miserable people. Everything was bowed down, dejected, oppressed, and broken. Habitations, fences, domesticated animals, men, women, children, and the soil that bore them – all worn out. [. . .]

For, in these times, as the mender of roads worked, solitary, in the dust, not often troubling himself to reflect that dust he was and to dust he must return, being for the most part too much occupied in thinking how little he had for supper and how much more he would eat if he had it – in these times, as he raised his eyes from his lonely labour and viewed the prospect, he would see some rough figure approaching on foot, the like of which was once a rarity in those parts, but was now a frequent presence. As it advanced, the mender of roads would discern without surprise, that it was a shaggy-haired man, of almost barbarian aspect, tall, in wooden shoes that were clumsy even to the eyes of a mender of roads, grim, rough, swart, steeped in the mud and dust of many highways, dank with the marshy moisture of many low grounds, sprinkled with the thorns and leaves and moss of many byways through woods. [. . .]

The night deepened. The trees environing the old château, keeping its solitary state apart, moved in a rising wind, as though they threatened the pile of building massive and dark in the gloom. Up the two terrace flights of steps the rain ran wildly, and beat at the great door, like a swift messenger rousing those within; uneasy rushes of wind went through the hall, among the old spears and knives, and passed lamenting up the stairs, and shook the curtains of the bed where the last Marquis had slept. East, West, North, and South, through the woods, four heavy-treading, unkempt figures crushed the high grass and cracked the branches, striding on cautiously to come together in the court-yard. Four lights broke out there, and moved away in different directions, and all was black again.

But, not for long. Presently, the château began to make itself strangely visible by some light of its own, as though it were growing luminous. Then, a flickering streak played behind the architecture of the front, picking out transparent places, and showing where balustrades, arches, and windows were. Then it soared higher, and grew broader and brighter. Soon, from a score of the great windows, flames burst forth, and the stone faces, awakened, stared out of fire.

A faint murmur arose about the house from the few people who were left there, and there was a saddling of a horse and riding away. There was spurring and splashing through the darkness, and bridle was drawn in the space by the village fountain, and the horse in a foam stood at Monsieur Gabelle's door. "Help, Gabelle! Help every one!" The tocsin[1] rang impatiently, but other help (if that were any) there was none. The mender of roads, and two hundred and fifty particular friends, stood with folded arms at the fountain, looking at the pillar of fire in the sky. "It must be forty feet high,"[2] said they, grimly; and never moved.

The rider from the château, and the horse in a foam, clattered away through the village, and galloped up the stony steep, to the prison on the crag. At the gate, a group of officers were looking at the fire; removed from them, a group of soldiers. "Help, gentlemen-officers! The château is on fire; valuable objects may be saved from the flames by timely aid! Help! help!" The officers looked towards the soldiers who looked at the fire; gave no orders; and answered, with shrugs and biting of lips, "It must burn."

[. . .]

The château burned; the nearest trees, laid hold of by the fire, scorched and shrivelled; trees at a distance, fired by the four fierce figures, begirt the blazing edifice with a new forest of smoke. Molten lead and iron boiled in the marble basin of the fountain; the water ran dry; the extinguisher tops of the towers[3] vanished like ice before the heat, and trickled down into four rugged wells of

1    The church bell, rung in French villages during the Great Fear of 1789 to warn that brigands were approaching and to call the men to arms.
2    The height of the flames reminds the reader why the château is being burnt: Gaspard was hanged forty feet high after murdering the Marquis for running over Gaspard's child.
3    The towers of French châteaux were cone-shaped, like extinguishers for candles or lamps.

flame. Great rents and splits branched out in the solid walls, like crystallisation; stupefied birds wheeled about, and dropped into the furnace; four fierce figures trudged away, East, West, North, and South, along the night-enshrouded roads, guided by the beacon they had lighted, towards their next destination. The illuminated village had seized hold of the tocsin, and, abolishing the lawful ringer, rang for joy.

## From Book III, Chapter 2: "The Grindstone"

The grindstone scene is one of the most memorable in the novel. Charles Darnay has returned to Paris to try and help his faithful servant, Gabelle, and has been arrested. Mr. Lorry, Lucie, and her father are in the Parisian office of Tellson's Bank, which has been set up in the old home of the Monseigneur who had insulted the Marquis earlier in the story. The Monseigneur has fled France disguised as his cook, as did many aristocrats. Charles Darnay is in La Force prison, in dire danger because the September Massacres are in progress and prisoners are being taken from the prisons and massacred (see Contextual Overview, **p. 11**). In this passage, Mr. Lorry and Doctor Manette are looking out of the window in horror at the scene below. The mingling of wine and blood in this scene recalls the spilling of the wine and Gaspard's use of it to write "BLOOD" on the wall (see Key Passages, **p. 126**). As a part of the Christian foundations of the novel (see Brooks, Modern Criticism, **pp. 90–3**), the reference here is to the Last Supper, when Christ told his disciples that the wine was his blood, shed for mankind. The Revolution has become a perversion of Christian compassion: the guillotine has replaced the cross, and is even worn as an ornament; religious observances were banned during the Revolutionary period. The images in this passage evoke hell and, as in the dancing of the Carmagnole (the wild Revolutionary dance described in Book II, Chapter 6), the men and women blend into an androgynous monster. Dickens's sympathy with the Revolutionaries is here obliterated in the viewer who would "petrify" the "frenzied eyes" of the crowd, an image that recalls the Gorgon that turned the Marquis to stone. The power of eyes and spying is a central motif in the novel and comments upon the interplay of private and public spheres of activity, from the Dover coach to the very public guillotine.

The grindstone image was a favorite of Dickens and Carlyle for any mechanical system of belief that reduced human beings to numbers (such as Utilitarianism, which took a statistical view of human nature) or denied the creative, spiritual aspect of mankind. The Revolutionaries had become such a mechanical force, and here, as in the Bastille scene, we see the dangers of mob thinking and action. Few individual men or women, thinking for themselves, would behave as they do in a crowd.

Looked out upon a throng of men and women: not enough in number, or near enough, to fill the court-yard: not more than forty or fifty in all. The people in possession of the house had let them in at the gate, and they had rushed in to work at the grindstone; it had evidently been set up there for their purpose, as in a convenient and retired spot.

But, such awful workers, and such awful work!

The grindstone had a double handle, and, turning at it madly were two men, whose faces, as their long hair flapped back when the whirlings of the grindstone brought their faces up, were more horrible and cruel than the visages of the wildest savages in their most barbarous disguise. False eyebrows and false moustaches were stuck upon them, and their hideous countenances were all bloody and sweaty, and all awry with howling, and all staring and glaring with beastly excitement and want of sleep. As these ruffians turned and turned, their matted locks now flung forward over their eyes, now flung backward over their necks, some women held wine to their mouths that they might drink; and what with dropping blood, and what with dropping wine, and what with the stream of sparks struck out of the stone, all their wicked atmosphere seemed gore and fire. The eye could not detect one creature in the group, free from the smear of blood. Shouldering one another to get next at the sharpening-stone, were men stripped to the waist, with the stain all over their limbs and bodies; men in all sorts of rags, with the stain upon those rags; men devilishly set off with spoils of women's lace and silk and ribbon, with the stain dyeing those trifles through and through. Hatchets, knives, bayonets, swords, all brought to be sharpened, were all red with it. Some of the hacked swords were tied to the wrists of those who carried them, with strips of linen and fragments of dress: ligatures various in kind, but all deep of the one colour. And as the frantic wielders of these weapons snatched them from the stream of sparks and tore away into the streets, the same red hue was red in their frenzied eyes; – eyes which any unbrutalised beholder would have given twenty years of life, to petrify with a well-directed gun.

All this was seen in a moment, as the vision of a drowning man,[1] or of any human creature at any very great pass, could see a world if it were there. They drew back from the window, and the Doctor looked for explanation in his friend's ashy face.

## From Book III, Chapter 9: "The Game Made"

Charles Darnay has been tried, released from prison, and rearrested. Fearing the worst, Sydney Carton prepares his plan with the assistance of John Barsad, whom he is able to blackmail into helping him. After a heart-to-heart talk with Mr. Lorry, who takes on the role of father to Carton (although he is not made privy to Carton's plan), he purchases the drugs required to render Darnay unconscious and spends the night wandering the streets of Paris, preparing for the end. The following passages have been written about extensively. Some commentators find the identification of Carton with Christ heavy-handed and unconvincing, but for many readers Carton's crossing of the river is a movement

1    Garrett Stewart relates this image to Carton's death. See Modern Criticism, pp. 87–8.

from death to life that prepares for his final redemptive sacrifice. The passage has many of the features of the "journey to the underworld" motif found in literature, in which a character, at the lowest ebb in his spiritual life, passes through the valley of the shadow of death and comes back renewed, with new faith and vision. We see this motif in Dickens's rendering of Carton's surroundings. The day comes "coldly, looking like a dead face out of the sky." The following night "turned pale and died, and for a little while it seemed as if Creation were delivered over to Death's dominion." These images of the valley of the shadow then give way to light and life as Carton sees his purposeless life as now a part of a great whole. For a detailed examination of this passage that gives full value to the resonance of the language see Chris Brooks, Modern Criticism, **pp. 92–3**. A different interpretation is offered by Cates Baldridge, who reads the imagery of Carton's absorption into the sea as identifying him with the Revolutionary mob (who are frequently described as a sea in full flood). See Baldridge, Modern Criticism, **p. 96**.

With a solemn interest in the lighted windows where the people were going to rest, forgetful through a few calm hours of the horrors surrounding them; in the towers of the churches, where no prayers were said, for the popular revulsion had even travelled that length of self-destruction from years of priestly imposters, plunderers, and profligates; in the distant burial-places, reserved, as they wrote upon the gates, for Eternal Sleep; in the abounding gaols; and in the streets along which the sixties rolled to a death which had become so common and material,[1] that no sorrowful story of a haunting Spirit ever arose among the people out of all the working of the Guillotine; with a solemn interest in the whole life and death of the city settling down to its short nightly pause in fury; Sydney Carton crossed the Seine again for the lighter streets.

Few coaches were abroad, for riders in coaches were liable to be suspected, and gentility hid its head in red nightcaps, and put on heavy shoes, and trudged. But, the theatres were all well filled, and the people poured cheerfully out as he passed, and went chatting home. At one of the theatre doors, there was a little girl with a mother, looking for a way across the street through the mud. He carried the child over, and before the timid arm was loosed from his neck asked her for a kiss.[2]

"I am the resurrection and the life, saith the Lord: he that believeth in me, though he were dead, yet shall he live: and whosoever liveth and believeth in me, shall never die."[3]

Now, that the streets were quiet, and the night wore on, the words were in the echoes of his feet, and were in the air. Perfectly calm and steady, he sometimes repeated them to himself as he walked; but, he heard them always.

The night wore out, and, as he stood upon the bridge listening to the water as it

---

1    In the previous paragraph, Carton has mourned the sixty-three people sent to the guillotine that day.
2    Saint Christopher carried a child safely across a stream and then found that he had been carrying Christ.
3    John 11:25–6.

splashed the river-walls of the Island of Paris,[4] where the picturesque confusion of houses and cathedral shone bright in the light of the moon, the day came coldly, looking like a dead face out of the sky. Then, the night, with the moon and the stars, turned pale and died, and for a little while it seemed as if Creation were delivered over to Death's dominion.

But, the glorious sun, rising, seemed to strike those words, that burden of the night, straight and warm to his heart in its long bright rays. And looking along them, with reverently shaded eyes, a bridge, of light appeared to span the air between him and the sun, while the river sparkled under it.

The strong tide, so swift, so deep, and certain, was like a congenial friend, in the morning stillness. He walked by the stream, far from the houses, and in the light and warmth of the sun fell asleep on the bank. When he awoke and was afoot again, he lingered there yet a little longer, watching an eddy that turned and turned purposeless, until the stream absorbed it, and carried it on to the sea. – "Like me!"

A trading-boat, with a sail of the softened colour of a dead leaf, then glided into his view, floated by him, and died away. As its silent track in the water disappeared, the prayer that had broken up out of his heart for a merciful consideration of all his poor blindnesses and errors, ended in the words, "I am the resurrection and the life."

## From Book III, Chapter 13: "Fifty-Two"

Charles Darnay is doomed to die for the sins of his fathers by Doctor Manette's testimony, written in the Bastille and found there by Ernest Defarge (see Synopsis of the Plot, **p. 113** and Hutter, Modern Criticism, **pp. 83–4**). In this chapter, Sydney Carton puts into operation the plan he has hatched to replace Darnay at the guillotine. Such substitutions were popular in the myths and stories surrounding the French Revolution in the nineteenth century, and Dickens would certainly have read of other accounts, including the one mentioned by Carlyle (see Contextual Overview, **pp. 17–8**). Cates Baldridge has drawn attention to the complete identification of Carton as Darnay here in his argument that Dickens is actually at odds with a liberal society's defence of the individual (see Modern Criticism, **pp. 96–7**).

'Of all the people upon earth, you least expected to see me!' he said.

'I could not believe it to be you. I can scarcely believe it now. You are not' – the apprehension came suddenly into his mind – 'a prisoner?'

'No. I am accidentally possessed of a power over one of the keepers here, and in virtue of it I stand before you. I come from her – your wife, dear Darnay.'

The prisoner wrung his hand.

---

4   The Île de la Cité is an island in the middle of the river Seine in Paris. On it are Notre Dame Cathedral and the Conciergerie Prison, in which Charles Darnay is imprisoned after his second trial.

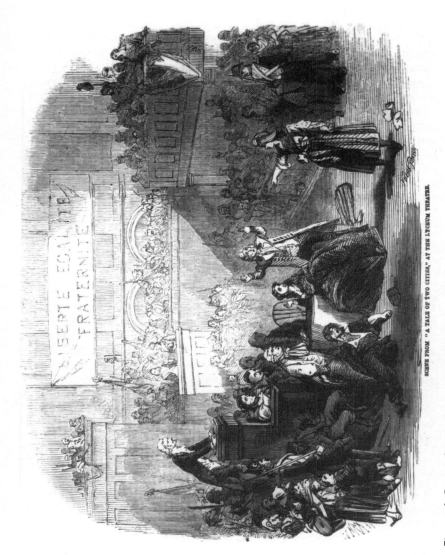

SCENE FROM "A TALE OF TWO CITIES," AT THE LYCEUM THEATRE.

**Figure 4 Court Scene from the 1860 Stage Production.**

'I bring you a request from her.'

'What is it?'

'A most earnest, pressing, and emphatic entreaty, addressed to you in the most pathetic tones of the voice so dear to you, that you well remember.'

The prisoner turned his face partly aside.

'You have no time to ask me why I bring it, or what it means; I have no time to tell you. You must comply with it – take off those boots you wear, and draw on these of mine.'

There was a chair against the wall of the cell, behind the prisoner. Carton, pressing forward, had already, with the speed of lightning, got him down into it, and stood over him barefoot.

'Draw on these boots of mine. Put your hands to them; put your will to them. Quick!'

'Carton, there is no escaping from this place; it never can be done. You will only die with me. It is madness.'

'It would be madness if I asked you to escape; but do I? When I ask you to pass out at that door, tell me it is madness and remain here. Change that cravat for this of mine, that coat for this of mine. While you do it, let me take this ribbon from your hair, and shake out your hair like this of mine!'

With wonderful quickness, and with a strength, both of will and action, that appeared quite supernatural, he forced all these changes upon him. The prisoner was like a young child in his hands.

'Carton! Dear Carton! It is madness. It cannot be accomplished, it never can be done, it has been attempted, and has always failed. I implore you not to add your death to the bitterness of mine.'

'Do I ask you, my dear Darnay, to pass the door? When I ask that, refuse. There are pen and ink and paper on this table. Is your hand steady enough to write?'

'It was, when you came in.'

'Steady it again, and write what I shall dictate. Quick, friend, quick!'

Pressing his hand to his bewildered head, Darnay sat down at the table. Carton, with his right hand in his breast, stood close beside him.

'Write exactly as I speak.'

'To whom do I address it?'

'To no one.' Carton still had his hand in his breast.

'Do I date it?'

'No.'

The prisoner looked up, at each question. Carton, standing over him with his hand in his breast, looked down.

' "If you remember," said Carton, dictating, "the words that passed between us, long ago,[1] you will readily comprehend this when you see it. You do remember them, I know. It is not in your nature to forget them." '

He was drawing his hand from his breast; the prisoner chancing to look up in his hurried wonder as he wrote, the hand stopped, closing upon something.

'Have you written "forget them"?' Carton asked.

1   Carton is dictating his own last words to Lucie, reminding her that he once promised to give his life to save a life she loved (Book II, Chapter 13).

'I have. Is that a weapon in your hand?'

'No; I am not armed.'

'What is it in your hand?'

'You shall know directly. Write on; there are but a few words more.' He dictated again. ' "I am thankful that the time has come, when I can prove them. That I do so, is no subject for regret or grief." ' As he said these words with his eyes fixed on the writer, his hand slowly and softly moved down close to the writer's face.

The pen dropped from Darnay's fingers on the table, and he looked about him vacantly.

'What vapour is that?' he asked.

'Vapour?'

'Something that crossed me?'

'I am conscious of nothing; there can be nothing here. Take up the pen and finish. Hurry, hurry!'

As if his memory were impaired, or his faculties disordered, the prisoner made an effort to rally his attention. As he looked at Carton with clouded eyes and with an altered manner of breathing, Carton – his hand again in his breast – looked steadily at him.

'Hurry, hurry!'

The prisoner bent over the paper, once more.

' "If it had been otherwise;" ' Carton's hand was again watchfully and softly stealing down; ' "I never should have used the longer opportunity. If it had been otherwise;" ' the hand was at the prisoner's face; ' "I should but have had so much the more to answer for. If it had been otherwise—" ' Carton looked at the pen, and saw that it was trailing off into unintelligible signs.

Carton's hand moved back to his breast no more. The prisoner sprang up, with a reproachful look, but Carton's hand was close and firm at his nostrils, and Carton's left arm caught him round the waist. For a few seconds he faintly struggled with the man who had come to lay down his life for him; but, within a minute or so, he was stretched insensible on the ground.

Quickly, but with hands as true to the purpose as his heart was, Carton dressed himself in the clothes the prisoner had laid aside, combed back his hair, and tied it with the ribbon the prisoner had worn. Then, he softly called, 'Enter there! Come in!' and the Spy presented himself.

'You see?' said Carton, looking up at him, as he kneeled on one knee beside the insensible figure, putting the paper in the breast: 'is your hazard very great?'

'Mr Carton,' the Spy answered, with a timid snap of his fingers, 'my hazard is not *that*, in the thick of business here, if you are true to the whole of your bargain.'

'Don't fear me. I will be true to the death.'

'You must be, Mr Carton, if the tale of fifty-two is to be right.[2] Being made right by you in that dress, I shall have no fear.'

'Have no fear! I shall soon be out of the way of harming you, and the rest will soon be far from here, please God! Now, get assistance and take me to the coach.'

---

2    Fifty-two people were condemned to die the next day. Tale: a tally or reckoning.

'You?' said the spy, nervously.
'Him, man, with whom I have exchanged.'

In this exciting passage, Dickens moves into the present tense to increase the sense of urgency and immediacy. More importantly, he shifts the pronouns from the third person "they" to the first person plural "we," the tense and person of most of Carlyle's *The French Revolution*. Critic Jeremy Tambling notes that Carlyle's use of the present tense does not allow the reader to be shielded by distance from the events. The sense of anxiety so created "suggests the ongoing power of a trauma."[3] The reader is swept along the road out of Paris in the carriage with the Manette family, Mr. Lorry, and a drugged Charles Darnay. Dickens's skill in writing this kind of passage is evident in the use of indirect speech (reported without comment rather than included in quotation marks) for Mr. Lorry's initial exchange and in the rhetoric of the escape that conveys the passengers' fear that they will be found out and brought back. The repetition of "leisurely," for example, heightens the sense of maddening delay felt by the family. One effect, however, of including the reader in the scene besides the obvious one of creating atmosphere and suspense is that it perhaps takes the reader's mind away from the fact that the inhabitants of the coach now know that Sydney Carton has gone to his death. A sense of guilt over their own good fortune should be accompanying their somewhat shameful flight from Paris with a hero who appears quite helpless and feeble in this scene, especially in comparison to the man who should be with them but isn't. Garrett Stewart suggests that in including the reader in the coach party, Dickens makes Carton's death a sacrifice for all of us (see Modern Criticism, **p. 87**).

The same shadows that are falling on the prison, are falling, in that same hour of the early afternoon, on the Barrier with the crowd about it, when a coach going out of Paris drives up to be examined.

'Who goes here? Whom have we within? Papers!'

The papers are handed out, and read.

'Alexandre Manette. Physician. French. Which is he?'

This is he; this helpless, inarticulately murmuring, wandering old man pointed out.

'Apparently the Citizen-Doctor is not in his right mind? The Revolution-fever will have been too much for him?'

Greatly too much for him.

'Hah! Many suffer with it. Lucie. His daughter. French. Which is she?'

This is she.

'Apparently it must be. Lucie, the wife of Evrémonde; is it not?'

It is.

'Hah! Evrémonde has an assignation elsewhere. Lucie, her child. English. This is she?'

3   *Dickens, Violence and the Modern State*, Houndmills: Macmillan; New York: St. Martin's Press, 1995, p. 140.

She and no other.

'Kiss me, child of Evrémonde. Now, thou hast kissed a good Republican; something new in thy family; remember it! Sydney Carton. Advocate. English. Which is he?'

He lies here, in this corner of the carriage. He, too, is pointed out.

'Apparently the English advocate is in a swoon?'

It is hoped he will recover in the fresher air. It is represented that he is not in strong health, and has separated sadly from a friend who is under the displeasure of the Republic.

'Is that all? It is not a great deal, that! Many are under the displeasure of the Republic, and must look out at the little window. Jarvis Lorry. Banker. English. Which is he?'

'I am he. Necessarily, being the last.'

It is Jarvis Lorry who has replied to all the previous questions. It is Jarvis Lorry who has alighted and stands with his hand on the coach door, replying to a group of officials. They leisurely walk round the carriage and leisurely mount the box, to look at what little luggage it carries on the roof; the country-people hanging about, press nearer to the coach-doors and greedily stare in; a little child, carried by its mother, has its short arm held out for it, that it may touch the wife of an aristocrat who has gone to the Guillotine.

'Behold your papers, Jarvis Lorry, countersigned.'

'One can depart, citizen?'

'One can depart. Forward, my postilions! A good journey!'[4]

'I salute you, citizens. – And the first danger passed!'

These are again the words of Jarvis Lorry, as he clasps his hands, and looks upward. There is terror in the carriage, there is weeping, there is the heavy breathing of the insensible traveller.

'Are we not going too slowly? Can they not be induced to go faster?' asks Lucie, clinging to the old man.

'It would seem like flight, my darling. I must not urge them too much: it would rouse suspicion.'

'Look back, look back, and see if we are pursued!'

'The road is clear, my dearest. So far, we are not pursued.'

Houses in twos and threes pass by us, solitary farms, ruinous buildings, dyeworks tanneries and the like, open country, avenues of leafless trees. The hard uneven pavement is under us, the soft deep mud is on either side. Sometimes, we strike into the skirting mud, to avoid the stones that clatter us and shake us, and sometimes we stick in ruts and sloughs there. The agony of our impatience is then so great, that in our wild alarm and hurry we are for getting out and running – hiding – doing anything but stopping.

---

4   This exchange contains good examples of what has been called "Franglais," the blending of English with French idiom that Dickens has used throughout the novel for the French-speaking characters. "Behold your papers," the use of the indefinite pronoun "one," and the direct translation of the French phrase "Bon Voyage" ("a good journey") are typical of this method that on the whole works well, although Sir James Fitzjames Stephen disapproved of it (see Early Critical Reception, p. 63).

Out of the open country, in again among ruinous buildings, solitary farms, dye-works, tanneries and the like, cottages in twos and threes, avenues of leafless trees. Have these men deceived us, and taken us back by another road? Is not this the same place twice over? Thank Heaven no. A village. Look back, look back, and see if we are pursued! Hush; the posting-house.

Leisurely, our four horses are taken out; leisurely, the coach stands in the little street, bereft of horses, and with no likelihood upon it of ever moving again; leisurely, the new horses come into visible existence, one by one; leisurely, the new postilions follow, sucking and plaiting the lashes of their whips; leisurely, the old postilions count their money, make wrong additions, and arrive at dissatisfied results. All the time, our overfraught hearts are beating at a rate that would far outstrip the fastest gallop of the fastest horses ever foaled.

At length the new postilions are in their saddles, and the old are left behind. We are through the village, up the hill, and down the hill, and on the low watery grounds. Suddenly, the postilions exchange speech with animated gesticulation, and the horses are pulled up, almost on their haunches. We are pursued!

'Ho! Within the carriage there. Speak then!'

'What is it?' asks Mr Lorry, looking out at window.

'How many did they say?'

'I do not understand you.'

'– At the last post. How many to the Guillotine to-day?'

'Fifty-two.'

'I said so! A brave number! My fellow-citizen here, would have it forty-two; ten more heads are worth having. The Guillotine goes handsomely. I love it. Hi forward. Whoop then!'

The night comes on dark. He moves more; he is beginning to revive, and to speak intelligibly; he thinks they are still together; he asks him, by his name, what he has in his hand. O pity us, kind Heaven, and help us! Look out, look out, and see if we are pursued.

The wind is rushing after us, and the clouds are flying after us, and the moon is plunging after us, and the whole wild night is in pursuit of us; but, so far, we are pursued by nothing else.

# From Book III, Chapter 14: "The Knitting Done"

The tension created in the previous chapter by Carton's exchange with Darnay and the flight of the others is maintained in Chapter 14, when Madame Defarge marches resolutely through the streets of Paris, intent on condemning Lucie and her child to the guillotine as family of her enemies, the Evrémondes. Dickens allows her considerable stature, however, singled out as she is from the mob, and she remains one of Dickens's most unforgettable women characters. In his letter to Edward Bulwer Lytton, Dickens discusses this scene and how he wanted Madame Defarge to die a "mean" death, not the heroic death she would have wanted (see Contemporary Documents, p. 49). For comment on Madame Defarge see Robson, Modern Criticism, pp. 98–101. There are many parallels between *A Tale of Two Cities* and *Hamlet*, and one thinks here of the contrast between Hamlet's death and the "mean" (because accidental) deaths of Polonius and Rosencrantz and Guildenstern. Dickens's ambivalence here— his attraction to Madame Defarge's power but his belief that she deserves only a "mean death"—is evident in the film versions of the novel, which are often uncertain how attractive to make Madame Defarge. Dickens emphasizes Miss Pross's Englishness in this scene, drawing to a conclusion the novel's developing sense that revolution is a foreign concept that would not be embraced by the levelheaded English. Tellson's bank, which at the beginning of the story was characterized by old-fashioned inefficiency (and even had some resemblances to the Bastille), has emerged as a haven of sense and security, especially in the grindstone scene.

When Miss Pross drops her basin and the water floods toward Madame Defarge's stained feet, the powerful Revolutionary metaphor of a relentless sea is concluded, now that Madame Defarge, the source of that sea for the Darnay family, is going to be washed away at last. There is also a sense of the cleansing power of water—at last the blood on those feet will be erased. The smallness of the basin, however, keeps the metaphor in perspective when weighed against the flood that is going to drown Sydney Carton in the next chapter.

There were many women at that time, upon whom the time laid a dreadfully disfiguring hand; but, there was not one among them more to be dreaded than this ruthless woman, now taking her way along the streets. Of a strong and fearless character, of shrewd sense and readiness, of great determination, of that kind of beauty which not only seems to impart to its possessor firmness and animosity, but to strike into others an instinctive recognition of those qualities; the troubled time would have heaved her up, under any circumstances. But, imbued from her childhood with a brooding sense of wrong, and an inveterate hatred of a class, opportunity had developed her into a tigress. She was absolutely without pity. If she had ever had the virtue in her, it had quite gone out of her.

It was nothing to her, that an innocent man was to die for the sins of his forefathers; she saw, not him, but them. It was nothing to her, that his wife was to be made a widow and his daughter an orphan; that was insufficient punishment, because they were her natural enemies and her prey, and as such had no right to live. To appeal to her, was made hopeless by her having no sense of pity, even for herself. If she had been laid low in the streets, in any of the many encounters in which she had been engaged, she would not have pitied herself; nor, if she had been ordered to the axe to-morrow, would she have gone to it with any softer feeling than a fierce desire to change places with the man who sent her there.

Such a heart Madame Defarge carried under her rough robe. Carelessly worn, it was a becoming robe enough, in a certain weird way, and her dark hair looked rich under her coarse red cap.[1] Lying hidden in her bosom, was a loaded pistol.

1    Red woollen caps were worn by the Revolutionaries to symbolize liberty. They were based on the Phrygian bonnets given to Roman slaves when they were freed.

Lying hidden at her waist, was a sharpened dagger. Thus accoutred, and walking with the confident tread of such a character, and with the supple freedom of a woman who had habitually walked in her girlhood, bare-foot and bare-legged, on the brown sea-sand, Madame Defarge took her way along the streets.

[. . .]

Afraid, in her extreme perturbation, of the loneliness of the deserted rooms, and of half-imagined faces peeping from behind every open door in them, Miss Pross got a basin of cold water and began laving her eyes, which were swollen and red. Haunted by her feverish apprehensions, she could not bear to have her sight obscured for a minute at a time by the dripping water, but constantly paused and looked round to see that there was no one watching her. In one of those pauses she recoiled and cried out, for she saw a figure standing in the room.

The basin fell to the ground broken, and the water flowed to the feet of Madame Defarge. By strange stern ways, and through much staining blood, those feet had come to meet that water.

Madame Defarge looked coldly at her, and said, 'The wife of Evrémonde; where is she?' [. . .]

'Those rooms are all in disorder, there has been hurried packing, there are odds and ends upon the ground. There is no one in that room behind you! Let me look.'

'Never!' said Miss Pross, who understood the request as perfectly as Madame Defarge understood the answer.

'If they are not in that room, they are gone, and can be pursued and brought back,' said Madame Defarge to herself.

'As long as you don't know whether they are in that room or not, you are uncertain what to do,' said Miss Pross to *her*self; 'and you shall not know that, if I can prevent your knowing it; and know that, or not know that, you shall not leave here while I can hold you.'

'I have been in the streets from the first, nothing has stopped me, I will tear you to pieces but I will have you from that door,' said Madame Defarge.

'We are alone at the top of a high house in a solitary court-yard, we are not likely to be heard, and I pray for bodily strength to keep you here while every minute you are here is worth a hundred thousand guineas to my darling,' said Miss Pross.

Madame Defarge made at the door. Miss Pross, on the instinct of the moment, seized her round the waist in both her arms, and held her tight. It was in vain for Madame Defarge to struggle and to strike; Miss Pross, with the vigorous tenacity of love, always so much stronger than hate, clasped her tight, and even lifted her from the floor in the struggle that they had. The two hands of Madame Defarge buffeted and tore her face; but, Miss Pross, with her head down, held her round the waist, and clung to her with more than the hold of a drowning woman.

Soon, Madame Defarge's hands ceased to strike, and felt at her encircled waist. 'It is under my arm,' said Miss Pross, in smothered tones, 'you shall not draw it. I am stronger than you, I bless Heaven for it. I'll hold you till one or other of us faints or dies!'

Madame Defarge's hands were at her bosom. Miss Pross looked up, saw what it was, struck at it, struck out a flash and a crash, and stood alone – blinded with smoke.

All this was in a second. As the smoke cleared, leaving an awful stillness, it passed out on the air, like the soul of the furious woman whose body lay lifeless on the ground.

## From Book III, Chapter 15: "The Footsteps Die Out for Ever"

Sydney Carton's dying words are probably the most famous last words in literature, and they have been subjected to relentless and microscopic examination over the years. The most complete account of the last chapter is found in Garrett Stewart's *Death Sentences* (see Modern Criticism, **pp. 87–90**). McWilliams, Jr., (Modern Criticism, **pp. 82–3**) also comments on the significance of Carton's death, and see Brooks (Modern Criticism, **pp. 90–3**) for a Christian reading. Carton does not go to his death alone. Although he is acting for Lucie, her place at his side is taken by the seamstress. When Carton shields her from the sight of the guillotine, the gesture recalls Darnay's similar shielding of Lucie from the sight of the Carmagnole (Book III, Chapter 6). Love, "always so much stronger than hate" (as Dickens says of Miss Pross's defeat of Madame Defarge), is for Dickens the only possible solution to human suffering and cruelty. The novel does not reveal how Carton's utopian vision will be achieved, how the "crushed" forms of a people oppressed by an unjust, inhuman feudal system will become whole again. The famous lines from the following passage sum up Dickens's warning to an England fraught by class tensions and injustice: "Crush humanity out of shape once more, under similar hammers, and it will twist itself into the same tortured forms." Fitzjames Stephen (Early Critical Reception, **pp. 63–4**) considered this message too obvious to be worth saying, but a century later George Orwell (Modern Criticism, **pp. 68–70**) considered it a message still worth repeating. The novel suggests that it is by individual action, by forgiveness rather than a "brooding sense of wrong" harbored by Madame Defarge, by duty and loyalty to each other, that social justice can be achieved. The novel also suggests that all but the most extreme of the Revolutionaries themselves were appalled by the violence of the Terror. Ernest Defarge does not share his wife's desire to punish Lucie and her child; he has had enough. Dickens firmly believed that we are not "naturally vicious," as Mr. Hubble would have it in *Great Expectations*. A wasted life can be redeemed; a crippled nation can be restored to health.

Along the Paris streets, the death-carts rumble, hollow and harsh. Six tumbrils carry the day's wine to La Guillotine. All the devouring and insatiate Monsters imagined since imagination could record itself, are fused in the one realization, Guillotine. And yet there is not in France, with its rich variety of soil and climate, a blade, a leaf, a root, a sprig, a peppercorn, which will grow to maturity under conditions more certain than those that have produced this horror. Crush humanity out of shape once more, under similar hammers, and it will twist itself into the same tortured forms. Sow the same seed of rapacious licence and oppression over again, and it will surely yield the same fruit according to its kind.

Six tumbrils roll along the streets. Change these back again to what they were, thou powerful enchanter, Time, and they shall be seen to be the carriages of absolute monarchs, the equipages of feudal nobles, the toilettes of flaring Jez-ebels,[1] the churches that are not my Father's house but dens of thieves, the huts of millions of starving peasants! No; the great magician who majestically works out the appointed order of the Creator, never reverses his transformations. 'If thou be changed into this shape by the will of God,' say the seers to the enchanted, in the wise Arabian stories,[2] 'then remain so! But, if thou wear this form through mere passing conjuration, then resume thy former aspect!' Changeless and hopeless, the tumbrils roll along. [. . .]

The supposed Evrémonde descends, and the seamstress is lifted out next after him. He has not relinquished her patient hand in getting out, but still holds it as he promised. He gently places her with her back to the crashing engine that constantly whirrs up and falls, and she looks into his face and thanks him.

'But for you, dear stranger, I should not be so composed, for I am naturally a poor little thing, faint of heart; nor should I have been able to raise my thoughts to Him who was put to death, that we might have hope and comfort here to-day. I think you were sent to me by Heaven.'

'Or you to me,' says Sydney Carton. 'Keep your eyes upon me, dear child, and mind no other object.'

'I mind nothing while I hold your hand. I shall mind nothing when I let it go, if they are rapid.'

'They will be rapid. Fear not!'

The two stand in the fast-thinning throng of victims, but they speak as if they were alone. Eye to eye, voice to voice, hand to hand, heart to heart, these two children of the Universal Mother, else so wide apart and differing, have come together on the dark highway, to repair home together, and to rest in her bosom.

'Brave and generous friend, will you let me ask you one last question? I am very ignorant, and it troubles me – just a little.'

'Tell me what it is.'

'I have a cousin, an only relative and an orphan, like myself, whom I love very dearly. She is five years younger than I, and she lives in a farmer's house in the south country. Poverty parted us, and she knows nothing of my fate – for I cannot write – and if I could, how should I tell her! It is better as it is.'

'Yes, yes: better as it is.'

'What I have been thinking as we came along, and what I am still thinking now, as I look into your kind strong face which gives me so much support, is this: – If the Republic really does good to the poor, and they come to be less hungry, and in all ways to suffer less, she may live a long time; she may even live to be old.'

'What then, my gentle sister?'

'Do you think:' the uncomplaining eyes in which there is so much endurance, fill with tears, and the lips part a little more and tremble: 'that it will seem long to

1   Shameless women, from 2 Kings 9:30.
2   A reference to the "Second Calender's (or Mendicant's) Tale" from the *Arabian Nights*, one of Dickens's favorite books.

me, while I wait for her in the better land where I trust both you and I will be mercifully sheltered?'

It cannot be, my child; there is no Time there, and no trouble there.'

'You comfort me so much! I am so ignorant. Am I to kiss you now? Is the moment come?'

'Yes.'

She kisses his lips; he kisses hers; they solemnly bless each other. The spare hand does not tremble as he releases it; nothing worse than a sweet, bright constancy is in the patient face. She goes next before him – is gone; the knitting-women count Twenty-Two.

'I am the Resurrection and the Life, saith the Lord: he that believeth in me, though he were dead, yet shall he live: and whosoever liveth and believeth in me, shall never die.'

The murmuring of many voices, the upturning of many faces, the pressing on of many footsteps in the outskirts of the crowd, so that it swells forward in a mass, like one great heave of water, all flashes away. Twenty-Three.

They said of him, about the city that night, that it was the peacefullest man's face ever beheld there. Many added that he looked sublime and prophetic.

One of the most remarkable sufferers by the same axe – a woman – had asked at the foot of the same scaffold, not long before, to be allowed to write down the thoughts that were inspiring her.[3] If he had given any utterance to his, and they were prophetic, they would have been these:

'I see Barsad, and Cly, Defarge, The Vengeance, the Juryman, the Judge, long ranks of the new oppressors who have risen on the destruction of the old, perishing by this retributive instrument, before it shall cease out of its present use. I see a beautiful city and a brilliant people rising from this abyss, and, in their struggles to be truly free, in their triumphs and defeats, through long years to come, I see the evil of this time and of the previous time of which this is the natural birth, gradually making expiation for itself and wearing out.

'I see the lives for which I lay down my life, peaceful, useful, prosperous and happy, in that England which I shall see no more. I see Her with a child upon her bosom, who bears my name. I see her father, aged and bent, but otherwise restored, and faithful to all men in his healing office, and at peace. I see the good old man, so long their friend, in ten years" time enriching them with all he has, and passing tranquilly to his reward.

'I see that I hold a sanctuary in their hearts, and in the hearts of their descendants, generations hence. I see her, an old woman, weeping for me on the anniversary of this day. I see her and her husband, their course done, lying side by side in their last earthly bed, and I know that each was not more honoured and held sacred in the other's soul, than I was in the souls of both.

'I see that child who lay upon her bosom and who bore my name, a man, winning his way up in that path of life which once was mine. I see him winning it

3   Madame Roland, a leading Girondist, one of the groups that comprised the Revolutionary movement in the National Convention (see Contextual Overview, p. 11). She wrote her memoirs in prison and was executed in November 1793. Her last words were said to be "O Liberty! What crimes are committed in thy name!"

so well, that my name is made illustrious there by the light of his. I see the blots I threw upon it, faded away. I see him, foremost of just judges and honoured men, bringing a boy of my name, with a forehead that I know and golden hair, to this place – then fair to look upon, with not a trace of this day's disfigurement – and I hear him tell the child my story, with a tender and a faltering voice.

'It is a far, far better thing that I do, than I have ever done; it is a far, far better rest that I go to, than I have ever known.'

# 4

# Further Reading

# Further Reading

## Recommended Editions of *A Tale of Two Cities*

The most useful edition of *A Tale of Two Cities* is Richard Maxwell's Penguin edition (2000). As well as providing detailed textual annotations, Maxwell, a specialist in French literature of the nineteenth century, includes extracts from a wide range of literature related to the French Revolution. Readers will find not just Dickens's well-known sources (Carlyle, Rousseau, Mercier) translated into English, but also extracts from Bastille memoirs, the de la Motte trial, French novelist Alexandre Dumas's writings on the French Revolution, and contemporary literature about victim substitution. An excellent introduction reveals Maxwell's thorough knowledge of French history. Useful also are his suggestions for further reading which include historical studies of the French Revolution as well as critical studies of the novel. The text is from the original *All the Year Round* weekly numbers, but the illustrations that appeared first in the monthly instalments are also included.

Another good edition is the Oxford World's Classics Edition (1988) edited by Andrew Sanders, the author of *The Companion to A Tale of Two Cities* (see below) and several studies of Dickens's sources for the novel. This edition makes use of Sanders' research, especially his study of the manuscript. It contains an introduction, annotations (less detailed than in the *Companion*) and chronologies. Lacking in this edition are headings on each page (indicating chapter title) and the illustrations. The text is that of the World's Classics edition of 1903.

The Everyman Edition, published by J.M. Dent (1994) and edited by Norman Page, contains a good introduction, annotations, a survey of the critical responses to the novel, suggestions for further reading, and a plot summary. Unfortunately the text, based on the Charles Dickens edition, contains some typographical errors. The original illustrations are included but are rather dark.

# Recommended Book-Length Studies Related to *A Tale of Two Cities*

Brannan, Robert Louis, ed., *Under the Management of Mr. Charles Dickens: His Production of "The Frozen Deep."* Ithaca, NY: Cornell University Press, 1966.
   This book is essential for anyone interested in the play that inspired Dickens's conception of Sydney Carton's sacrifice. Although Brannan does not comment much on *A Tale of Two Cities*, his excellent introduction provides much valuable information on Dickens's management of the play.

Glancy, Ruth, *A Tale of Two Cities: Dickens's Revolutionary Novel*, Twayne's Masterwork Studies No. 89, Boston, Mass.: G.K. Hall, 1991.
   This study for students includes the literary and historical context and critical reception up to 1990 as well as a detailed reading of the novel.

Glancy, Ruth, *A Tale of Two Cities: An Annotated Bibliography*, New York: Garland, 1993.
   This bibliography provides a very complete annotated listing of materials relating to the novel published or performed between 1859 and 1992. It includes editions, adaptations, criticism, study guides, and bibliographies.

Newlin, George, ed., *Understanding A Tale of Two Cities: A Student Casebook to Issues, Sources, and Historical Documents*, London and Westport, Conn.: Greenwood Press, 1998. In the Greenwood Press "Literature in Context" Series.
   Newlin's useful and unusual selection of source materials includes passages from Dickens's sources such as Carlyle and Arthur Young as well as contemporary documents relating to the French Revolution. Newlin comments on related issues such as capital punishment, prison systems, and resurrection men. There is a glossary and detailed index as well as a chronology of the French Revolution and a listing of the major historical figures. The book includes illustrations and is attractively organized.

Sanders, Andrew, *The Companion to A Tale of Two Cities*, London: Unwin Hyman, 1988. Reprinted Mountfield: Helm Information, 2002.
   Sanders' annotations for the novel include not just literary, historical, biblical, and other references, but also information on the manuscript and quotations from Dickens's sources. Unfortunately, the transcription of Mercier's French is often incorrect, so either Sanders' or Maxwell's well-annotated editions (see above) are probably preferable as offering as much annotation as most readers need.

# Collected Essays on *A Tale of Two Cities*

*Charles Dickens's A Tale of Two Cities*, Modern Critical Interpretations, ed. by Harold Bloom, New York: Chelsea House, 1987.
   Eight major studies of the novel are included in full in this volume, (including

Hutter and Stewart from the Contexts section of this sourcebook) but without their footnotes. Bloom's introduction concentrates on Madame Defarge.

*Critical Essays on Charles Dickens's A Tale of Two Cities*, ed. by Michael A. Cotsell. Critical Essays on British Literature Series. New York: G.K. Hall, 1998.

This volume is the most useful of the collections. A detailed introduction by Cotsell (marred by typographical errors) puts the included material in context. As well as ten major studies of the novel, this edition contains extracts from Carlyle, Dickens's *American Notes*, and the historians Walter Bagehot, Georg Lukács, and George Rudé. Unlike the other selections of critical essays, this volume includes all the original footnotes.

*Readings on A Tale of Two Cities*, ed. by Don Nardo. San Diego, Calif.: Greenhaven Press, 1997 In the Greenhaven Press Literary Companion Series.

Sixteen well-known essays on *A Tale of Two Cities* are extracted with short introductory notes to each one. There are no footnotes. A detailed index makes it possible to find specific references to themes, characters, and topics.

*Twentieth Century Interpretations of A Tale of Two Cities*, ed. by Charles E. Beckwith. Englewood Cliffs, NJ: Prentice Hall, 1972.

Extracts from ten studies of the novel are grouped into biographical criticism, studies of sources, and definitive assessments.

# Recommended Reading for the French Revolution

Schama, Simon, *Citizens: A Chronicle of the French Revolution*, New York: Alfred A. Knopf, 1989.

This long but very readable, in fact exciting, account of the Revolution is an excellent accompaniment to the study of *A Tale of Two Cities*, providing a comprehensive and clear account of the events and people involved in the Revolution. A detailed index makes it easy to find specific references relating to the novel.

# Selected Criticism

The following is just a selection from the many articles published on *A Tale of Two Cities*. Not listed here are the essays excerpted or referred to throughout the sourcebook.

Alter, Robert, "The Demons of History in Dickens' *Tale*," *Novel*, 2 (1969), pp. 135–42.

Alter examines the visual elements of the novel – particularly light and darkness – to argue that the novel allegorically dramatizes how people become slaves to impersonal forces.

Druce, Robert, "*A Tale of Two Cities* to *Mam'zelle Guillotine*: The French Revolution Seen through Popular Fiction," in C.C. Barfoot and Theo D'haen, eds, *Tropes of Revolution: Writers' Reactions to Real and Imagined Revolutions 1789–1989*. Amsterdam and Atlanta, Ga.: Rodopi, DQR Studies in Literature, 9. 1991, pp. 324–50.

This essay usefully places *A Tale of Two Cities* in the context of other representations of the French Revolution in England to argue that they were all in keeping with the British Government's policy of distancing the Revolution and denying its relevance to British class issues.

Friedman, Barton R. "Antihistory: Dickens' *A Tale of Two Cities*," in *Fabricating History: English Writers on the French Revolution*. Princeton, NJ: Princeton University Press, 1988, pp.145–71.

This essay is a useful starting place for students as Friedman reviews much of the criticism prior to 1988 as well as relating the Christian elements to Dickens's view of history. He draws attention to elements of Gothic romance in the novel.

Kucich, John, "The Purity of Violence: *A Tale of Two Cities*," *Dickens Studies Annual*, 8 (1980), pp. 119–37. Reprinted in Bloom, Nardo, and Cotsell, above.

This influential essay examines Carton's sacrifice in terms of Kucich's other studies of the tension in Dickens between energy and limits. Kucich argues that Carton's "chaste suicide" liberates him from self-hatred while resolving the Revolutionaries' desire for freedom that has become lost in their pursuit of revenge. Kucich answers the critics who find Carton's sacrifice unrelated to the Revolution.

Simon Petch, "The Business of the Barrister," *Criticism*, 44, 1 (2002), pp. 27–42.

Simon Petch, an expert in the presentation of the law in nineteenth-century literature, is the first to consider in detail the novel's analysis of professional and business relations in eighteenth-century England and France and the England of 1859. Petch places Carton's "morbid alienation" in the context of a barrister caught up in a competitive system at odds with the professional man's sense of duty.

Rance, Nicholas, "Charles Dickens: *A Tale of Two Cities* (1859)," in *The Historical Novel and Popular Politics in Nineteenth-Century England*, London: Vision Press; New York: Barnes & Noble, 1975, pp. 83–101. Reprinted in Cotsell, above.

Rance usefully places the novel in the context of other English writings on the Revolution in the 1850s to argue that Dickens and his contemporaries saw it as both a warning and an historical monstrosity that could not happen again.

Stange, G. Robert, "Dickens and the Fiery Past: *A Tale of Two Cities* Reconsidered," *English Journal*, 46 (1957), pp. 381–90.

This thoughtful essay succinctly discusses many of the major themes and motifs of the novel, including doublings, patterns of imagery, and the allegorical use of water.

# Index

# Related titles from Routledge

## William Shakespeare's King Lear
### Edited by Grace Ioppolo

This sourcebook clearly introduces the many critical issues surrounding this complex and haunting play. Ioppolo examines sources, from Holinshed to Spencer, and looks at critical readings and notable performances of the play. Examining *King Lear* within its literary and cultural contexts, this book brings together:

- contemporary documents surrounding King Lear

- performance history

- early critical reception from major critics

- twentieth-century criticism

- key passages from the play itself.

The volume concludes with a list of recommended editions and further reading, allowing students to pursue their study in the areas that interest them the most. This is the ideal introduction for undergraduates, providing a clear guide to the play, its reception and the critical material which surrounds it.

Hb: 0–415–23471–9
Pb: 0–415–23472–7

Available at all good bookshops
For further information on our literature series,
please visit www.routledge.com/literature/series.asp
For ordering and further information please visit:

## www.routledge.com

# Related titles from Routledge

## Jane Austen
### Robert P. Irvine
### Routledge Guides to Literature

Jane Austen is one of England's most enduringly popular authors, renowned for her subtle observations of the provincial middle classes of late eighteenth- and early nineteenth-century England.

This guide to Austen's much-loved work offers:

- an accessible introduction to the contexts and many interpretations of Austen's texts, from publication to the present

- an introduction to key critical texts and perspectives on Austen's life and work, situated within a broader critical history

- cross-references between sections of the guide, in order to suggest links between texts, contexts and criticism

- suggestions for further reading.

Part of the *Routledge Guides to Literature* series, this volume is essential reading for all those beginning detailed study of Jane Austen and seeking not only a guide to her works, but a way through the wealth of contextual and critical material that surrounds them.

Hb: 0–415–31434–8
Pb: 0–415–31435–6

Available at all good bookshops
For further information on our literature series,
please visit www.routledge.com/literature/series.asp
For ordering and further information please visit:
## www.routledge.com

# Related titles from Routledge

## William Shakespeare's Hamlet
Edited by Sean McEvoy
Routledge Guides to Literature

William Shakespeare's *Hamlet* (*c*.1600) is possibly his most famous play, in which the motives of revenge and love are entangled with the moral dilemmas of integrity and corruption.

Taking the form of a sourcebook, this guide to Shakespeare's remarkable play offers:

- extensive introductory comment on the contexts, critical history and many interpretations of the text, from first performance to the present

- annotated extracts from key contextual documents, reviews, critical works and the text itself

- cross-references between documents and sections of the guide, in order to suggest links between texts, contexts and criticism

- suggestions for further reading.

Part of the *Routledge Guides to Literature* series, this volume is essential reading for all those beginning detailed study of *Hamlet* and seeking not only a guide to the play, but a way through the wealth of contextual and critical material that surrounds Shakespeare's text.

Hb: 0–415–31432–1
Pb: 0–415–31433–X

Available at all good bookshops
For further information on our literature series,
please visit www.routledge.com/literature/series.asp
For ordering and further information please visit:

# www.routledge.com